THE
LAST
NARCO

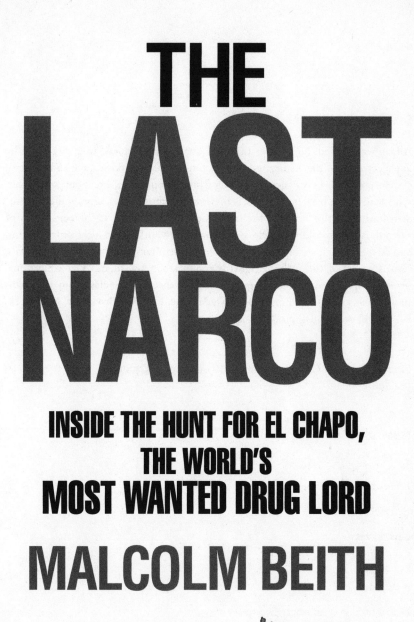

THE LAST NARCO

INSIDE THE HUNT FOR EL CHAPO, THE WORLD'S MOST WANTED DRUG LORD

MALCOLM BEITH

WITHDRAWN

Grove Press
New York

First published in Great Britain in 2010 by Penguin Group,
London England

ISBN: 978-0-8021-1952-0

Printed in the United States of America

Grove Press
an imprint of Grove/Atlantic, Inc.
841 Broadway
New York, NY 10003

Distributed by Publishers Group West

www.groveatlantic.com

10 11 12 13 14   10 9 8 7 6 5 4 3 2 1

'I'm a farmer'

Joaquin Archivaldo Guzman Loera, a.k.a. 'El Chapo'

10 June 1993

Contents

MEXICO: THE WAR FOR NARCO-TERRITORY

Sinaloa/
Remnants
of Tijuana
Cartel

U.S.A.

Sinaloa vs.
Juarez Cartel

Sinaloa
Cartel,

Gulf of
Mexico

Disputed
territory

Gulf Cartel,
Los Zetas,

Gulf Cartel,
Sinaloa
Cartel

Sinaloa Cartel/
La Familia

Sinaloa Cartel

Pacific
Ocean

Los Zetas

The Narcos

'El Chapo'
Joaquin Archivaldo Guzman Loera
Born on 4 April 1957 in La Tuna de Badiraguato, Sinaloa. The head of the Sinaloa cartel, he is Mexico's most wanted man.

'El Padrino'
Miguel Angel Felix Gallardo
Born in Culiacan, Sinaloa, on 8 January 1946. El Padrino – literally, the Godfather – is widely considered to be the founder of the modern Mexican drug trade.

Rafael Caro Quintero
Born on 24 October 1954, in Badiraguato, Sinaloa. Was a leading drug trafficker in the 1970s and 1980s.

'Don Neto'
Ernesto Fonseca
Born in 1942, in Badiraguato, Sinaloa. Was a leading drug trafficker in the 1970s and 1980s.

'El Guero'
Hector Luis Palma Salazar
A former car thief, reportedly born in California. El Guero began working for Felix Gallardo as a gunman. He is widely credited for having trained Chapo.

'El Mayo'

Ismael Zambada Garcia
Born in El Alamo, Sinaloa, on 1 January 1948. El Mayo is a key ally of Chapo.

Amado Carrillo Fuentes
Born in Guamuchilito, Sinaloa. He became head of the Juarez cartel in the early 1990s. He has two brothers, Rodolfo and Vicente.

'El Azul'

Juan Jose Esparragosa-Moreno
Born in Badiraguato, Sinaloa, on 3 February 1949. El Azul served as a senior adviser to Chapo.

The Beltran Leyva brothers

The five Beltran Leyva brothers, Marcos Arturo ('El Barbas'), Alfredo ('Mochomo'), Hector, Mario and Carlos, were all drug traffickers born in Badiraguato.

The Arellano Felix brothers

The Arellano Felix brothers, Francisco Rafael, Benjamin, Carlos, Eduardo, Ramon, Luis Fernando and Francisco Javier were born in Culiacan, Sinaloa, and later ran the Tijuana cartel.

Juan Garcia Abrego
Born in Matamoros, Tamaulipas, on 13 September 1944. Garcia Abrego founded the Gulf cartel.

'El Mata-Amigos'

Osiel Cardenas Guillen
Born in Matamoros, Tamaulipas, on 18 May 1967. Cardenas Guillen became the head of the Gulf cartel in the late 1990s and created Los Zetas.

Los Zetas
A paramilitary wing comprising thirty-one former Mexican special forces soldiers who deserted to work for Cardenas Guillen and the Gulf cartel.

La Familia
A group of drug traffickers based in Michoacan, which rose to prominence around 2006.

Jose de Jesus Amezcua Contreras
Founder of the Mexican methamphetamine industry.

Glossary of Terms

Capo: a drug kingpin

Gatillero: a gunman, sometimes written in other texts as 'gavillero'

Narco: anyone affiliated with the drug trade, from couriers to kingpins. In this book, the term in its singular is largely used to denote a high-level narco.

Narco-corrido: a song commemorating exploits of drug traffickers

Narco-manta: a banner hung in public, either taunting rival narcos or denouncing authorities for complicity in drug trafficking

Sicario: hired assassin, or killer. Usually part of the capo's inner circle, but sometimes contracted out.

AFI: Federal Investigations Agency, Mexico's equivalent to the FBI

DEA: US Drug Enforcement Administration

CNDH: National Human Rights Commission

FBI: US Federal Bureau of Investigation

PAN: National Action Party

PGR: Mexican Attorney General's Office

PRD: Democratic Revolution Party

PRI: Institutional Revolutionary Party

Sedena: Mexican Defence Secretariat (ministry)

SIEDO: Organized Crime Investigation Unit

SSP: Public Security Secretariat

Prologue

'You tell everyone, you spread the word – Chapo is in charge here. Chapo's the law. There is no law but Chapo. Chapo is boss. Not Mochomo, not El Barbas. Chapo is the law.'

Carlos's eyes glazed over as he spoke about his boss, Joaquin Archivaldo Guzman Loera, a.k.a. 'El Chapo'. In the hills beyond the town of Badiraguato, Sinaloa, in the distance over Carlos's shoulder, was Mexico's most wanted man. Just over there, beyond the river, past the lush vegetation, perhaps a little further amid the green peaks covered in dark grey clouds, was the nation's most powerful drug lord.

Nothing but steep, rocky dirt roads lead from Badiraguato to Chapo's mountain lairs; a grinning Carlos said he would take me to his boss. Then he thought better of it. He frowned. There was no way we'd be allowed to pass in a *cuatrimoto*, as all-terrain vehicles are known in this part of north-western Mexico, in the mountain range called the Sierra Madre Occidental. Riding a donkey through wouldn't disguise the fact that I was a *guero*, or blond, either; they might just kill him for bringing me along, Carlos mumbled.

It was only eight in the morning, and his breath reeked of beer and tequila from the night before. It looked like he had slept in the red plaid shirt, jeans and cowboy boots he was wearing, if he had slept at all.

Carlos lit a cigarette. He appeared to be sobering up. He looked me in the eye, and continued in his gravelly monotone.

'You really want to meet Chapo? Everyone wants to meet him. To find him. You won't. They won't.'

★

Since a dramatic escape from a maximum-security prison in the central Mexican state of Jalisco in 2001, Chapo, the head of the Sinaloa drug cartel, has been on the run.

The US Drug Enforcement Administration (DEA) is offering a $5 million reward for information leading to the whereabouts of the man it claims has built a multi-billion-dollar fortune through the drug trade since the 1990s, killed hundreds of enemies in the process, and earned the reputation as the most powerful *capo*, or drug lord, in Mexico and Latin America.

The Mexican authorities want Chapo dead or alive. So does the United States. 'They have him squarely in their crosshairs,' said former DEA Chief of Operations Michael Braun, who still maintains contact with his law enforcement counterparts in Mexico. 'That will ultimately lead to his apprehension and his death. He won't walk out of prison again.'

Chapo's enemies – of which there are thousands, working for rival cartels and upstart criminal organizations throughout Mexico – want him out of the picture, too. Since December 2006 the Mexican government has been engaged in a fully fledged battle with the nation's drug traffickers, Chapo and his Sinaloa cartel chief among them. At the same time the 'narcos', as the drug traffickers are known, have been battling it out among themselves over immensely profitable smuggling corridors to the US – the world's biggest consumer of illicit drugs – and the production of marijuana, methamphetamine and heroin on Mexican soil.

Even Chapo's former allies – the Beltran Leyva brothers, who also hail from the sierras of Sinaloa – have turned on him.

The war's toll on Mexico has been heavy: about 25,000 deaths since the end of 2006. Killings have always been common in Mexico, but the horrific brutality that has besieged the country is not. In Sinaloa it now costs a mere $35 to have a rival murdered.

In September 2006, five heads were rolled on to a dance floor in the central state of Michoacan. By late 2007, beheadings had become commonplace, barely even making the evening news. Throughout 2008, innocents were being gunned down, addicts in rehab centres were being massacred, and dozens of bodies were turning up every day on Mexico's highways and overpasses, mutilated, naked, humiliated.

By 2009, when a man known as 'El Pozolero' – the Stewmaker – confessed to having dissolved more than 300 bodies in caustic soda for one drug cartel, the public had grown accustomed to horror, brutality and gore. There were more than 300 beheadings in Mexico in 2009 alone; there are still no signs of the violence ebbing.

Chapo was responsible for starting the war.

He grew up in the Sierra Madre Occidental of the north-western Mexican state of Sinaloa, in a small hamlet known as La Tuna de Badiraguato, about 3,000 feet above sea level and sixty miles from Badiraguato, the county seat. Born into a farming family in 1957, neither education nor gainful employment were options. But as a teenager he got a job working for a local drug boss, and, blessed with an entrepreneurial spirit and a penchant for sheer brutality, Chapo rose rapidly to become the head of the Sinaloa cartel by the 1990s.

Today, he is considered one of the world's richest men, and one of its most-wanted. In 2009 the leading wealth and business magazine *Forbes* included Chapo on its annual Billionaires' List, provoking a fierce reaction from those who accused it of glamorizing drug smuggling.

But later the same year, *Forbes* drew up another list – this time of the world's most powerful people. The magazine considered several criteria – influence, control of financial resources, and power across multiple spheres. They had only sixty-seven slots: one for every 100 million people on the planet. At the summit was Barack Obama, with Rupert Murdoch and Bill Gates in the top ten. At number forty-one was Joaquin Guzman.

Forbes wrote:

Believed to have directed anywhere from $6 billion to $19 billion in cocaine shipments to the U.S. over the last eight years. His specialty: importing cocaine from Colombia, smuggling it into U.S. through elaborate tunnels. Diminutive nickname 'El Chapo,' or Shorty, belies fearsome behavior: as power behind struggle with government forces to control transport corridors to U.S., responsible for thousands of deaths. In 1993, arrested in Mexico on homicide and drug charges; escaped prison in 2001, reportedly through the laundry; seized back control of organization.

Forbes would controversially include Chapo on its list again in 2010. This much we know: Chapo's empire, the Sinaloa cartel, channels tons of marijuana, cocaine, heroin and methamphetamine into the United States each year. It operates in at least seventy-eight US cities. He is believed to control 23,000 square miles of Mexican territory.

But Chapo's reach is global. His cartel is believed to be increasingly responsible for the distribution of much of the cocaine consumed in Europe; Chapo's organization is also thought to own properties and other assets throughout Europe, in a bid to spread the money-laundering base.

Chapo's organization is believed to own properties and other assets throughout Europe, too, in a bid to spread its money-laundering base. The cartel receives methamphetamine ingredients from Asia, and in recent years it has spread its tentacles throughout Latin America and all the way to West Africa.

The Sinaloa cartel is the largest in Mexico and the oldest. It is a complex structure with many layers and levels of tens of thousands of operatives and gangs, but the man behind this vast empire is Chapo.

And even though he is on the run from the law, most believe he still lives in the hills of Sinaloa or Durango, not far from where he spent his childhood. That part of the Sierra Madre – where the states of Chihuahua, Sinaloa and Durango meet – is known as the Golden Triangle. But when it comes to Chapo, it might as well be the Bermuda Triangle.

Finding him and catching him have so far proven impossible.

I spent a day and part of the evening wandering around Badiraguato, asking about Chapo and the drug trade as discreetly as

I could. At night in the centre of town, a young man approached me; he told me he knew someone who knew Chapo.

Carlos and I met at 7.30 the next morning, on the outskirts of Badiraguato. We sat on the back porch of a small one-storey house, looking out across the Sierra in all its splendour. Millions, perhaps billions, of dollars' worth of raw drugs lay out there.

Sinaloa's mountains are home to many potential hiding places – if one can even get there. Clandestine landing strips in the area and a fleet of private planes and helicopters have made Chapo's getaways that much easier.

Badiraguato is effectively the last stop on the map of civilization before Chapo country. From this town of about 7,000 inhabitants, it's a five-hour drive on steep, winding dirt roads to La Tuna and the other hamlets which he calls home. When heavy rains don't make passage inaccessible (they often do between June and September), military roadblocks stand in the way.

This is a land that is awkwardly – and often dangerously – inhabited by the forces of law and lawlessness. So there are also the checkpoints set up by Chapo's own people, which are the most feared. After all, the *gatilleros*, or hired guns, don't ask many questions. On the rare occasion an outsider ventures further than he or she should, they tend to shoot first.

I met Omar Meza, a resident of Badiraguato in his thirties, in the town during Independence Day festivities. I was keen to learn more about the drug trade in the area, I told him, and to see more of the surrounding countryside, where Chapo roams and reigns. Meza, who goes by the nickname 'El Comandante', agreed to show me around. Proud of his county but, at the same time, well aware and honest about its reputation for drugs and violence, he would make a good guide.

As Meza and I drove through a winding section of the Sierra Madre still accessible in a standard vehicle, the vegetation began to change. Pines began to replace the shrubs. There were no more real towns at this point, just a few settlements on either side of the road, by the river, each about five miles apart. One had been abandoned

just a year earlier, after an hours-long shootout claimed the lives of
nearly everyone who inhabited the area. We passed a row of houses,
built out of wood and scraps of metal – nothing more than shacks.

As we rounded another bend, avoiding rubble from a recent
landslide, I saw a gunman standing in a clearing that had been
carved into a hillside overlooking the road. Meza was eager for me
to see more of the countryside. But upon my noticing the armed
man, he realized it was best to turn around.

'They don't like us being here.'

Meza knows the repercussions of treading on someone else's
turf. A few weeks earlier, a friend of his, also from Badiraguato,
had been killed in Ciudad Juarez, near the American border. The
friend worked in the drug trade, for lack of other options. He had
gone to Ciudad Juarez to work on behalf of Chapo; Ciudad Juarez
wasn't Chapo's turf, but the Sinaloan drug lord wants control of it.
Meza's friend quickly became just another casualty of war.

His killers cut off his arms and legs, and chopped them up into
small pieces. The authorities were kind enough to send the remains
home to Badiraguato, where he was given a proper burial.

The young men of Badiraguato have little choice but to become
narcos, as there is legitimate work for only about a thousand
people. Outside the county seat, there's not much apart from marijuana, poppy and methamphetamine labs. Only the lucky few can
find work in the local government, or health and education. Some
head to the nearby city of Culiacan; most stay in Badiraguato and
its environs and turn to drugs.

Carlos from Badiraguato got a diploma in education, only to
find there was no work available. So he turned to the drug bosses.
'Everything is narco here,' Carlos said, his eyes glazing over again.

About 97 per cent of the county's residents are thought to work in
the drug trade, in some way or another. From the farmers and their
families – even the kids – who cultivate the opium poppy and marijuana, to the young armed men who act as enforcers, the drivers
and pilots who shift the product, and local politicians and police,
almost everyone is involved.

Residents of Culiacan talk about Badiraguato as if it's the last place on earth they'd ever want to go to. Some, the curious few, say they've always wondered what it's like 'out there' – but they'd never go themselves.

I'd ridden the bus from Culiacan to Badiraguato without much ado. The scorching heat blasted through the open windows of the twenty-seater, and I got a few glances from other passengers – it's not every day that a white man or any foreigner rides this bus into the hills; moreover, locals are generally wary of anyone from the city to begin with – but the two-hour trip went without alarms.

When I had changed buses in the town of Pericos, a stout man in his forties wearing a cowboy hat had wandered over to a pay-phone near by. An informant perhaps, I thought. Or just a man making a phone call.

By the time I hopped off the bus, I was sweating profusely; not really from nerves – it was over 90 degrees Fahrenheit outside. At least the humidity had dropped since we'd left Culiacan and the coast far behind.

I walked into town, down a road lined with houses, into the main square. I made straight for the mayor's office on the south side. I had been to the town before, uninvited, and felt that this time around it might be best to alert the authorities to my presence. I walked up the stairs to the mayor's office building, the Palacio Municipal, just opposite the church. The door was open; a lone policeman leaned against the wall next to it, half asleep under the afternoon sun. I walked in.

'How odd that you should come here to Badiraguato,' said the mayor's secretary, eyeballing me, as we sat down in his sparse office just inside the main entrance. I could hear laughter coming from the mayor's door opposite.

Here was another journalist, looking for Chapo, hoping to learn more about organized crime in the area, hoping beyond hope to nab an interview with the man himself, appearing to want to portray the positive side of this notorious region, but in reality, absorbed by its mystique as a hotbed of criminality.

Badiraguato had never been so famous. Badiraguato – 'rivers of the mountains' – remains off the beaten path; it entertains few visitors. Most locals didn't particularly like the attention Chapo and the drug war were drawing. We've got this bad reputation, they said, and it's impossible to change that. Few wanted to talk openly about the drug lord – it was taboo, too dangerous. In 2005 one local official completely denied any knowledge: 'We do not know in the slightest whether or not this famous Chapo even exists.'

The mayor's secretary was welcoming, however. He thanked me for coming to his town, and in that pleasant, traditional Mexican way, told me he was 'at my service'.

'How odd that you should come here to Badiraguato,' echoed the mayor, or *presidente municipal*, Martin Meza Ortiz, just minutes after my encounter with his secretary.

He smiled, ever so suspiciously. But when I explained that I was curious about the region, its history, its narco-lore, he opened up. His family – his mother, his wife and children, brother, cousins, everyone – sat down for an impromptu taco lunch around his big pine desk, while he explained how it all worked. Badiraguato goes about its own business, he said, while the Sierra remains under the law of the narcos. Although they are ostensibly in charge of security throughout the 3,500-square-mile county, Badiraguato's thirty or so policemen do not leave the town – ever.

Neither do the politicians. Portraits of every mayor of Badiraguato line the walls of a dining room adjacent to the mayor's office; many of them look just like the sort of *pendejo* (ass) a party leadership might hire ostensibly to maintain order in a region where order is an impossibility. Meza Ortiz himself is likeable, and is no-nonsense with his staff, wife and children. Still, it's pretty clear that if the narcos started to cut up rough, he'd either get with the programme or just get going. Meza Ortiz last went deep into the Sierra during his campaign for mayor. He probably won't go again. His administration is trying to develop the area a little, attempting to bring basic necessities to the deepest parts of the Sierra. Education, he told me, is key to preventing the people of his county from falling into drugs. Employment is the next step.

The mayor is also trying to change the way people perceive Badiraguato – or 'Marijuanato', as some Sinaloans like to call it. 'The reality is undeniable, our origin . . . [But] I've always been an impassioned defender of my county, of my people. Badiraguato is not all as bad as they say. It's full of people [who are] full of hope, people who work every day. Dedicating oneself to drug trafficking is a circumstance of life. No one should be blamed for where they are born.'

Meza Ortiz denies any links to drug trafficking. Some residents of Badiraguato, meanwhile, quietly lament the fact that their mayor earns 650,000 pesos ($46,000) a year, drives a BMW, and lives in a two-storey gated house that's 'good enough for a narco'. All this, in one of the 200 poorest counties in Mexico.

The whole town of Badiraguato is quite surreal in this sense: rather than the unpaved roads, homes with dirt floors, and dilapidated public buildings that are something of a trademark of rural Mexican pueblos, this town is clean, well lit, and boasts freshly paved streets, driven by SUVs and other top-of-the-range vehicles. The majority of residents dress stylishly and well – far too well for inhabitants of a traditional and typically impoverished Mexican mountain town.

The streets of Badiraguato are nearly always empty, unlike in many mountainside pueblos where everyone gathers in the streets at all hours to chat or simply pass the time. To an outsider, the ghost-town effect appears to be a consequence of the narcos' presence; Meza Ortiz claims it's simply due to the fact that the people of Badiraguato have a deep appreciation for their privacy, and prefer to stay indoors most of the time.

In Badiraguato and its environs, there's little resentment regarding where the money comes from. Although narcos like Chapo may be criminals in the eyes of the Mexican and US governments, the Sinaloan people are largely proud of their drug bosses, and operate on a code of secrecy that is often likened to the Omerta of the Sicilian Cosa Nostra.

There's honour in protecting and revering outlaws, as evidenced by a shrine set up in the Sinaloan city of Culiacan to Jesus Malverde, a mythical nineteenth-century bandit who supposedly robbed from the rich and gave to the poor. Through their own exploits, the region's drug traffickers have also created Robin Hood-like auras.

But with the drug war in full swing, the sentiments of some are changing. Locals reminisce about the days when it was just Chapo in charge, not the young upstarts of today who are hellbent on violence and appear to have no allegiances. Simply uttering 'Chapo' makes most locals remember a time when the drug trade was controlled – sure, it was violent, but the violence was controlled by him.

Some – a minority, most likely – are happy to see what they perceive as the downfall of any narco, whether Chapo or the young thugs. During an earlier visit to Badiraguato, I had sat on a bench in the town square, chatting with an elderly gentleman; he refused to talk about Chapo, or even utter the drug lord's name. He did, however, dare to whisper his negative opinions about the local 'mafia'.

When one of the bad guys is caught or killed by soldiers, 'they cry'. He grinned, and went silent again.

Four SUVs with tinted windows pulled up into the square. They slowly made their way around. They circled three more times.

'You had better leave now,' the old man said.

1. The Great Escape

Prison guard Jaime Sanchez Flores made his usual rounds at 9.15 p.m. at Puente Grande. Nothing was amiss, everyone was in his place.

There was reason to be especially vigilant. Earlier that Friday, 19 January 2001, a group of high-ranking Mexican officials had visited the maximum-security facility, located in the central state of Jalisco. Leading the delegation was Jorge Tello Peon, the nation's deputy police chief, and high among his concerns was one inmate in particular: Joaquin Archivaldo 'El Chapo' Guzman Loera.

Chapo had been in Puente Grande since 1995, having been transferred there two years after his capture in Guatemala. Although he had been behind bars for nearly eight years, and had never tried to break out, there was good reason for Tello Peon to be worried. Just days before the officials' 19 January visit, the Mexican Supreme Court had ruled that criminals tried in Mexico could be more easily extradited to the United States.

Chapo, facing drug trafficking indictments north of the border, could soon find himself on the way to a maximum-security prison in the United States.

No drug trafficker wanted to face such a fate, and Tello Peon knew it. So did Chapo. Within the towering whitewashed walls of Puente Grande, Chapo could still run his business with little difficulty. Corruption in the prison was rampant, and Chapo's status as one of Mexico's most formidable narcos was indisputable – even if he was locked away in a Mexican jail.

But in the United States, Chapo would face real justice, with real consequences. It was every narco's fear, to be cut off from his closest cronies, his network – to be moved out of the Mexican system that was so riddled with corruption. During the 1980s, Colombia's drug lords had fought a terror campaign in order to beat down extradition laws; Mexico's drug lords were of a similar mindset. Chapo would not go to the United States.

Minutes after Sanchez Flores did his last rounds, the lights went out in the cells at the facility, which held 508 prisoners. At the time, Puente Grande was one of three maximum-security penitentiaries in Mexico, equipped with 128 of the best closed-circuit TV cameras – they monitored every corner of the jail – and alarm systems available. The cameras were all operated from outside the prison itself, and no one on the site had access to the controls. In the hallways, only one door could be open at a time – each was electronically controlled.

Between forty-five minutes and an hour after Sanchez Flores last checked up on the drug lord, a guard named Francisco Camberos Rivera, a.k.a. 'El Chito', opened Chapo's electronically locked cell.

The high-priority prisoner waltzed down the hall and hopped into a laundry cart, which El Chito wheeled right out of Cell Block C3. They took a right, and headed down to the next level of the prison. Most of the electronic doors opened easily, as the circuits had been cut. Others were broken and didn't work anyway, so they just swung open. One door had been propped open with an old shoe – hardly the epitome of maximum security that the government claimed.

El Chito and Chapo – still in the cart – turned towards Cell Block B3, but the guard quickly realized that was a bad move. There were still people in the dining area, probably guards having a late meal. So El Chito chose a seemingly risky route, going through the hallway lined with observation rooms – which was normally also filled with guards – towards the main exit.

They passed into the area in which visitors and all those who enter the prison during daylight hours are searched from head to toe. The on-duty guard asked El Chito where he was going.

Taking out the laundry, like I always do, the guard replied.

The on-duty officer stuck his hands deep in the cart – but not deep enough. All he felt were clothes and sheets. He waved them through; Chapo was wheeled out of the gates.

Only one guard was monitoring the car park, and he was indoors behind a glass pane with his nose buried in paperwork at his desk. Chapo shed his beige prison jumpsuit and shoes and hopped out of the cart, into the boot of a nearby Chevrolet Monte Carlo.

El Chito dropped the cart off just inside the main gate, as he always did when taking out the laundry, and got behind the wheel of the getaway car. They began their drive out of Puente Grande.

A guard stopped them as they tried to leave the car park. But his shift was about to end, and he was in no mood to do his job thoroughly. He had a quick look inside the vehicle, ignoring the boot, and waved El Chito through. The guard and Chapo drove away down Zapotlanejo Avenue.

Chapo was free.

El Chito's role wasn't finished yet. Chapo got into the passenger seat, and told his young accomplice that he would be better off fleeing with him, given that the ensuing newspaper and television headlines, not to mention the manhunts, would all include him.

Worried, El Chito mulled this over as he kept driving. When they arrived on the outskirts of Guadalajara, Chapo told the guard he was thirsty. El Chito went into a shop to buy him a bottle of water.

When he got back to the car, Chapo was gone.

Throughout the whole affair, no alarms in Puente Grande had sounded. The guards in the looming towers of the prison, with their 360-degree view of the area, had seen nothing. Inside, their colleagues carried on their night-time inspections as if nothing had occurred.

At 11.35 p.m., prison warden Leonardo Beltran Santana received a phone call. Chapo wasn't in his cell, a guard told him. Panic ensued among the prison staff, and they began a search of the facility, cell by cell, room by room, closet by closet. It would be another five hours before Tello Peon would be informed of the break.

Tello Peon's first thought – rightly – was that the system had broken down. Corruption had long been rampant within Mexico's prison walls, and only corruption could have allowed Chapo to escape so easily. That had been the precise reason for his visit – to check the prison for signs of guards' collusion with Chapo and his narco cohorts. Prior to 19 January, there had been rumours that Chapo would try to break out, but no concrete evidence of a plan being put into action. As a result, Tello Peon had ordered that Chapo be transferred to a different wing of the prison after his visit, but this order had not yet been carried out.

'This is treason against the security system and the country,' Tello Peon declared that Saturday morning, as the nation woke up to headlines of Chapo's Hollywood-style escape. Fuming, livid, the police official vowed to launch a nationwide hunt for this man, to catch Chapo no matter what, to punish all those responsible.

He began at Puente Grande. Seventy-three guards, custodians and even the warden were detained for questioning. Under Mexican law, they would be held for forty days by decree of a judge, in order for the Attorney General's Office to investigate them thoroughly for alleged complicity in the escape.

In towns near by, the police and Army began their searches. They ransacked houses, ranches, even government buildings, but found little – traces of drug traffickers, guns, money, drugs, but not Chapo.

The hunt spilled over into Guadalajara, Mexico's second-largest city, located just over five miles away. There, at the home of one of Chapo's associates, federal police found military-issue weapons, phones and computers, and $65,000 in cash – but still no Chapo. Anonymous tips led them to Mazamitla, a few miles south of Guadalajara, where they searched seventeen houses and four ranches from top to bottom. The people of Mazamitla were harbouring Chapo, or so the authorities had been told, but no, he wasn't to be found there either.

Within days, it was clear that Chapo must have fled the immediate area. The hunt would have to be extended nationwide, with hundreds of federal police and soldiers scattering everywhere from major cities to tiny pueblos in the sierras and dusty border towns, all searching for the one man who had so embarrassed the government with his escape. As far north as Tamaulipas and all the way to the southern border with Guatemala, checkpoints were reinforced.

Authorities in Guatemala were put on alert. US agencies – the FBI among them – were called in to help in the manhunt north of the border, on the offchance the drug kingpin had made it safely into the United States in the confusion following the breakout. The public was laughing at newly elected President Vicente Fox over Chapo's disappearance. Fox, meanwhile, was furious and frustrated, as his prison system had been proven useless. No resource would be spared to catch the fugitive.

Chapo, meanwhile, was throwing a party in Badiraguato with his old partners in crime.

The DEA was furious. Cooperation between Mexico and the United States had begun to improve during the Fox administration – Chapo's escape was 'an affront to the efforts to strengthen and honour the rule of law', fumed then-DEA Administrator Asa Hutchinson.

Some DEA agents took his evasion personally, too. They and their Mexican counterparts had lost lives trying to capture drug kingpins, and now Chapo had simply been allowed to walk out of jail. It was a 'huge discouragement to law enforcement efforts'.

Good Life within the Gates

The day Chapo set foot into Puente Grande on 22 November 1995, he laid down the law. He would approach prison guards and employees, often individually, and ask if they knew who he was. Has your supervisor told you about me? Would you be willing to work for us? It wasn't really a question, and they would be compensated well. Even cleaners and kitchen personnel were paid off, receiving anywhere between $100 and $5,000 for their collaboration.

Money was no object: Chapo's allies in Sinaloa were sending him regular quantities of cash. Soon, Chapo and his cronies had set up a system whereby prison staff would even do the recruiting for them. 'I present you another person who is going to work for us,' the guard would tell Chapo upon introducing a new recruit. The names and roles were duly noted by one of Chapo's secretaries, who were also prisoners.

Although Chapo's men kept a log with details on each person's role, specific jobs weren't always assigned to those on the payroll. Sometimes they were paid per job; almost always, the sum was delivered monthly. One of Chapo's cohorts would write down a code ('I have a delivery from the school principal,' was one such message, which meant the guard was to pick up his pay at a pre-designated spot in Guadalajara) on a napkin, and hand it over to one of their employees.

The idea was to have the whole prison at the drug lord's beck and call. Chapo wanted to run Puente Grande as if it were his, and nothing would stop him. He would bide his time until the moment came to leave.

And bide his time he did. At first, prison guards recall, the demands were small – more like requests. Chapo and his cronies wanted a little special something for dinner: could the cooks whip something up? A ladyfriend was visiting: would they be allowed a little extra time for a conjugal visit?

Gradually, Puente Grande became Chapo's personal playground. Parties in the cell block housing him and his main cohort, Hector Luis Palma Salazar, a.k.a. 'El Guero' (the Blond), became commonplace. They wandered wherever they liked within the walls of Puente Grande, also known as the Cefereso No. 2, and enjoyed smuggled alcohol, cocaine and marijuana, not to mention conjugal visits by women other than their wives and girlfriends. Chapo had a fondness for whiskey and Cuba Libres (rum and cokes).

They feasted on specially cooked meals – the kitchen staff were his employees, after all – and paid little attention to the rules of the maximum-security facility. Two cooks in particular, Oswaldo Benjamin Gomez Contreras and Ofelia Contreras Gonzalez, were responsible for preparing 'feasts' for Chapo, according to the

Mexican Attorney General's Office, which is commonly referred to by its Spanish acronym, the PGR. The cooks would later be charged with drug-related crimes, in which they had become involved while at Puente Grande under Chapo's command.

On at least one occasion, a mariachi band was brought in to perform for Chapo and his fellow prisoners. For a Christmas Eve party, recalled one prison guard after Chapo's escape, more than 500 litres of wine were trucked in for a similarly private fiesta. They dined on lobster soup, filet mignon and a selection of cheeses, and drank whiskey and soda long into the night.

Sometimes the fun and games were competitive: Chapo liked to play chess with one inmate in particular, a former member of the presidential guard who had succumbed to corruption. He also played basketball and volleyball. 'He was good at everything,' recalls the inmate. Chapo was in top physical shape for a man in his early forties; he was also blessed with 'astonishing willpower'.

Chapo apparently had a lighter side, too. Sometimes musical groups that played Sinaloan *banda* would turn up at the prison; an avid dancer, the drug lord adored them. On occasion, Puente Grande's dining hall would be converted into a cinema; Chapo and other inmates would watch film after film on a big screen while eating popcorn, ice cream and chocolates. Chapo was a bit soppy at times, according to one inmate. 'We watched *Cinderella* together, eating popcorn. Just imagine.'

Word began to leak out about the parties and goings-on at Puente Grande, which became something of a national joke in a country where the prison system was already in dire need of reform. To this day, there exist unconfirmed reports that Chapo was regularly allowed to leave the prison at weekends, to visit friends, cohorts and family near by. Jose Antonio Bernal Guerrero, a local human rights official, has insisted publicly that Chapo was allowed to enter and exit the prison whenever he liked during his internment.

Mexico's prisons have never been famous for being securely run institutions, but Puente Grande in the 1990s was a farce. When

Chapo arrived, 'security and discipline in the Cefereso 2 fell apart', recalls prison guard Claudio Julian Rios Peralta. There was discipline of a kind, but not from the prison staff.

On the offchance money wasn't enough to convince a guard or fellow inmate to comply with Chapo's every whim, threats would ensure they did. Those who didn't want to work for Chapo were reported to Jaime Leonardo Valencia Fontes, a prisoner who operated as the drug lord's closest 'secretary'.

Valencia would approach the reluctant prisoner or guard: 'Listen, they say you are annoyed and don't want our friendship. Don't worry, here we have . . .'

He would then take out a laptop and a hand-held electronic organizer, and show it to the offender. Then he would continue: '. . . the details of your residence and your family. There's no problem.'

After that, almost everyone complied. A baseball-bat-wielding group of thugs known as 'the Batters' took care of those who didn't.

Chapo and his crew were also supplied regularly with women, from both inside and outside Puente Grande. There was a procedure for picking up prostitutes. Someone on Chapo's payroll would head to the bars in Guadalajara at night, and select several women, who would be driven back to a meeting point near Puente Grande. There, a senior guard, who was paid $3,000 a month for his role as a pseudo-pimp, drove them into the prison in a truck. His presence meant there would be no search, but he carried extra money just in case he needed to bribe his subordinates to bring in extra alcohol or drugs.

For two hours in the evenings, Chapo and the other narco-inmates would close off the dining hall and have sex with their chosen women. The dining hall was converted into a 'hotel', according to testimony from one prison employee. Sometimes, the women would be allowed up to their cells. The rooms designated for conjugal visits were rarely used.

Women inside Puente Grande were fair game, too, and it appears

Chapo actually had a charming side. In a 2001 interview, kitchen worker Ives Erendira Arreola recalled how the drug lord had wooed her. It was June of the year before, and she was working in Cell Block 2. According to his fellow inmates, he had first spotted thirty-eight-year-old Erendira about a month before, and enquired about her. Where was she from? Did she have family, kids? Was she married? Could she be transferred to work in Cell Block 3, where he was housed?

When he finally walked up to the shy kitchen employee in June and introduced himself, Erendira's boss knew exactly what he was after. She and her colleagues encouraged Erendira – it was, after all, a way to make money, and Erendira was a single mother from a poor town near by. Left unsaid was the fact that turning Chapo down could only lead to trouble.

Erendira knew, however, that consorting with Chapo could lead her down a dangerous road, too. So when he finally asked her to come to his cell during pre-arranged hours for conjugal visits, she declined. 'I won't go up,' she said politely. 'I have children, I live alone and I don't want people to talk about me . . . Even if I just come up to talk, people will say I've been with you.'

Chapo appeared to take it well, offering his friendship and nothing more. But the next day, Erendira arrived home to find a bouquet of roses. There was no card, but Erendira knew who they had come from. Then he called her – on her mobile phone, a number she had not given out. 'Did you like the roses?' Chapo asked.

The flowers kept coming, and by July, Erendira would succumb to Chapo's charms. They had sex for the first time in a prison cubicle reserved for visiting lawyers, psychologists and priests. For several months, the trysts would continue, and although Chapo was the perfect gentleman (he would make sure his cell, or whatever room they happened to meet in, was in the best state; he would order clean sheets, flowers and curtains for privacy), Erendira was fearful of repercussions. By September, she realized it would be best to leave her job at Puente Grande, and resigned.

Chapo wouldn't let her go that easily. I'll buy you a car. No, came Erendira's reply. A house? Still no. Chapo promised to set her up with a small business of her own – her children would be well cared for. Still, Erendira refused.

But even if she could turn down the money, there was something she couldn't resist – Chapo himself. After leaving her job, she continued to visit him in Puente Grande, where they would spend the night together. They became close. On her birthday, 11 November, there was a knock on Erendira's door. Chapo had sent one of his men to give her a gift of $1,000. It wasn't much for a man of his means, but it was the thought that counted.

There were other women, many other women. His wives Alejandrina and Griselda had code names and special mobile phone numbers through which they could be reached – and summoned – at a moment's notice. Chapo even received regular deliveries of Viagra to maintain his libido.

And then there was Zulema.

Even as he was pursuing Erendira and entertaining his wives, Chapo was falling in love with an inmate, twenty-seven-year-old Zulema Yulia Hernandez, a former cop from Sinaloa who had been convicted of drug-related offences.

Hernandez had begun her career as an exemplary policewoman, with top grades and glowing assessments from her superiors. But the temptations of the narco world had become too much, and she had been seduced by both the lifestyle and the money. She had wound up in Puente Grande, one of a mere five female inmates in the maximum-security penitentiary. But she was the inmate who stood out: five-foot-five, slim with chestnut hair, light skin, dark brown eyes and a 'near perfect body', as one journalist put it. She was the prize.

Both she and Chapo were from Sinaloa. Both knew of the grinding poverty in the Sierra that destroyed lives even before they had begun. Both were involved in the drug trade. Both had wound up in Puente Grande, stuck within the same dreary prison walls. She and Chapo connected. She found solace in his arms, as he did in hers.

'Joaquin and I identified with each other, because I was in the same place as he was,' recalled Hernandez in an interview with Mexican author Julio Scherer in 2001. 'I was living the same [hell] as he was. I know of the walk from side to side in one's cell. I know what it's like to lie awake and wait, I know of this insomnia, I know of this . . . wanting to burn oneself in sex, burn one's hands, one's mouth, smoke the soul, smoke the time away . . . And he knew that I knew.'

The love affair played out. The two would often sleep together in his cell, sometimes making love, sometimes just lying there. They would talk, hold each other, share their most intimate secrets. '[Often] we didn't have [sex], but he wanted to feel me near him,' she recalled. 'He wanted me to be naked, to feel me next to his body. We didn't have sex, but we were together. And I understood him, and knew he wanted to cry. I knew he had had it up to here with this prison . . .'

Hernandez recalled that after the first time they had made love, 'He sent a bouquet of flowers and a bottle of whiskey to my cell. I was his queen.'

Although he could not write, Chapo also sent Hernandez cards, penned by a fellow inmate, expressing his thoughts.

'Hello, my life! Zulema, my dear,' Chapo wrote on 17 July 2000, as the authorities were planning to transfer his paramour to another correctional facility. 'I have been thinking of you every moment and I want to imagine that you are happy . . . because your transfer will soon take place . . . The other prison will be much better for you, because there will be more space, more movement and time on the days that your family visits.

'When one loves someone, as I love you, my heart, one is happy when there's good news for this person who one adores, even though I will be more emotional for the days following your transfer . . . Precious, if before you are transferred we might see each other (God willing, tomorrow) I want to give you a sweet kiss and take you in my arms to preserve this memory every time I think of you and that way, endure your absence until God allows us to be together again under different conditions, and somewhere other that this difficult place.'

He signed the letter simply – 'JGL'.

Zulema wasn't transferred. Chapo wrote again a few days later.

'Love of my loves! How are you, precious? I hope you are well, calm and optimistic as you should be, you probably are a bit anxious because you haven't been transferred yet but don't despair, it will happen, it's only a matter of time, just a few days according to the lawyer . . .

'. . . My heart, now that you're going and I will be staying a while longer, I will miss you very much . . . When you are [gone] I will suffer much, I have become very fond of you, you've figured out how to win my sentiments and with frankness and honesty I can tell you that I love you, that you are a beautiful person, a pretty girl who has awoken within me the passion of love . . . I am comforted because I think of how you have behaved with me, I remember your face with that smile which pleases me so, I remember everything we've talked about, the joys, the sadnesses, but above all for me, remembering every moment, every instant, that we were a couple – man and woman – has special value . . . Zulema, I adore you . . .'

After seven years behind bars, five of them spent at Puente Grande, it was clear that Chapo had found a true companion. Hernandez's transfer never came through, and they continued their relationship.

Chapo sent more letters.

'Hello my love!. . . My love, yesterday I dreamed of you and it was so real, so beautiful that when I woke up I felt as if I had something good in me, but at the same time [I felt] a little sadness as I realized it was just a dream . . . At the moment I don't know the exact details but yes . . . next week, God permitting, I'll see you and have the opportunity to look into your eyes and at the same time tell you how much I love you, [tell you] what you represent in my life and [tell you about] the plans that I have for us in a future.'

One night in late 2000, when they were together, Chapo spoke to Hernandez of his plans to flee.

'We had finished making love,' recalls Hernandez. 'He hugged me: "When I leave, you will be better off; I'm going to help you with everything. I've given instructions to the lawyer . . . Don't worry, nothing will go wrong, everything is OK."'

Chapo would keep his promise. In 2003 Hernandez was released from Puente Grande, and joined a small gang of drug traffickers. Within about a year she was caught, but Chapo's lawyers helped cut short her sentence.

Chapo's relations with women inside Puente Grande weren't all roses, however, or even dressed up as love. Some of the goings-on were far more sinister. Reports of abuse and rape during Chapo and his associates' trysts with the hookers abounded, and on more than one occasion, human rights officials and state authorities investigated the complaints.

Little was ever proven, of course: everyone was on Chapo's payroll, and few would talk.

Warning Signs

Even though Chapo was a prisoner (of sorts) he was still a major drug trafficker. He was able to continue running his business from inside Puente Grande. Before his capture, he had given some money to a top lieutenant to make sure everything ran smoothly while he was inside. Chapo and his men all had several mobile phones and could conduct their affairs that way; they also apparently used laptops for some accounting tasks.

According to the DEA and PGR, one of Chapo's younger brothers, Arturo, had been granted operational control of the Sinaloa drug trade by 1995, around the time Chapo was transferred to Puente Grande. But through his lawyers, who would give Arturo instructions, Chapo was apparently still ordering the construction of drug smuggling tunnels under the US border – which, by then, had become his trademark – and making sure his brother had a firm handle on the business.

He even appeared to be gaining clout. In 1996 the DEA's top administrator, Thomas Constantine, told the United States Congress that Miguel Caro Quintero, based in the northern state of Sonora, was in charge of Sinaloan drug trafficking. But by 1997 Constantine had changed his tune, reminding the government of Chapo's existence.

'Presently, he is incarcerated in Mexico; however, Mexican and United States authorities still consider him to be a major international drug trafficker,' Constantine told Congress. 'The [Sinaloa] organization has not been dismantled or seriously affected by Guzman Loera's imprisonment . . . Guzman Loera's elements and close associates are active in Mexico, along the south-west [US] border, in the western and midwestern regions of the United States, and in Central America.'

The following year, Constantine once again warned of Chapo's might. 'Guzman Loera is still considered a major threat by law enforcement in both the United States and Mexico,' he declared.

To this day, it's unclear why Chapo chose to remain in Puente Grande for so long, given that he probably could have escaped earlier without too much trouble.

In 1995 he had undergone intensive psychological testing and counselling. Although diagnosed with antisocial personality disorder, he apparently responded to counselling. During sixty-three sessions with a therapist in his cell, he had opened up about his family and expressed an interest in changing his behaviour if it were necessary.

Both his ability to handle frustration and control his patience improved during the course of the therapy; Chapo also learned to control his impulses, the psychological assessment said. His capacity for introspection was increasing; his judgement was improving. He learned from experiences. Chapo had also come up with a plan for the future, the therapist said: he would work in agriculture, legitimately.

According to Zulema Hernandez, Chapo knew the risks of leaving Puente Grande. During their night-time liaisons, he talked of the fate that awaited him on the outside.

He had many enemies all over the country. The Arellano Felix brothers in Tijuana wanted him dead, and relations between Chapo's Sinaloa cartel and his rivals from the Gulf of Mexico were always a source of tension. 'He knew that if he escaped, he was exposed . . . they might kill him,' Hernandez recalled. 'He knows that in this business one [might] lose one's whole family. And he knew what he would face. It isn't so easy to say "I'm going . . . and that's that." Because it's fleeing for the rest of one's life, it's hiding one's entire life, it's being alert one's entire life.'

Apart from his brothers and close kin, it wasn't even clear whether Chapo could really trust his own people in Sinaloa – even the Beltran Leyva brothers, Juan Jose Esparragosa-Moreno, a.k.a. 'El Azul' (the Blue) and Ismael 'El Mayo' Zambada Garcia. The Sinaloa group had never been a close-knit brotherhood, instead operating in a loosely organized fashion that would later earn them and their allies the name 'the Federation'. But the Beltran Leyva brothers were sending Chapo money in Puente Grande, helping him maintain his lifestyle through corruption, and through messages relayed to him in prison, the Sinaloa capos eventually conveyed their wish for him to rejoin their ranks.

He had to trust that.

There were also indications that Chapo did not have full control inside Puente Grande, as some have claimed. In his letters to Zulema, the drug lord sometimes acknowledged that things were not totally in his power. Sometimes he would write that arranging meetings with her and other affairs were 'only a matter of $', while at other times he couldn't see his love because 'we must be prudent'.

It's quite possible that Chapo was simply leading Hernandez on while he cavorted with other women. He was certainly a smooth operator for a man of such a simple background. He was also extremely gushing for a man believed to be so emotionally detached; some of his words (as transcribed by a fellow inmate) sounded like those of a conman, not a lover: 'I send you a kiss of honey and a hug that makes you shake from emotion,' he wrote in October 2000.

One interesting theory surrounding Chapo's escape was that he had so much dirt on federal government ties to his organization and to his enemies that he had to be set free. Some say that Chapo was going to blow the lid off the new administration of President Vicente Fox, which in 2000 had become Mexico's first democratically elected government. Another theory has it that Chapo knew a change in governance would help his situation, given that the Arellano Felix brothers had allegedly been so tight with the Institutional Revolutionary Party (PRI).

Chapo hinted in one of his letters to Hernandez that he was waiting until Fox took power to sort out matters: 'they will be able to arrange many things in affairs that are not as straightforward as yours . . .'

Former federal anti-organized crime prosecutor Samuel Gonzalez Ruiz believes it was Chapo's brains and savvy – not to mention official corruption – that got him out, asserting that the escape plan was some four years in the making. Chapo, he says, sent a brother-in-law to both the Mexican government and the DEA to try to strike a deal. What can I give you? the brother-in-law asked. 'There were serious negotiations, serious pressure,' said Gonzalez Ruiz.

Chapo eventually offered to give them the Arellano Felix brothers, he claims. 'The North Americans fell into the trap,' said the former prosecutor. 'Chapo won over the [US] Embassy. He's smart.'

American officials dismiss these claims as bogus.

Whatever the reason, by the dawn of the new millennium, Chapo was ready to go, and his allies in the Sinaloa cartel apparently wanted to bring him back into the fold. They would help get him out.

Nearly a year before his escape, Chapo had set the plan in motion. The original idea was to stage a *motin*, or uprising, and escape during the chaos. Such brazen prison breaks had been executed before – not from Puente Grande, but from other Mexican penitentiaries – and Chapo knew it could work. But there was always the risk of an immediate federal police or military crackdown as soon as the riot broke out.

The Mexican underworld got wind of these rumours quickly; at least one prisoner phoned the Puente Grande authorities anonymously and tipped them off. There was talk that Chapo was planning to escape; perhaps he had even done so already, and the government was simply covering it up. There was also speculation that federal judges had been paid to let Chapo off the hook.

In 1995, two years after his arrest, Chapo had been convicted of three crimes: possession of firearms, crimes against health – or drug trafficking – and involvement in the murder of Cardinal Juan Jesus Posadas Ocampo on 24 May 1993. The trial had taken place as most serious Mexican trials do – behind closed doors, with a judge but without a jury. Chapo had been tried and sentenced in a 'courtroom' inside the gates of the federal prison on the outskirts of Almoloya de Juarez, State of Mexico.

After Chapo had served several years in prison, another judge had ruled that he was not guilty of the murder charge. Clearly, Chapo had paid him off, the cynics cried; soon, he'd buy his way out of jail entirely, they prophesied.

On 12 October 2000 the PGR spoke out. '[Rumours that] Mr Joaquin Guzman Loera could soon gain his freedom are absolutely false and inaccurate. Mr Joaquin Guzman Loera . . . is confined in the maximum-security federal prison in Puente Grande, Jalisco, where he is serving a [sentence] of 20 years and nine months,' the federal law enforcement body said in a statement.

How wrong the PGR was. By this time, Chapo had already put Plan B into action. Although the prison was effectively on his payroll, Chapo had especially befriended the guard known as El Chito. He and El Chito had become close – the guard was, on occasion, employed as a go-between, delivering flowers and gifts from Chapo to Erendira.

Just months later the time came to go. The escape would reputedly cost Chapo $2.5 million; dozens of guards would have to be bribed. Police in Jalisco would be paid off, so that he would have at least twenty-four hours to get out of the state and stay far enough ahead of the inevitable military manhunt.

The official story, told to the Puente Grande guards being bribed, would be that Chapo was smuggling some gold out of the prison. The gold, ostensibly extracted from rock at the inmates' workshop, was contraband, but it wasn't so serious that the guards would be severely punished for overseeing its exit. Only El Chito would know it wasn't gold in the laundry cart.

It was one of the oldest (but best) tricks in the book: admit to an illegal activity, but keep your real intentions a secret. Just as spies had long crossed borders posing as smugglers, and Mexican drug traffickers had headed to the United States pretending to carry other – less harmful – illegal goods, Chapo would sneak out under the cover of illegal gold. It was practically foolproof.

Only Tello Peon stood in the way. On 15 January 2001 the deputy police chief received a phone call from the national human rights commission. Conditions at Puente Grande were deteriorating by the day, he was told. Something must be done about the corruption in the facility. Tello Peon realized that Chapo was at least partly to blame. The drug lord had to be moved immediately to a new cell block, where his movements and interaction with other inmates would be far more restricted. That would be an adequate first step; perhaps later he could be transferred to another facility.

It would never happen.

El Chapo Guzman escaped
[*Journalist Joaquin Lopez*] Doriga gave the news [*broadcast*]
It was a very powerful story
for the government that day
They had never imagined

that El Chapo would escape
They had him sentenced
in Puente Grande prison
Chapo had big problems ahead of him . . .

How beautiful these escapes are
when there's no violence involved
My compa [*friend*] beat them fair and square
They had to pay many millions of greenbacks
to the director of the prison and his 32 colleagues
They handed in their papers
and now they're in prison

Where is El Chapo Guzman
they're looking for him all over . . .
If one day they do catch him
many people will die

Goodbye, Puente Grande
for me, it was never a jail
I felt like I was in my home
but still I couldn't get used to it
Goodbye, compa 'Guero' Palma
outside, I'll wait for you

'La Fuga del Chapo' ('Chapo's escape'), narco-corrido sung
    by El As de la Sierra

2. The Blame Game

As more than 500 agents from the PGR and members of the federal police and military scrambled throughout Mexico to find Chapo, the blame game went into full swing. State human rights officials pointed the finger at the National Human Rights Commission (known as the CNDH), saying they had ignored claims of corruption within Puente Grande. The PGR attacked the federal Public Security Secretariat, or SSP, which oversees the nation's penitentiary system, among other things.

Tello Peon wondered why it had taken so long for the prison to notify him of the escape, but received no answers. Press reports contradicted one another; the reliable newspaper *Reforma*, for instance, reported that the Army and federal police learned of the escape at 10 p.m., hours before Tello Peon was told — leading to more talk of large-scale complicity. *Reforma* even alleged that Chapo had been allowed to vanish by federal mandate, because he had so much information implicating high-ranking officials.

Some prison guards testified that the escape had occurred earlier in the evening, others claimed Chapo had fled several days before Tello Peon's visit. Holes in the story would remain, even after subsequent investigations. Confusion was the only certainty.

The search and arrests weren't without their own troubles, either. The jail guards who had been detained filed complaints, claiming to have been both abused and deprived of their rights. Mauricio Limon Aguirre, the governor of Jalisco, was livid that Tello Peon had not included state troopers in the hunt for this most notorious escaped convict. (The Army and federal police had taken over the chase, in large part because of worries that state police had been bought off by Chapo already.)

At a press conference on 22 January, Limon blasted the federal police chief: 'I believe there is a series of contradictions between what the federal authorities are saying and what they are doing,' he declared. 'Mr Tello Peon has [publicized] a telephone number for the public to call [with tip-offs on Chapo's whereabouts]. However, he has not asked for support from the state government, formally or informally.' Representatives of the PGR in Sinaloa made the same complaint. The public had been asked to help, but the local authorities had been sidelined.

Those locals may have been suspect in the federal government's eyes, but the phone number set up for the public wasn't exactly working miracles, either. In the days immediately following Chapo's escape, the federal police received about ten calls every five minutes through their hotline. Callers' anonymity was guaranteed, but no reward was offered, even though almost everyone who called asked about one. Some leads were followed, but the majority of calls, it turned out, were just kids having a laugh. 'Lamentably, people are interpreting this as a game, to joke around,' one police source told a local newspaper.

Tello Peon was having none of the jokes. 'What happened in Jalisco,' he pronounced, 'is evidence of the capacity of corruption – shall we say, the structural erosion of national institutions by organized crime, particularly drug trafficking. The prison bars and millions of pesos [invested] in security systems won't do anything if prisoners leave through the doors. They say that Mr Guzman didn't escape, that they let him out. They're right.'

Tello Peon again vowed to hunt Chapo down. 'It's all of our responsibility,' he said. 'We all have to work for the security of Mexico, we have to make the lives of people like [Chapo] impossible, whether they are known as a criminal fugitive or complicit civil servant.'

From that day, Chapo has been Mexico's most wanted man.

In 2001 alone, dozens of Chapo's associates were arrested in the cities of Reynosa, Puebla, Toluca and the nation's capital. Sinaloa and the neighbouring state of Nayarit would also experience a wave of busts.

In late summer of that year, Esteban Quintero Mariscal, a cousin and hired killer of Chapo's, was arrested and thrown into the Cefereso No. 1, Mexico's highest-security prison. The next day, El Chito, the prison guard who had helped Chapo escape, was captured and locked up in Mexico City's Reclusorio Preventivo Oriente.

Back in Guadalajara, in the immediate aftermath of the escape, El Chito had suffered a moment of serious panic. He had returned to the car with a bottle of water, only to find that Chapo had fled into the night. What should he do with the car? Should he take Chapo's advice and go on the run? He didn't have a way to contact the drug lord – could he manage to evade capture on his own?

El Chito had decided to leave the Chevrolet outside a girl-friend's house; she was fast asleep, so wouldn't ask any questions. He then took a taxi into the centre of Guadalajara, where he bought a bus ticket for Mexico City. He would be anonymous there; nobody would know or recognize him.

Still, the authorities caught up with him. Once in their hands he talked.

El Chito's testimony appeared to contradict much of what the government had thus far claimed. For one, El Chito claimed he had acted alone; he was the only person responsible for what 'El Senor' did, he told a judge in the prison. Furthermore, the escape had not been planned, El Chito said. He had been doing his rounds with the laundry cart when Chapo had summoned him into his cell.

Will you help me? the drug lord had asked. I can't face extradition, I need to get out of here right now.

El Chito estimated the entire escape had taken precisely fifteen minutes from that moment. He had wheeled out the laundry cart simply to help Chapo, with whom he sympathized. 'I wasn't paid one peso for the favour I did for Mr Guzman Loera.'

The authorities didn't buy it. Although there were still plenty of holes in their own reconstruction of the escape, they simply didn't believe that El Chito had been the only one involved in such a complicated, not to say embarrassing, affair.

The hunt continued. On 7 September the authorities' luck changed.

After a raid on a stash house in the eastern Mexico City neighbourhood of Iztapalapa, federal agents chased a trio of suspects all the way to the south of the city in Taxquena where they caught them. Among those detained was Arturo Guzman Loera, a.k.a. 'El Pollo' (the Chicken). They had nabbed Chapo's brother, the man who had run the Sinaloa drug business while his older sibling was locked up inside Puente Grande. Perhaps even more importantly, they had been led to Arturo by the captured cousin, Quintero Mariscal. If family was turning on family, they could be in luck.

That autumn of 2001, the dominoes would keep on falling. Big bust would follow big bust. In November military intelligence pinpointed Chapo's location to somewhere between the cities of Puebla and Cuernavaca. Federal agents moved in.

But by the time they got there, Chapo was once again long gone. They did capture a key accomplice, however, in Miguel Angel Trillo Hernandez. (He would later be transferred to Puente Grande, which by this point had jokingly come to be known as 'Puerta Grande', or Big Door.) Trillo had helped Chapo in the immediate aftermath of the escape, too, renting houses that the drug lord could hide in.

The authorities had more leads, but still no Chapo. On occasion, following tip-offs provided by detainees and anonymous locals, they had come within a whisker of catching him. They had discovered that Chapo was hiding out on a ranch outside the town of Santa Fe, Nayarit. The military deployed helicopters to close in on the area, but his cohort 'El Mayo' Zambada provided a chopper of his own to spirit Chapo away to safer ground in the Sierra.

They had also missed Chapo when he was hiding out in Toluca, about an hour outside the nation's capital. On one occasion Chapo's convoy had been travelling on the Mexico City–Toluca highway. One of their four cars had been stopped at a checkpoint. Chapo was in one of the other three that had been allowed through just moments before.

In the aftermath of his escape, he wasn't continually on the run. One federal police official revealed that Chapo had spent June to September hiding out in Zinacantepec, a town of about 130,000 outside Mexico City, prompting federal authorities to re-examine once again the possible complicity of local officials and police forces.

Two incidents in Nayarit, the state just south of Sinaloa, had proved to be the most disturbing. After his escape, Chapo had apparently hosted a big party in Nayarit, which was also considered his territory at the time. Such exposure should have allowed the authorities to catch him.

On another occasion the Army had received word that Chapo was in the hills in the state, near where the soldiers were busy destroying marijuana plantations. As they were preparing to close in, a Mexican Air Force plane flew directly over the area where Chapo was said to be hiding. If he had indeed been there, the plane had provided ample warning: by the time the soldiers arrived, he was nowhere to be found. Having someone in the Air Force on his payroll would be easy enough for a kingpin like Chapo, but such complicity was deeply worrying.

Rumours still abounded that Tello Peon had played a role in Chapo's escape. Only a high-level government insider such as he could have orchestrated the break, the cynics whispered; he must be in Chapo's pocket.

Tello Peon denied the allegations. But they took their toll. Towards the end of 2001 he resigned from his post, and from public office, citing personal reasons.

But as the year came to a close, the authorities still had hope. They had learned that Chapo had taken the capture of his brother hard; informants who had been with the narco in Puebla in October said he had considered suicide for some time following the capture of Arturo.

The fall of nearly a handful of Chapo's top logistics and security men had also apparently pummelled his morale. He would fall soon, the authorities maintained; the only place for such criminals was in jail.

But Chapo ignored the rhetoric. He was still free.

3. From Gomeros to Gods

When he was born, the midwife asked
what will they call him
By last name, he'd be Guzman Loera
and he'll be called Joaquin
As a boy he sold oranges over there in the Sierra
just so he could eat
He was never ashamed of this
on the contrary, he said it was a matter of pride

For those who don't know who Guzman Loera is
with pleasure I'll talk to you
Supported by El Mayo, by Nacho and Juanito
and friends from around there
He's part of the cartel
the strongest that exists
It's pure Culiacan
I wear the shirt with pride
I am El Chapo Guzman

'El Hijo de La Tuna' ('The Son of La Tuna'), narco-corrido sung
    by Roberto Tapia

The hills around La Tuna de Badiraguato, Sinaloa, rise steep and
fast. Dirt roads lead out of town; in the distance, the red bulbs of
opium poppy dot the high-altitude terrain. There are purple bulbs,
too; and some hillside fields are filled with white bulbs that from
the air look like snow.

It was here, in the north-west of Mexico, that Chinese mer-
chants first introduced opium to the western hemisphere in the

nineteenth century. And it was here, in this tiny hamlet of just a few hundred inhabitants, that Joaquin Guzman Loera was born on 4 April 1957.

La Tuna had about 200 residents back then, all crammed into little more than a dozen small homes scattered below a ridge that peaks at 1,400 metres above sea level. La Tuna still has about 200 inhabitants today; apart from a large *finca*, or ranch, that Chapo built for his mother, the lie of the land remains largely the same. There are two roads heading into the town, two roads leading out of it. An airstrip on the outskirts is the principal means of getting there and away.

Like every other man in La Tuna, Chapo's father Emilio Guzman Bustillos was, at least officially, a cattle rancher and farmer. Save a few tomato and orange patches in the pueblo, the local economy ostensibly revolved around cattle. Life was tough in this part of the Sierra, as it still is today. Most of La Tuna's inhabitants live in small, two-room homes with dirt floors. There is no clean, drinkable water in the area. There is no sewage system of any kind. Children walk barefoot through the town and up the hillsides. Hospitals and schools are luxuries not afforded to the people of this part of the Sierra.

A decent education was not in the cards for Joaquin, who as a young boy had earned the common Sinaloan nickname 'Chapo', meaning 'short and stocky'. The nearest real school was about sixty miles away, so he and his sisters Armida and Bernarda, and his brothers Miguel Angel, Aureliano, Arturo and Emilio, were taught by visiting teachers. They were largely volunteers, and would spend three to six months in La Tuna before rotating out. School supplies and books were scarce, and the children would study until the age of only twelve, at best. Then they would have to work land so unforgiving that most could barely afford to live, and could only hope and pray for a better life than the lot they'd inherited.

Hamlets like La Tuna are neglected backwaters. There is no government, just one citizen of the town who ostensibly reports back to the municipal authorities. There's a famous story of a newly elected state congressman who visits one of the more far-flung villages in his district. Addressing the locals in the square he pulls no punches. 'Take a good, long look at my face . . . because this is the last time you are going to see it in this shithole of a pueblo.' As the tale goes, the congressman stuck to his promise.

Most people in Badiraguato look down their nose at the deep Sierra, much like residents of Culiacan sniff at Badiraguato. One member of the mayor's staff was particularly blunt in his assessment of the village where Chapo grew up: 'Why would you want to go to La Tuna? It's fucked there.'

Domestic violence is rampant in the Sierra, as is child abuse. Young girls are sometimes raped by their fathers and uncles; women effectively have no rights. Mothers are revered by their sons, but once those sons marry, the cycle of abuse continues with their new wives. The majority of the Sierra's population is illiterate. Alcoholism is rampant. Life has little value. When they are young, locals snap the necks of chickens; when they grow older, some don't hesitate to snap the necks of their fellow men.

Sinaloa's politicians admit that the situation is bad in the Sierra, but that doesn't mean they're doing anything about it. 'People in the Sierra who work in drug trafficking – [it's because] we haven't offered them opportunities for development so that people will realize crime doesn't pay,' lamented Sinaloa congressman Aaron Irizar Lopez, a former mayor of Culiacan, as we talked over breakfast in the lobby of a hotel in the city on a hot summer morning. 'People over there are born into drug trafficking. [And] people are like computers – what you put in is what they do.'

As the congressman spoke, a group of narco-wives eating brunch in the hotel laughed loudly at a long table behind him. Dolled up with painted nails and hair-dos straight out of a mafia movie, they would spend the next three hours sipping champagne and chatting, before finally leaving in their sports cars and SUVs – some of which didn't have licence plates. The hotel staff served them quietly, waiting for them to leave before whispering about them. Most of the narcos' wives come from Culiacan and its environs; it's common knowledge that talking publicly about them – particularly in a negative light – carries a high price.

Irizar, a kind-looking man in his fifties who clearly knows the limits of politics, is well respected in Sinaloa. As mayor, he pledged to crack down on certain illicit activities – prostitution, for instance – and received death threats as a result. But he persevered, in spite of his fear. 'To say I wasn't scared would be lying. But we need a change of attitude. We're living in a time when democracy isn't meeting the expectations of the public.' During our meeting, several passers-by came up to him and greeted him; shaking his hand, they wished him the best of luck in turning things around. He smiled, and wished them the best of luck as well.

Irizar is pushing particularly hard for a programme to instil values in the Sierra – where 'the drug bosses will kill fathers and kidnap mothers' – and is extremely eager to get youth projects off the ground throughout his home state. The congressman grew up in a small town about fifty miles from Culiacan; he admits that some of his peers from his schooldays became narcos. 'Some are in jail, some are dead,' he said, smiling sadly. 'Others are rich.'

Like most Mexicans who grow up in this impoverished mountain region, the young Chapo wanted out. His father beat him regularly and, when he was in his teens, kicked him out of the house. He went to live with his grandfather. Day and night he worked the fields. It was no childhood of any kind, he would recall to Zulema Hernandez while in jail. When he recounted his stories to her, Chapo would back himself up against the cold, concrete walls – 'as if it was something he just wanted to forget, and yet at the same time, it had him imprisoned every moment of his life'.

But unlike his predecessors, he would have an escape. As Chapo was growing up in Sinaloa, another industry was growing quietly and quickly around him. In the aftermath of the Second World War, with US war veterans requiring medicinal morphine and others seeking out illicit heroin to ease their postwar pain, Sinaloa's agricultural sector was diversifying. Opium was becoming a quick ticket out of abysmal poverty; acceptance of marijuana in the United States in the 1960s and 1970s was creating demand for another illicit product the Sinaloans could grow.

Chapo's father may have officially been a cattle rancher, but according to locals who remember La Tuna back then, he was actually a *gomero*, or opium poppy farmer, like everyone else in the town. Although they worked for higher-ups – at that time, the bosses were the local politicians, law enforcement operators and their kin – the gomeros ran their operations as family businesses.

Everyone worked: every morning at dawn, the sons – at least, those between the ages of eleven and about eighteen – would hike a couple of hours up the hillside to their poppy patch and begin work on the harvest. Carefully, they would cut the bud of the poppy, from which the prized opium gum would ooze like molasses. (A kilo of gum would earn the family about 8,000 pesos, or $700, today.) All the while, the mother and daughters would cook lunch, which any younger sons would then hoist on their backs and carry up to their brothers in the early afternoon.

The father's role wasn't only that of a farmer, but also of a businessman. He would negotiate the sale of the harvest with the next link in the chain, and the opium would be hauled off to Culiacan or another nearby city like Guamuchil. The industry works much the same way today.

Chapo's own father was lucky enough to be connected to the higher-ups in the Sinaloan capital of Culiacan through a relative, Pedro Aviles Perez. A key player in the Sinaloa drug business, Aviles Perez is seen as a pioneer, finding new methods of transporting the rural produce to the urban areas for shipment. He was also reputedly the first to make use of planes to fly cocaine to the United States.

For a family of *campesinos*, or peasant farmers, that was a mighty step. By the time he was in his twenties, the young Chapo would have a window to escape the horrific poverty that entrapped his predecessors and peers.

Roots of Rebellion

'If you confuse the sky and the earth, green with red; if you've forgotten how to figure out a square root and you don't know what to do with your compass, the morning or love, you've arrived in Sinaloa.'

– Elmer Mendoza, Sinaloan writer

Sinaloa wasn't always about drugs, but even before the narcos and US demand for illicit substances, it had been about lawlessness. It has always been lawless – and violent. 'The character of the Sinaloan is that of an angel and a devil,' said local historian and sociologist Martin Amaral.

Often throughout history, the angel has been well hidden; sometimes, it's been completely buried.

During the pre-Hispanic period – prior to 1519 – various indigenous groups lived in the Sierra. The region was isolated and they rarely came down to the valleys. Some nomadic groups passed through the region, including the Aztecs, and the mountains were often safer, in spite of the harsh conditions. Still, one group known as the Huey Colhuacan eventually settled in the area that is now Culiacan, its three rivers and the vegetation of the valley far more attractive than the difficult life in the mountains.

For several hundred years, the Huey Colhuacan lived undisturbed on the banks of the three local rivers now known as the Humaya, Tamazula and Culiacan. Their settlement was known as Colhuacan, which loosely translates as 'Those who worship the god Coltzin'. The Huey Colhuacan numbered only a few hundred, and lived a largely peaceful existence.

Then, in 1531, the Spanish came. Having finally conquered the Aztecs in 1521, they were expanding their reach. On 29 September

1531, Nuno Beltran de Guzman, a conquistador who had set out two years before from the capital of New Spain to colonize the west, renamed the area San Miguel de Culiacan. It rapidly became a strategic point for the Spanish conquerors, who were now seeking not only to extend the reaches of New Spain but to introduce God.

They would have their work cut out for them. Just four years after the founding of San Miguel de Culiacan, a smallpox epidemic killed hundreds of indigenous locals and Spaniards alike. While they set about founding cities like Mazatlan on the coast and Sinaloa de Leyva in the foothills of the Sierra Madre, and building missions and forts throughout what is now the state of Sinaloa, the Spaniards quickly discovered that imposing their idea of order on the indigenous groups in the area would be difficult, if not impossible.

Although dispersed, the indigenous tribes were fiercely united on one front: a hatred of outsiders. As a result, a majority of Spaniards simply moved on – a large part of their quest, after all, was to head north and expand – while those who stayed on interbred with the locals despite facing the imminent prospect of death.

Locals even killed two friars – 'the indians didn't want more Spanish on their lands,' wrote one historian – and the Spanish gradually withdrew their presence from this hostile territory.

Then, on 6 July 1591, the Jesuits arrived. A Catholic order that had been sanctioned by the Pope to lead the Counter-Reformation, they founded missions in the Sierra and throughout the lowlands along the coast. It was the Jesuits who would come closest to imposing order on Sinaloa. Avoiding the Spanish approach of colonization by enslavement, they sought to gain the confidence of the indigenous peoples. The missionaries learned the language and regularly visited communities.

Within a year, more than 1,000 indigenous people in San Miguel de Culiacan and its environs had been converted, and the Jesuits hoped for many more. They were betting on what they optimistically perceived to be the 'docility' of the Sinaloans – even if they rather timidly surrounded themselves with Spanish soldiers when visiting the pueblos in the Sierra. The locals didn't mind listening to their spiel, the Jesuits realized; they even appeared open to change.

Walking through Culiacan today is like navigating a maze of the unknowable. The city centre bustles like any other: the faithful file in for mass as the church bells ring; the elderly sit in the park and discuss the news of the day or the weather; young school kids walk along the streets teasing each other and flirting; taxi drivers yell out of their cab windows.

But the underworld is ever present: near the city's small yet teeming market, young men loiter on street corners. Some of them sell drugs, others are simply hanging around. At market stalls and in shops, locals welcome outsiders politely; but nearly everyone is clearly wondering why you are there.

Turning your back and ignoring your instincts in Culiacan is tantamount to suicide, according to one DEA agent.

'The indigenous weren't as docile as the Jesuits had believed,' said historian Sergio Ortega Noriega. In 1594, just three years after the Jesuits had arrived, those tensions came to a head. An indigenous man named Nacabeba rounded up a group of fellow rebels. They killed a missionary.

Miguel Ortiz Maldonado, effectively the Spanish governor of Sinaloa, gathered his troops and captured the insurgents. They were executed. But to prevent the rebellion from spreading further throughout the region, Ortiz Maldonado also effectively expelled the Jesuits, ordering them to retreat to San Miguel de Culiacan.

Missions were still maintained, but the Jesuits adopted a lower-key approach. As one Culiacan history student puts it, 'The Jesuits were the best rulers Sinaloa ever had – they let us rule ourselves.' Jesuit relations with the Spanish, meanwhile, only deteriorated. In July 1767 the Spanish expelled the Jesuits from Sinaloa altogether.

Over subsequent decades, Sinaloa became lawless again, subject only to the whims of its own people and their hot-blooded temperament. Tumultuous times followed. The Spanish who remained in charge grew accustomed to an easy, less law-abiding life in the New World.

In late 1810, with Mexico in the midst of its war of independence from Spain, the indigenous population of Badiraguato took up arms, too. Within months their homeland was rid of the Spanish; on 25 February 1811 the locals declared their independence.

Since then, the Mexican Army, local government and tribal-like rulers (strongmen, smugglers and narcos) have rarely been on the same page, almost always at odds, but somehow coexisting.

The worst sort of criminal has always found himself welcome in Sinaloa. An accessible coastline and mountains in which to hide are the main draw for smugglers, while the lack of proper governance is an equally appealing trait to Mexico's *bandidos*.

In the early part of the twentieth century, even the legendary revolutionary Francisco 'Pancho' Villa made his home in the Sierra Madre, in the foothills of what is now the state of Chihuahua. On the run from both Mexican and US forces throughout his life, Villa hid out in the Sierra, and eventually met his maker in the mountain town of Hidalgo de Parral.

By the 1960s the culture of illegality was so entrenched in Sinaloa that the mythical bandit Jesus Malverde enjoyed cult-like status among locals. Legend had it that the moustachioed bandit had robbed from the rich and given to the poor in the late 1800s, before he was supposedly caught and hanged on 3 May 1909.

Malverde's legacy would flourish. Even today, a century later, thousands of devout followers flock to his shrine in Culiacan every month to commemorate his life and death, and to appeal for his assistance just as they might to the Virgin of Guadalupe, the nation's most revered symbol.

Criminals consider Malverde a sort of 'narco-saint', while the authorities denounce his celebration as a blight on society. 'Often, the government doesn't give to the people, so they turn to the narcos,' said law student Jesus Manuel Gonzalez Sanchez, who has run the Malverde shrine in Culiacan since his father, the founder, passed away. 'Malverde is just a symbol of this.'

Violence is rife in Sinaloa. In the 1960s, just as in centuries past, land disputes in the Sierra often ended up with killings. Machetes were still a popular weapon among campesinos (today, modernity has arrived; easily obtained guns tend to be the weapon of choice). Old-fashioned duels – disputes resolved through shootouts at dawn, with pistols – still occur.

While there is no doubt that the absence of the rule of law plays a big part in this culture, some locals put it down to the temperament of the people (*caliente*, or hot-blooded) while others simply blame the climate (equally hot). Psychoanalyst Luis Ricardo Ruiz, who works with Sinaloan drug addicts today, is blunt in his assessment of the roots of his people's violence. 'Drugs won't bring out something that isn't already in you. A butcher is a butcher.'

It was on these foundations that both Culiacan and the drug trade grew. Culiacan had maintained its geographic isolation until the 1940s, only then accepting a wave of Greek and Chinese immigrants arriving on Sinaloan shores. But in the mid-twentieth century a new train line from Mexico City, which passed through Guadalajara, would prompt an influx of Mexicans of all types. Culiacan became a boom town, growing at a pace that has yet to slow.

By the 1960s, ranches outside the city owned by the wealthy were being surrounded by middle- and lower-class housing. Industry was giving the city a financial boost, and agriculture was flourishing. So was smuggling; locals who grew up in Culiacan in the 1960s remember vividly how vendors would sell goods from the United States – which were banned from import by the federal government – all along the streets and in the markets of the city. Whereas even in a cosmopolitan capital like Mexico City such items such as clothes and shoes were still hard to come by, up north they were all the rage in Sinaloa. Middle-class kids wanted for little.

There was no social condemnation of illegal activity in Sinaloa, so why would growing or trafficking in drugs be deemed wrong? Even the United States hadn't really begun its war on illicit narcotics yet. (Conspiracy theories persist today that after the Second World War, the Mexican and US governments came to an agreement through which the Sinaloans would extra-legally provide the US with heroin, but most experts dispute their veracity.) The men in charge of the drug trade were largely politicians or members of a social elite. Some were in agriculture, some were in imports. They were businessmen, not narcos.

The word 'narco' didn't even exist back then. Those who worked in the drug trade – the men and women who got their hands dirty growing or transporting marijuana and opium – were either known as gomeros or the more derogatory *buchones*. Living in the Sierra, the buchones rarely ate salt, a hard-to-come-by commodity. So they often developed gout, which can lead to a swollen neck – hence *buchon*, which is a play on the pouch some birds have on their throats to store food. Today, the word has come to be associated simply with anyone who makes money illegally; many younger Sinaloans even believe it derives from the gold chains worn around the narcos' necks.

Back in the 1960s and 1970s the gold chains and flashy clothes, so often spotted today in cities like Culiacan, were nowhere to be seen. While the buchones went about the hard work, the capos simply went about their business. Of course, they had their sports cars and designer clothes, and some threw lavish parties at opulent mansions. But by now the wealth displayed was classy, and the parties were held in governors' residences, empresarios' ranches. There was nothing ostentatious or sinister about it, in large part because the government and big business effectively endorsed it.

Miguel Angel Felix Gallardo, a former policeman-turned-politician's bodyguard who by the 1980s would become the godfather of the drug trade (earning him the nickname of 'El Padrino'), walked the streets of Culiacan. Ernesto 'Don Neto' Fonseca, from Santiago de los Caballeros in the hills beyond Badiraguato, kept a quiet home in the city. They were just businessmen.

Chapo and his future partners, the Beltran Leyva brothers (Marcos Arturo, Alfredo, Hector, Mario and Carlos), meanwhile, were eking out a living in the Sierra, another bunch of buchones. They were nobodies.

The War on Drugs

By the 1970s the Sinaloa drug trade had become the dominant part of a national business. It was flourishing. Cocaine was brought in from Colombia on boats and planes, and the Sinaloans would haul it up across the American border in trucks. Sometimes they used light planes. Marijuana and cocaine were rapidly becoming acceptable in liberal America, and the drug trade was booming.

It was also attracting a lot of attention. The US government was rapidly awakening to the growing drug consumption within its borders, which it perceived as a threat to the fabric of society. On 17 June 1971 President Richard Nixon declared that drug abuse had 'assumed the dimensions of a national emergency'. He appealed to Congress for $155 million to combat drug use and trafficking (domestically and internationally), his goal being to turn back a 'tide which has swept the country in the past decade and which afflicts both the body and soul of America'.

Within two years, the DEA would be created. In 1974, having warned that 'Mexican mud', or heroin, was 'suddenly in great demand', the DEA would declare that Mexican traffickers controlled 75 per cent of the US heroin market. 'An all-out global war on the drug menace' had begun.

The Sinaloa drug trade – and, by some counts, Sinaloa itself – would only just survive the initial stages of this US-led onslaught. On 26 January 1974 Operation SEA/M (Special Enforcement Activity in Mexico) was launched in Sinaloa to combat opium and heroin trafficking. In 1976 the DEA and the Mexican government launched a larger joint poppy eradication programme in the Golden Triangle. (The CIA was also rumoured to be involved.) Helicopters, donated by the American State Department, were employed to dump herbicides throughout the hills of Durango, Chihuahua and, of course, Sinaloa, which was the primary focus of the operation. After a year, about 22,000 acres of poppy – enough to produce eight tons of heroin – had been completely destroyed.

The DEA hailed the success of Operation Trizo, as it was known. 'By 1979 the purity of Mexican heroin fell to just five per cent, its lowest level in seven years,' stated the official history of the counter-drug initiative. 'In addition, 4,000 members of organizations in Mexico were arrested. Operation Trizo lessened the demand for Mexican heroin in the US market.'

But many residents of the Sierra remember *la limpieza* (the cleansing) less fondly. It coincided with a Mexican anti-drug operation, Condor, and wiped them out. In fact those '4,000 members of organizations' were mostly buchones or other residents of the Sierra unfortunate enough to be lumped in with them. As some American agents would admit years later, not one major trafficker was arrested. And the consequences of the spraying and arrests in the Sierra were too drastic. As many as 2,000 communities were abandoned or destroyed.

People displaced from the Sierra migrated to the city, where they formed 'great lines of misery', recalls 'El Padrino' Felix Gallardo. 'The lack of space and employment pushed them into crime or they died of hunger, the kids didn't go to school, they were social rejects and they took jobs in whatever they could . . . Working in the city was different from what they knew how to do.'

Those who chose to stay on in the Sierra suffered immensely. Thousands of soldiers patrolled the area unchecked, allegedly stealing whatever crops or animals those who stayed behind had managed to nurture. Homes were searched and destroyed. In many cases, small towns were decimated; only a few dozen elderly residents remained behind.

Eventually bowing to public pressure, the Mexican government temporarily broke off its partnership with the DEA, and in 1978 Operation Trizo was put permanently on hold. Sinaloa's principal traffickers hadn't come close to seeing the inside of a prison. They had won the first of many battles.

Shortly after Operation Trizo, El Padrino took control of the Sinaloa drug business. With the help of 'Don Neto' Fonseca and Caro Quintero, he would run the show. El Padrino was the point man for all of the drugs coming through and going out of Mexico, from every corner of the fifth-largest nation in the western hemisphere.

But he was only the point man: the Colombians were still in charge of it all.

Even well into the 1980s there were two major drug cartels in Latin America – the Medellin and Cali groups, both named after cities in Colombia. The DEA and Interpol (and, in some cases, US military special forces) were focused on these two major suppliers of cocaine and heroin to the United States. The Mexicans involved in drug trafficking were still largely just 'mules'. The Colombians would ship tons of their illegal drugs to Mexican shores, and the Mexicans would simply move them across the border to the United States.

Moving the drugs across the 2,000-mile border wasn't such a difficult task, it just required manpower and bribery. Thousands of trucks cross the US–Mexico border each day, at dozens of key routes. There was no way that even normally watchful border guards could monitor all the contraband coming in; for the right amount of money, their counterparts on the Mexican side would simply look the other way. On the rare occasion the authorities did crack down, clandestine airstrips and light planes ensured that the drugs would get across just as easily.

This was eventually to be Chapo's job. In the late 1970s Sinaloan capo 'El Guero' Palma Salazar gave Chapo his first big break, placing him in charge of transporting drugs from the Sierra to the cities and the border and overseeing shipments.

According to local lore, Chapo was ambitious.

He was eager to increase the quantities of drugs being transported north, and would press his bosses to allow him to do so. He was also no-nonsense. If a delivery wasn't made from the Sierra, or was delayed for some reason (even heavy rains, which would wash away entire roads, were no excuse), he would execute the employee himself.

He didn't lose his temper, he just shot the man in the head. The gomeros in the Sierra, too, knew better than to try and rip Chapo off by selling their drugs to another buyer, even if a higher price was being offered.

The bosses noted his style, and in the early 1980s Chapo was introduced to El Padrino himself. He was put in charge of logistics – effectively, coordinating plane flights, boat arrivals and trucks coming from Colombia into Mexico. El Guero continued to make sure the deliveries travelled safely by land to clients in the United States.

Soon, Chapo would prove worthy of working directly with El Padrino himself.

4. The Godfather

Born on the outskirts of Culiacan on 8 January 1946, El Padrino rose rapidly through the ranks of the drug trade. A policeman until his mid-twenties, he left the force to serve as a security escort for the then-Sinaloa governor Leopoldo Sanchez Celis. It was in that position he is believed to have learned about the drug trade in the state, which was governed by Celis's Institutional Revolutionary Party (PRI).

The PRI, which ruled Mexico with an iron grip between 1929 and 2000, is widely blamed for allowing the drug trade to flourish, as its governance was tainted by corruption of the most insidious kind. The current government of Mexico is a conservative one led by the National Action Party (PAN); but the PRI still controls more than half of Mexico's state governorships, prompting widespread accusations from other parties that it continues to look the other way (at the very best) from drug trafficking. 'Sinaloa is a symbiosis of crime and politics,' said Manuel Clouthier Carrillo, a descendant of one of Culiacan's first wealthy families and an impassioned member of the PAN, which his father helped found.

US officials have lamented the situation, too. 'Political protection is difficult to prove [in Mexico],' a US border state prosecutor explained. 'If we could prove it, we'd have them all under indictment. There's a big difference between knowing something and proving it in a court of law . . . You have extremely reliable intelligence sources, but unless you can prove it, why burn your sources? You'd have their body parts spread all over Sonora.'

El Padrino rose through this politico-criminal system. And not content with being just a lackey, he sought to build his own empire. Through his connections with a major Honduran trafficker, Juan Ramon Matta-Ballesteros, El Padrino became the main man in

Mexico for the Medellin cartel, which was run by Pablo Escobar. Through his political connections, El Padrino ensured that the right people all the way up Mexico's Pacific coast were in his pocket, from politicians to policemen. He also oversaw the distribution of local marijuana and opium, which could easily be shipped north along with the Colombians' produce. He was the lord of Mexican drug lords – he oversaw everything in the country. 'There were no cartels' at that time in Mexico, recalls El Padrino now. There was just him, his cronies and the politicians who offered him protection.

El Padrino was a soft-spoken man, devoted to his family. Almost always working, and travelling throughout Mexico frequently to keep an eye on his business, he lived in one house while his eighteen children lived in two others near by. He owned properties in every state of Mexico, most of which were used for business. Obsessed with electronics – he had every new type of gadget on the market – he lived a relatively quiet life.

Aside from his huge collection of Italian designer shoes and clothes, and a few sports cars, he appeared to be just like everyone else – at least, everyone else who was wealthy. His ranch complex on the outskirts of Culiacan was splendid, but not ostentatious. He collected fine watches but never wore them. He knew not to attract too much attention. While still living in Culiacan, he shifted the centre of his operations to Guadalajara; it would be less conspicuous there, given all the heat on Sinaloa after Operation Trizo.

Chapo learned how to survive and thrive in the drug trade from El Padrino. He was already living quietly, without much fanfare or extracurricular activity. In 1977 he married Alejandrina Maria Salazar Hernandez, in a small wedding in the town of Jesus Maria, Sinaloa. It wasn't even covered by the local tabloids, which at the time routinely reported on society activities in the area, including those of the big-time traffickers.

Chapo had three children with Salazar Hernandez: Cesar, Ivan Archivaldo and Jesus Alfredo. He set up a home on a ranch in the small town, about sixty miles outside of Culiacan on the road to

Badiraguato. The family didn't host big parties, and were rarely seen in the big city. Chapo may have been drawn to the wealth that drug trafficking offered, but he was not interested in becoming part of the social elite, preferring instead to spend his non-working hours drinking whiskey with his closest confidants or caring for his family. Like his mentor El Padrino, he is believed to have spent the majority of his time working, travelling to oversee shipments and doing deals.

By the mid-1980s Chapo had remarried, this time to Griselda Lopez Perez, with whom he had another four children: Edgar, Joaquin, Ovidio and Griselda Guadalupe. At the same time, according to the DEA, the young man from La Tuna de Badiraguato had not only become a family man, he had established himself as one of El Padrino's right-hand men. Indeed, he was ready to become a *patron* or boss in his own right.

Chapo was ready to be in charge. He had developed a keen sense of business and a ruthless manner of executing it. Incompetence or mistakes were not tolerated; anyone who crossed him was simply crossed off the list. He and his associate 'El Mayo' were purportedly making strong connections, too, with the mayor of Culiacan, for instance.

By the mid-1980s – the vehemently anti-drug Reagan era – Mexico was ready to become its own boss, too. Anti-drug efforts by the Colombian authorities with US support would soon topple Escobar and his Medellin cartel. Colombian cocaine was still flowing fast to the United States, but the previously well-organized, tight-knit Colombian groups were losing their clout, and the Mexicans saw an opportunity – at least, that's how the Sinaloans remember it. The DEA maintains that it was the Colombians who realized it would be more profitable to give the Mexicans more control, as they would no longer have to risk monitoring shipments all the way to the American border and watch over every move the Mexicans made themselves.

For years, the Mexican narcos had followed the Colombian model and worked for their counterparts, smuggling as much as twenty tons of cocaine a month into California and similar amounts into Texas, to be taken up to the east coast of the United States. Now, the Mexicans were capos in their own right. They could also produce their own marijuana and heroin (later, meth-amphetamine would appear on the menu) and smuggle that into the United States in the same way they were moving the cocaine. They could run Mexico and the western hemisphere, rather than have the Colombians run it for them.

But as the Mexicans obtained more clout, the DEA would once again emerge as a threat to the Sinaloan bosses.

The DEA in the Fray

At the time, the DEA's work on the ground in Mexico was laden with risk. Corruption on the Mexican side was rampant, and no one in the DEA knew whom to trust. The agents had orders to go undercover and nurture trustworthy sources and informants, but they were largely operating alone, without diplomatic protection or immunity. They simply headed over into Mexico from Arizona, or whatever border state they were stationed in, and made contact with local police forces. They hoped for the best; their modus operandi was to do 'as much damage as you possibly can', according to Michael Vigil, a former DEA agent who was stationed in Mexico for more than a decade.

There was 'no protection at all', Vigil recalls. 'It was basically analogous to iron-man football. We had no padding . . . we had no protection, and we took tremendous hits on both sides of the border politically.'

On one occasion, Vigil and another agent, Enrique 'Kiki' Camarena, organized a raid on an isolated marijuana ranch in Sonora. They had received reliable intelligence that there were armed guards on the ranch, so they rented a truck and requested about thirty soldiers from the Mexican military. When they got there, bullets began 'flying all over the place'. The soldiers returned fire, and all but one of the narcos fled. After about thirty minutes of resistance, the last man eventually fell.

The Mexican military, much as it does today, had a take-no-prisoners approach; it cared even less for the judicial process. To erase any doubt prosecutors might have over whether the dead man was linked to drug trafficking, a group of soldiers stuffed his pockets with raw marijuana. Such was the way of justice at the time. 'Mexico knew that it had a war on its hands,' recalls Vigil. 'At that time there were no human rights . . . per se. They did what was necessary in terms of stemming the drug-related violence . . . It was a very harsh rule of law.'

The DEA's modus operandi then as now meant putting its best men's lives at risk, as the groundwork had to be done in person by someone trustworthy. The agent would meet with a trafficker, sometimes in broad daylight, in border cities like Nogales, Sonora. He would go out to the man's home – or to an unknown location – and procure the heroin or marijuana. The agent had no real backup, and because his meetings often took place out in the open at the dealer's request, he could easily be compromised once arrests were made on the other side of the border, if word of DEA involvement got out.

'The times were very tough,' according to Vigil. But the DEA had its best men in Mexico, he adds; they had 'intestinal fortitude and . . . a lot of ingenuity. This was like a human chess game.'

In late 1984 the tensions came to a head. Camarena, an eleven-year DEA veteran by that point, had become particularly intrepid. Based in Guadalajara, he managed to infiltrate deep into the drug trafficking world of the Golden Triangle. He had even become close with some of the country's major traffickers, El Padrino among them.

Acting on information provided by Camarena, 450 Mexican soldiers backed by helicopters closed in on a 1,000-hectare marijuana plantation known as 'Rancho Bufalo', just on the eastern side of the Sierra Madre in the northern state of Chihuahua. More than 10,000 farmers worked these fields, the annual production of which was later valued at $8 billion. The drug lords were outraged and apprehensive about what they saw as not only a security breach but also perhaps even a betrayal from within.

These fears were not unwarranted. Unlike in the past, when some DEA agents had simply been content with the Mexicans locking up the usual suspects (low-level farmers), Camarena wanted to take down the top guys. He was working on projects aimed at identifying the country's top narcos and pinpointing their whereabouts. One was called 'Operation Godfather' – targeting El Padrino.

But on 7 February 1985 Camarena took a break from work to meet his wife for lunch in Guadalajara. A car pulled up and five men jumped out. One identified himself as a Mexican police officer. They grabbed Camarena and shoved him inside. He was never seen alive again.

The abduction prompted DEA outrage. Mexican police had apparently been involved in the incident, yet Los Pinos – the presidential residence in Mexico City, akin to the White House – was doing nothing. Washington pressed the anti-drug agency to simply accept what had happened – 'You will do nothing about it because the politics of Mexico and the US are too important,' the DEA was effectively told. 'A DEA agent is expendable in the overall political game.'

The anti-drug boys weren't about to give in so easily. 'Nobody's gonna kill a DEA agent and have some other agency say to us it doesn't matter in the overall political scheme of things,' recalls one former DEA man.

So the DEA acted, through Operation Leyenda – the largest DEA homicide investigation ever undertaken. A special DEA unit was dispatched to coordinate the investigation in Mexico – where corrupt officials were being implicated – and twenty-five special agents were sent to Guadalajara to search independently. For the next month, they stormed ranches and quizzed locals and informants for intelligence. They followed any leads they could. The DEA soon came to its conclusion, and asked the Mexican federal police to 'consider' Rafael Caro Quintero, 'El Padrino' Felix Gallardo and 'Don Neto' Fonseca as the primary suspects in the kidnapping.

The search led to a field in the central state of Michoacan, where they found two bodies; an American pathologist and forensic team performed an autopsy. Their conclusion: one of the dead was Camarena. He had been tortured for at least two days and eventually died from 'blunt force injuries to the head', resulting in a 'crushed skull'.

Additional arrests – including five police officers who admitted to being part of a conspiracy to kidnap and torture Camarena – laid the blame squarely on the shoulders of Caro Quintero and Fonseca. They were quickly detained, too, and gave statements admitting the DEA agent's abduction – but not his murder. That was the work of El Padrino, they claimed.

El Padrino still enjoyed political protection. But he was wanted by the US authorities for 'the kidnapping and murder of Camarena, racketeering, violent crimes in aid of racketeering, conspiracy to commit violent crimes in aid of racketeering, possession and conspiracy to possess with intent to distribute cocaine . . .': the Department of Justice's list went on. The arrest of Caro Quintero and Fonseca was proof enough that the DEA could crack the whip on the Mexicans if it wanted, and that the Mexicans could and would make arrests when they really wanted to as well.

So in 1987 El Padrino moved with his family to set up camp permanently in Guadalajara. He moved into a house in a nondescript residential neighbourhood, while his wife, mistress and their children occupied two others near by. Guadalajara offered more anonymity than Culiacan or any other Sinaloan city.

El Padrino also decided to divide up the trade he controlled – it would be more efficient, more organized and more self-sufficient – and less likely to be brought down in one fell law enforcement swoop.

In effect he was privatizing the Mexican drug business and opening up the market. But he was also sending it back underground, to be run by bosses who were less well known and not yet on the Americans' radar. None was implicated in the killing of Camarena. None had a long, publicized history of criminality. All of them could develop new ties with the Mexican political system and police (money was no problem, after all), and if they remained local, sticking to their respective patches of turf, they could control the business even more tightly.

El Padrino convened the nation's top narcos at a house in the southern resort city of Acapulco, and laid out his plans for the future. The divvying up of the *plazas*, as the drug routes are known, was pretty simple.

The Tijuana route would go to the Arellano Felix brothers, who contrary to subsequent press reports and government statements were not El Padrino's nephews; they were, however, originally from Culiacan and he had known the family during his life there. Ciudad Juarez, with its all-important trucking routes into Texas, would go to the Carrillo Fuentes family, from Guamuchilito, Sinaloa, under the supervision of a high-ranking security force contact of El Padrino's.

Rafael Caro Quintero's brother Miguel, originally from La Noria in the hills of Badiraguato, would run the Sonora side of the business – in other words, the key trucking/smuggling routes through Arizona. In their early days, Miguel and his brothers had shown real entrepreneurial vision, rising from being just local marijuana growers to partners with 'Don Neto', and El Padrino knew he could trust Miguel to run Sonora without there being much conflict with Sinaloa just to the south.

Over on Mexico's north-east coast in Matamoros, Tamaulipas, Juan Garcia Abrego would retain control of operations. Having forged close ties with the Colombians since 1985, the man who would be credited with having founded the Gulf cartel was a capo in his own right, and would not be disturbed.

Meanwhile in Sinaloa, Chapo and 'El Mayo' Zambada would take over Pacific coast operations. They would bring 'El Guero' Palma Salazar back into the fold (he had fallen out with El Padrino in the 1970s, and had sought to establish his own operation). Working with their fellow Sinaloans to the north in Sonora, they would move their drugs through into Arizona and parts of California. Chapo was given control over the smuggling corridor of Tecate.

El Padrino still planned to oversee national operations; he had the contacts, so he was still the top man. But he would no longer control the entire business as a one-man show.

On 8 April 1989 El Padrino arrived at the home of a friend in Guadalajara, ahead of a lunchtime appointment with a high-ranking police officer called Guillermo 'Memo' Calderoni, a contact of his.

El Padrino entered the house. Five federal agents stormed in right behind. They threw El Padrino to the ground. He knew them all from way back. Then Calderoni arrived.

'What's happening?' asked El Padrino.

'I don't know you,' the cop replied.

Now in his sixties, languishing in a cell in a maximum-security facility outside Mexico City and suffering from poor health, El Padrino continues to blame Calderoni – who was later linked to Garcia Abrego on the Gulf coast – for turning on him.

Shortly after his capture, stories emerged that El Padrino's own protégés had betrayed him. In the early 1990s Chapo and El Guero even ordered the killing of El Padrino's loyal lieutenants and lawyers, prompting widespread belief that Chapo had turned on his mentor. But El Padrino has never addressed such speculation, choosing instead to blame Calderoni, the cop, for the betrayal.

The New Guard

So the Arellano Felix brothers inherited Tijuana, a city founded in the late nineteenth century. For decades following its founding, Tijuana consisted of a few ranches scattered from the countryside to the coast. A few hundred farmers called Tijuana home. Then came the Prohibition Era. Between 1920 and 1933 the prohibition of alcohol in the United States would transform Tijuana into a den of disrepute. Bars opened; smuggling operations boomed. The PRI government looked the other way, as everyone from American soldiers to Hollywood stars to members of the mafia came south for a good time at the brothels, bars, casinos and racetracks.

Tijuana also became a central gathering point for migrants aspiring to a life in the United States. Known as *la esquina de Latinoamerica* (the corner of Latin America, due to its location on the north-western tip of Mexico, right next door to the United States), the city attracted migrants from as far south as Argentina. Those who made it across the border created new lives in California; those who didn't started anew in Tijuana.

Even before the drug trade arrived, Tijuana was a smuggling hub. Booze and other cheap goods were shipped north, and migrants were led over the border on foot across the nearby desert, or trucked across by the dozen at Tijuana's regulated crossings. The Tijuana River offered another possible route into the US. By the 1980s, child-exploitation had become rampant, adding to the city's list of blights. Good government and policing have always been a fantasy.

Tijuana now has a population of about 1.2 million; its surrounding suburbs and settlements sprawl almost all the way to Mexicali, 135 miles away. This was the city that the Arellano Felix brothers took over at the beginning of the 1990s. Many of the city's public figures and politicians at the time were already believed to be involved in the sleazier side of the city – gambling and money laundering – and within months of their arrival, the Arellano Felix brothers were part of the social circuit. They went to all the right parties, knew all the right people.

They became close to Jorge Hank Rhon.

No tale about Tijuana is complete without Jorge Hank Rhon; no story about Mexican corruption or politics is complete without his father, Carlos Hank Gonzalez, a former kingmaker of the Institutional Revolutionary Party who allegedly used his political position to enrich himself and developed strong ties with drug trafficking. As Hank Gonzalez himself famously put it: 'A politician who is poor is a poor politician.'

A senior Mexican law enforcement source once called Hank Gonzalez the 'primary intermediary between the multinational drug trafficking enterprises and the Mexican political system.'

It quickly became clear that Hank Rhon, his second son, was neither the politician nor the businessman his father had been. Hank Rhon had moved to Tijuana in 1985, when he was twenty-nine. He became a leading figure in the city, taking over Agua Caliente, a racetrack with a proud history. Hank Rhon's alleged mismanagement led to its demise: within five years, the track went under and the horses retired to their stables. But he was still a multimillionaire by inheritance, and his activities in Tijuana continued to make the gossip pages.

Although it was never proven that Hank Rhon was connected to drug trafficking in Tijuana, he was never shy of appearing to live like a narco. He held lavish, raucous parties at his ranch outside the city; sometimes the Arellano Felix brothers were present, it was said. He wore his hair long and sported cowboy boots made from the skins of exotic species.

The man who later would become mayor of Tijuana and run for governor of Baja California always loved his animals. As a child he played with show horses and pedigree dogs at his father's ranch outside Mexico City. He keeps two she-wolves as pets. He has been known to have pythons in his home, and bring tigers into the office to liven things up. In the infield of the Agua Caliente racetrack, which is now just a dusty dog track, sits what might well be Hank's greatest accomplishment: a private zoo, filled with 20,000 animals of all shapes and sizes – zebras, lions, giraffes, wolves, emus, owls, bears. Caged along the track's eastern flank dwell Hank's pride and joy, his white tigers. Only 200 or so exist throughout the world – and Hank owns fourteen of them.

A father of eighteen children from three wives and a girlfriend, Hank Rhon once told a reporter that women were his favourite animals.

Hank Rhon's alleged connections to the Arellano Felix brothers would garner much more attention than his animals or outrageous quotes. A leaked US National Drug Intelligence Center report, 'The White Tiger' paper, once accused him, his father and brother Carlos of involvement in the Mexican drug trade. Specifically, it claimed that he was 'reportedly a close associate' of the Arellano Felix brothers. 'The Hank family represents a significant threat to the United States' because of its money laundering and cocaine distribution activity, stated the report. And he 'is more openly criminal than either his father or his brother . . . [He] is regarded as ruthless, dangerous and prone to violence.'

The Arellano Felix brothers carved out a similar reputation for themselves. They showed themselves to be the most powerful of the new cartels; they were certainly the most violent. Tijuana registered more than 300 killings a year from 1994 until 1999, when it hit 637. The majority of these homicides were attributed to the brothers from Sinaloa.

Killing was sometimes all part of the business; on other occasions, the Arellano Felix brothers wanted a power trip. They would be out drinking at a bar or eating at a restaurant, for instance, and Ramon Arellano Felix would suddenly 'have the urge to kill', recalls former DEA Special Agent Errol Chavez, who was based in San Diego at the time. 'So they would just drive off down the road – and kill somebody.'

The brothers instilled a climate of fear and unpredictability in the northern border city. Their men would dress in police uniforms and roam Tijuana's streets, kidnapping anyone they no longer trusted or who posed a threat. Gangs employed by the brothers made sure the streets remained loyal. These gangs even worked their way to San Diego. If someone owed money for a drug shipment on the US side, they would be hunted down; some offenders were kidnapped for ransom, some were dissolved in vats of acid.

Police and investigators did nothing. The climate in Tijuana – not to mention the Arellano Felix brothers' political connections – made for such impunity.

In 1994 an ambitious young PRI politician and presidential candidate, Luis Donaldo Colosio, pledged to combat corruption and shake up the system. He even made promises to combat drug trafficking. While campaigning in Tijuana, he was shot in the head. Some have accused the Arellano Felix brothers of Colosio's assassination; no evidence has ever been brought before a court.

Without thorough investigations, evidence of illicit activity in Tijuana was virtually impossible to come by. Hank Rhon, for one, maintains that he and others have been the targets of smear campaigns, nothing more.

'I've always [said], "Don't pay attention to gossip, just find the proof, then come back," ' he said during an interview in his Tijuana offices, just after he had taken over as mayor. Indeed, shortly after the report was leaked, the then-US Attorney General Janet Reno disavowed it, saying its claims had never been accepted.

Still, in a city like Tijuana, dark accusations tend to hold more weight than their denial, or, even on the rare occasion that it exists, proof of innocence. One allegation in particular continues to haunt Hank Rhon. Hector Felix Miranda, a journalist for a respected Tijuana weekly, had long had a relationship with him; the two would meet at parties, the reporter would cover the latest goings-on in a roundabout way, without going into too much detail about Hank Rhon's private and social life. He also wrote frequently about the Arellano Felix brothers, who attended some of the same functions.

But it is said that, on one occasion, Hank Rhon felt Felix had betrayed his trust. The reporter had published material about Hank Rhon that was meant to be confidential. It wasn't anything incriminating, but Hank Rhon apparently felt it was personal information that didn't belong in a newspaper column.

On a rare rainy morning, 20 April 1988, Felix was gunned down at the wheel of his LTD Crown Victoria. The autopsy found nineteen bullets, which had ripped apart his chest, breaking eleven ribs. According to reports from the forensic experts who examined the corpse, even Felix's heart had been shattered. The culprits were three of Hank's bodyguards from Agua Caliente. Two were convicted, the third was found dead in Tijuana shortly after their trials.

Hank was never charged in connection with the murder. Still, the accusation seems to touch a nerve. When I asked him directly about Felix, Hank Rhon slumped deep into his chair and placed his right hand to his forehead.

'The truth is, it's what happens when you're starting to become too popular and you step on someone's foot . . .' he began. 'They find a way to neutralize you. But it's always been allegations.' Indeed, in Mexico few politicians or businessmen rise up the ladder without having continually to fend off allegations of corruption; it has even become part of the game for the media to throw out allegation and see what sticks.

Throughout the rise of the Arellano Felix brothers such allegations would swirl around the city. They would never be proven. The DEA and Mexican authorities maintain that the brothers had free rein and killed at will. Between 1990 and 2000 they smuggled hundreds of tons of drugs through to California.

'Lord of the Skies'

While the Arellano Felix brothers were settling into Tijuana, Amado Carrillo Fuentes was establishing himself as chief of the Ciudad Juarez drug corridor.

The eldest of six brothers, Carrillo Fuentes had learned the drug trade from none other than 'Don Neto' Fonseca in Sinaloa. As a young man, Carrillo Fuentes had been sent to Ojinaga, a small city located 190 miles to the west of Ciudad Juarez, to coordinate cocaine smuggling there.

He learned fast, and by the time he inherited the Ciudad Juarez plaza he was a master. He proved adept at nurturing contacts, and was known nationwide as a diplomatic narco, preferring peace to war, and corruption to chaos.

At that time, Mexico and the United States were working on a radar network that would improve the tracking of planes coming in from Colombia. A former Army general was placed in charge of the new radar network.

Carrillo Fuentes got to him quickly, US officials claimed.

The former military man denied any cooperation with drug traffickers, but there was no doubt Carrillo Fuentes had succeeded in gaining access to the air. He owned several airline companies, and began using them to fly cocaine straight from Colombia to Chihuahua, and on to the United States. The planes would land at an airstrip in the Chihuahua desert, where the Carrillo Fuentes crew and as many as seventy security personnel awaited the load. Within mere minutes the drugs would be offloaded, and the Colombian plane could return home. Another plane was then used to fly the drugs into Texas.

The planes Carrillo Fuentes used were fast – exceeding 500 nautical miles an hour – and could outrun the radar planes used by US Customs. They would land in the middle of the desert, where the haul – sometimes as much as twelve tons of cocaine – was picked up by the American contact. The flight back to Mexico would carry the proceeds: up to $60 million in one trip.

Carrillo Fuentes came to be known as 'El Senor de los Cielos' – the Lord of the Skies.

Carrillo Fuentes was also keen to expand within Mexico. He set up operations in Hermosillo, Sonora, which he planned to use as a key transit point for drug shipments. (Located in the desert just south of a remote stretch of the US–Mexico border, Sonora had long been a crucial shipping route from Sinaloa.) Carrillo Fuentes moved into a pink stucco mansion near the American consul's residence, and had construction resumed on an unfinished home known locally as 'The Palace of 1,001 Nights' on account of its onion-like domes. According to DEA agent Wilburn Sears, at one point the head of the Hermosillo station, Carrillo Fuentes managed to get federal protection for flights going in and out of the city. 'They were doing everything out there except kick-starting the narcos' airplanes.'

Carrillo Fuentes would face some opposition: in 1991 the governor of Sonora, Manuel Fabio Beltrones, ordered the seizure of several of the drug lord's properties – including his palace. But the DEA alleged that Beltrones was simply seizing a few of the properties in order to appear on the right side of the law. The governor, the Americans believed, was in deep with Carrillo Fuentes.

Nothing was ever proven, and Beltrones vehemently denied it, claiming that intelligence reports linking him with the drug lord were fabricated by political rivals. 'This sounds like a novel, filled with horror and error,' he told the *New York Times*. 'At what time of the day do I govern, if I'm spending my time on all these crimes?'

Carrillo Fuentes was even linked to Raul Salinas de Gortari, the brother of former President Carlos Salinas de Gortari. This, too, was denied and was never proven.

Carrillo Fuentes, it would turn out, had a weak spot. But for the majority of the 1990s, he would remain all-powerful in the area surrounding Ciudad Juarez.

5. Chapo's Rise

The arrangement with the Colombians had evolved by the early 1990s. Ninety per cent of Colombian cocaine consumed in the United States was now coming through Mexico; Colombia's traffickers were now paying their Mexican counterparts up to 50 per cent of profits for each shipment.

The Mexicans were effectively equal partners with the Colombians. But without the oversight and authority of El Padrino, that also meant the Mexicans were in serious competition with each other.

Chapo decided that he had to be better than the rest.

While his compadres were making names for themselves in Tijuana and Ciudad Juarez, Chapo was continuing to do things El Padrino's way – gradually, methodically, with less fanfare but with unyielding ambition. He was determined never to return to the poverty from which he had emerged scarred, but alive. He had risen through the ranks from the bottom, and vowed never to lose his position of power.

Chapo constructed an inner circle in the tradition of the mafia. He employed relatives he could trust – brothers and cousins, though later he would expand this circle to include nephews and nieces. (His father had since died, and his mother would stay out of the fray.) His closest associates were largely from the Sierra, not outsiders he didn't know well.

His main adviser – equivalent to the Italian mafia's *consiglieri* – was Juan Jose Esparragosa-Moreno, a.k.a. 'El Azul'. Much darker-skinned than Chapo and his relatives – they were *mestizo*, in that their bloodline had mixed with that of Spaniards at some stage – Esparragosa was given his nickname because his dark hue at times appeared almost blue.

Born in Badiraguato, Esparragosa had narco-connections that went way back. He had worked with El Padrino, 'Don Neto' Fonseca and Rafael Caro Quintero in the early days (first in Sinaloa, then in Guadalajara), and had allegedly been complicit in their conspiracy to kill the DEA agent 'Kiki' Camarena. Of the original Sinaloan capos, Esparragosa was the only one still free. A former police officer like El Padrino, he had extensive connections. He had also married into Chapo's clan – he wed his fellow narco's sister-in-law.

Esparragosa was discreet, reserved and not prone to losing his temper. He would also act as a mediator between Chapo in Sinaloa and Carrillo Fuentes in Ciudad Juarez. Something of an independent adviser, he was also considered the No. 2 in Carrillo Fuentes' organization. Esparragosa had an ability to play both sides yet represent their interests equally; when he entered the room, egos would be cast aside for profit.

Chapo employed *sicarios*, or killers. Some were military deserters in their thirties, experts in using weapons like AK-47s and M-16s, grenades and rocket launchers. They recruited young men throughout the country to work on their behalf. They wore military or military-style clothing, and used weapons that in Mexico are reserved for the Army; mistaking these men for the military itself was not uncommon.

Chapo wanted efficiency, and would not tolerate mistakes or unnecessary bloodshed.

On one occasion a female employee lost Chapo some money on a shipment. The boss ordered Luis Rolando Llanos Romero, a.k.a. 'El Chilango', one of his younger sicarios, to kill her. Llanos Romero, however, killed the wrong woman. When Chapo found out, he was livid, according to a protected witness who later testified before the PGR.

Chapo ordered a meeting at which Llanos Romero would be reprimanded. A group of Chapo's men – Llanos Romero included – gathered in a house used by the network, and discussed his mistake. The meeting adjourned and with Llanos Romero apparently bloodied but unbowed, they grabbed their guns off the table and made for the door.

On his way out, another of Chapo's sicarios put a bullet in the back of Llanos Romero's head.

Chapo may have got angry when betrayed, but he never let his temper get the better of him. 'One of his strengths is his tolerance for frustration . . . revenge is not something that he exacts with the immediacy of an impulsive person,' reads a psychological analysis of the drug kingpin conducted by the PGR. 'His response is calculated, intentional, his vision is to hurt his adversary using his weaknesses to produce the most harm possible.'

Whenever violence flared between low-level gangs, it was Esparragosa who stepped in, reminding everyone that uncalculated killings – and subsequent attention – were bad for business.

Chapo, too, controlled his emotions when it came to business. Whatever the situation, according to the PGR, Chapo would reason it through. 'When it comes to his revengeful actions, he is obsessive but measured . . . so that [any action undertaken] strengthens [his] structure.'

Chapo was egocentric, the PGR concluded, making sure everyone always knew who was boss. But he also understood his responsibilities in that position, and would on occasion take the blame when something went wrong. Chapo, in spite of it all, was 'an emotionally stable person'.

Early on, Chapo was based in Guadalajara, where 'El Padrino' Felix Gallardo also lived until his arrest; but his 'command and control centre' was actually further north, in Agua Prieta, a border city in Sonora. This enabled him to monitor his organization's smuggling activities personally.

As El Padrino had done, Chapo bought dozens of homes in various cities throughout Mexico; he employed trustworthy proxies to make the purchase and register the properties under false names. The houses were nothing special, usually one- or two-storey structures with a gate and a driveway, sometimes a yard, located in residential neighbourhoods. The homes were scattered throughout cities like Culiacan, Mexicali, Tecate and Guadalajara. The nation's capital was also used, as a hiding place; it offered Chapo and his men anonymity they couldn't find elsewhere. (They called Mexico City 'the Smoke'.) The properties largely served as stash houses for operatives, guns, drugs and money.

Usually, three to five men would operate from one stash house; any more than that would draw unwelcome attention. Inside each house, it wasn't uncommon to find dozens of machine guns, grenades and thousands of rounds of ammunition. Operatives carried tens of thousands of US dollars and Mexican pesos in cash; often it would be necessary to bribe policemen or customs officers.

Chapo acquired ranches, too, throughout Mexico, but particularly in Sinaloa, Sonora, Chihuahua and Durango. There, local gomeros would grow poppy and marijuana. Sometimes Chapo paid for the ranches; sometimes he simply seized them through force.

According to the PGR, Chapo liked to delegate, so that he would be able to sit back and enjoy his money without having to pay attention to the minutiae of every drug transaction. Even recruitment was carried out locally. A prospective employee would be introduced to a local boss; that man would then report to another superior, and so on up the ladder. Chapo stayed in the shadows; few met the man himself.

The men in Chapo's 'cells' largely stayed put, overseeing operations in their designated area. Their main objective was to receive, guard and distribute Chapo's drugs to the next link in the chain. They would also kill on behalf of their boss.

Although they worked for Chapo, it appears these operatives were sometimes given leeway to run side-operations like car theft and trading in counterfeit goods. As long as they weren't attracting attention their activities were condoned. Even in Sinaloa, Chapo didn't mind a little moonlighting; he apparently allowed outsiders to operate as long as they paid him a levy.

All activities – receipts of shipments and cash, transactions, unpaid debts – were logged into accounting books. Cell operatives were given fake IDs (passports and Mexican identity cards) and, on occasion, armoured vehicles. They usually communicated by walkie-talkie, just as Chapo's people in the Sierra did. Later mobile phones would be used more frequently. Chapo would bribe senior staff in the telecommunications companies to ensure the phones used by his people wouldn't show up on the central database. Each member of the organization would receive a mobile phone (or, for some employees, as many as three phones) and a code by which to identify himself.

After his escape from prison, Chapo would also make a smooth transition into the Internet age. He hired an accountant to digitalize all of his organization's paperwork. It is believed that he always travelled with a laptop and used e-mail to send instructions to subordinates. He arranged meetings via chat rooms, preferring codes sent online to codes over the phone. In the mountains of Sinaloa, his people now scour the Internet for the latest stories about their boss.

In the Sierra the gomeros still use walkie-talkies, too. They also whistle and make other natural noises (owl sounds, for instance) to each other when they hear soldiers or trespassers coming.

Beneath the Veneer

From the outset one of Chapo's main challenges was to remain mobile. When travelling outside his own home area, Chapo surrounded himself with an entourage of his best men. Sometimes, dozens of armed men would accompany him; he almost always drove in convoy. He employed a chauffeur, who was more like a trusted bodyguard. Chapo had several of these chauffeurs scattered throughout the country, always on call.

Occasionally Chapo would even don a disguise. He had a preference for impersonating a priest or an Army officer: after all, in Mexico, few were as untouchable as these figures. Travelling in clerical or military garb would guarantee a journey without any disturbances.

Beneath the disguises, the entourages and the layers of security, lay the real Chapo, a man who was always more comfortable in a baseball cap and jeans than the flashy gold jewellery and designer suits worn by the other narcos.

Chapo is '*puro* Badiraguato' – born and raised in the hills. The only ostentatious thing about him has always been his penchant for gold-plated pistols engraved with the initials J.G.L. He has a back-country twang that is common to the Sierra. His voice is also somewhat nasal, but calm – it's not high-pitched enough to squeak; rather, it seems to softly sing. His left eye is seemingly paralysed, giving him a stare that is at once kind and chilling.

Shortly after he arrived at Puente Grande in 1995, Chapo was paraded in front of the cameras. He stood there in the rain, hand-cuffed, as the guards looked on. He wore a baseball cap and a beige puffer jacket. He grinned at the cameras, but said little. The look on his face said it all: I am in charge here. I own this moment. I own you all – the guards, the press, the government.

Chapo always has to be in charge, according to the authorities; he has an obsessive need to 'control' his environment. But he is also self-assured, pleasant, courteous and polite to those in his presence. He is straightforward and can come across as simple, but the wheels are constantly turning inside his head; he is extremely sharp, those who know him say.

Chapo is a charmer, a man with a reputation for seduction – whether it be of a fellow drug trafficker for business purposes or a woman for sexual ones. 'His affable character allows him to natur-ally convince those he interacts with, especially those who . . . protect him,' the authorities said.

He stands only 5ft 6ins tall. The PGR contends that this has been one driving factor in Chapo's success. His 'tenacity' seems to stem from an underlying sense of inferiority linked to his height, causing him to compensate through 'intellectual superiority' and 'disproportionate ambition for power'.

His small stature is an asset in another way: it helps keep him at the level of his employees. With his nasal voice, his childishly devilish smirk and his down-to-earth style of dressing, Chapo looks like any other low-level narco, not an ego-inflated superior. Such is his style.

Miguel Angel Segoviano, an accountant, remembers the first time he met Chapo. He had been summoned to meet the drug lord at a party – the launch of a front company called Servicios Aero Ejecutivos. Segoviano walked into the room and witnessed a man dressing down another – who he presumed to be the boss. Segoviano butted in. 'Why don't you leave him alone? Why are you scolding him?' Another man quickly grabbed the accountant, ushering him upstairs. He was at a loss; he couldn't think what he had done wrong.

The man he had berated was Chapo himself. 'I never thought that Joaquin Guzman – well, Joaquin Guzman looked like a normal person, like any employee,' he would later recall in a US court.

Segoviano survived the mishap, and rose through Chapo's organization until he was finally caught.

Chapo certainly has a way with people, even with those on the opposite side of the law. Jose Antonio Ortega Sanchez, a Mexico City-based lawyer, met the drug lord in 2000, in Puente Grande. Ortega Sanchez had come to the prison to take Chapo's testimony, on behalf of the federal government.

The appointment was scheduled for 10 a.m. Ortega Sanchez arrived on time, and was led to a room inside the prison itself – not the standard cubicles near the entrance reserved for lawyers or visitors. Ortega Sanchez waited and waited. A guard came in; Chapo was delayed, he said. The hands of the clock on the wall continued to tick by. Ortega Sanchez waited some more. Before he knew it, night had fallen. Chapo still hadn't shown.

At 11 p.m., the drug lord finally entered the room. He was smiling. He looked content, calm. He apologized to Ortega Sanchez for making him wait, and extended his hand.

'Look, *licenciado*,' he said, using the common Mexican courtesy for addressing professionals. 'I had a conjugal visit. Afterwards, I took a bath. Then I had a short nap . . . in order to be ready for you.'

Chapo's charm worked on Ortega Sanchez, who would ignore the fact that he'd been kept waiting for nearly twelve hours, and hang in there for five hours more to take the drug lord's testimony.

During that time, he noted Chapo's control.

There was no glass window separating Ortega Sanchez and the drug lord. All that rested between the two was a table, on which a guard had placed coffee and a selection of cakes. The only other person in the room was a federal prosecutor. Chapo wasn't handcuffed. No one was supervising him. He was alone with the prosecutor and the lawyer.

He was calm, in good spirits, recalls Ortega Sanchez; the guards who brought in the refreshments treated him as if he were their boss. 'That's how you see the power of Chapo in prison,' said the lawyer.

Ortega Sanchez remembers being impressed by Chapo's intelligence, by just how sharp he was. The drug lord may have spoken in his Sierra accent – he called Ortega Sanchez 'signor' instead of 'senor', for instance – and on the surface appeared to be just another locked-up gomero, but he was alert and in command. At every point during the testimony, Chapo knew where the lawyer's questions were headed. He anticipated then reacted – much faster than the prosecutor, the lawyer recalls. Although he was being asked the questions, Chapo steered the conversation. Only once, during the whole five-hour affair, did Chapo reveal any semblance of frustration. Ortega Sanchez had asked him a question that he hoped would lead to more insight into Chapo's crimes; Chapo objected quickly and said, 'We're not supposed to be talking about this.'

Otherwise, Chapo was calm. 'He felt at home,' Ortega Sanchez recalls. 'He felt as if he had control.'

He did.

For five hours, the drug lord looked the lawyer straight in the eyes, blinking only when necessary and never disconnecting his gaze. Not once did Chapo look down or away, as if in denial or to avoid the lawyer's penetrating questions. Even when he was lying – or at least contradicting previous testimony – Chapo looked directly at Ortega Sanchez.

'His eyes . . .' recalls the lawyer, staring ahead, eyes wide open, as if impersonating the drug lord. 'They never left me. They were alive. Very alive.'

Few people have looked directly into those eyes. At any one time, Chapo has as many as 150,000 people working for him and his drug operation. Not many have met him in person. Even in the early days, Chapo rarely communicated directly with employees; he hired a *vocero* (literally, a spokesman) to relay his orders. Other orders come from intermediaries, lower links down the chain of command.

Isaac Gastelum Rocher, a thirty-six-year-old born and raised in Culiacan, worked for the Sinaloa cartel as a street dealer. His brown eyes darting back and forth, beads of sweat beginning to form on his brow, he begins to tell his story.

In his mid-twenties, he began using *hielo*, as methamphetamine is known in these parts, on an occasional basis. Within a few years he was using it daily, and adding cocaine, marijuana and alcohol to the mix. Some peers approached him: would he like to transport drugs to Nogales, on the border with Arizona? 'They said: "We know you need money, you have a family, you want to move up,"' recalls Gastelum. He was open to the idea, so went with them to a house in Culiacan. 'Are you in or out?' they asked a group of young men just like him.

Scared, he realized he was in over his head, but told them that if there was lower-scale work to be done, he would be game. They gave him eight chunks of methamphetamine to sell on the streets of Culiacan and Navolato. 'They saw me as trustworthy.'

As Gastelum talks, he sits upright, eyes shifting from side to side. For two years the relationship with his new employers blossomed; he could get meth easily from his suppliers because they were hoping he would join their ranks. They gave him bundles of cash to keep him afloat even when the addicts weren't buying. But Gastelum's luck finally ran out. One evening, he was driving, slightly drunk, to a local supermarket in Navolato, when the police stopped him. He looked suspicious – they searched him and the car. They found 100 grams of meth in a bag.

The police accused him of planning to distribute drugs on behalf of the Sinaloa cartel to the local prison, which was located right next to the supermarket. He was given a prison term of just over ten years for *delitos contra la salud*, an all-encompassing Mexican judicial euphemism for serious drug-related charges or drug trafficking.

Gastelum never met anyone higher up in the Sinaloa cartel than the men who had originally approached him. He certainly never met the boss.

Jose Luis Garcia Puga was also born and raised in Culiacan. The twenty-nine-year-old had a pilot's licence, so had better prospects than many in his *barrio*, or neighbourhood. Squinting his eyes in the midday sun and fidgeting constantly, he tells how he got his start by flying local businessmen to other airports in Sinaloa and neighbouring states.

One day at the airport in Guamuchil, where the plane he rented was grounded, he was approached by one of the businessmen he regularly flew. Would he be willing to take some marijuana up to Nogales?

To Garcia Puga, it was a no-brainer. They would pay him $15,000 just to load up the plane with marijuana and fly it north to an airport with minimal security. He wouldn't have to cross borders, or do anything too risky. For several years, he would transport the drugs in his plane. He was never caught for doing it. He and a friend tried to steal a plane belonging to the PGR, and after their unsuccessful mission, got into a fight. In the heat of the moment he shot his friend and was sentenced to twelve years' imprisonment.

Garcia Puga looks tortured as he talks. He knows the risks. As he reveals parts of his story, he squints and slams his fist down on the table. In confessing his so-called sins, he betrays not only his bosses but his beliefs. When he eventually gets out of prison, he shrugs, he hopes to become a legitimate pilot again. But he now has a criminal record and the narcos are the ones with all the money and power. Garcia Puga gets up and walks away.

He has never met anyone higher up in the Sinaloa cartel than the man who originally approached him.

Jesus Manuel Beltran Zepeda, a.k.a. 'The Horse', and Gerardo Maximiliano Coronel del Razo, a.k.a. 'El Max', were picked up in Ciudad Juarez. They were carrying 200 kilos of marijuana, military uniforms, bullet-proof vests, two handguns, a grenade, cartridges and a variety of electronic equipment. According to the PGR, they were part of a nine-member cell commanded by Chapo.

They have never met the boss.

Armando Guzman Nares, Benjamin Dosal Rodriguez and Luis Carlos Villa Rosales were arrested by soldiers in a house in the rundown neighbourhood of San Isidro, also in Ciudad Juarez. The Army seized four stolen vehicles, seven kilos of marijuana, 230 grams of crack, eight rifles, three handguns, and 1,987 cartridges of various calibres.

The men were part of a cell working for Chapo, assigned to kill members of a Ciudad Juarez-based gang. According to the military, the cell of about ten men was responsible for at least twelve executions in Ciudad Juarez and its environs. They had also burned down at least three houses belonging to members of the rival gang.

They, too, have never met their boss.

Master Strategist

From the outset, Chapo knew his goals and the ways in which he would achieve them. 'Planning, organization, negotiation and looking to the future' were Chapo's strengths, according to the PGR.

Unlike the other capos, based in their allocated smuggling hubs, Chapo had to concern himself with transportation from the source. So, in order to move the drugs from the mountains of Sinaloa, Chapo's people bought or stole whatever planes they could get their hands on. Sometimes, they even stole government-owned aircraft. They hid drugs in vehicles and paid off truckers to haul their goods up north. Secret compartments in the floor of a standard car could conceal several kilos of cocaine; sometimes the drugs were stashed in the tyres.

Chapo established pickup points along the Pacific coast, as far south as Chiapas. There, the Colombians could deliver their cocaine, which would then be moved straight up the coast to the US border. Law enforcement officers up and down Mexico's coastline were paid off. So were politicians.

Chapo wanted to be 'directly responsible for the planning of his actions in order to successfully achieve his objectives', according to the PGR, but he also knew he couldn't control every business deal if his operation was to expand. So he linked up with senior figures he could trust, throughout Mexico.

Chapo employed a team of lawyers to approach public figures, high-ranking military men and other officials on his behalf.

In Oaxaca, Pedro Diaz Parada became Chapo's main man. A local *cacique*, or strongman, with unrivalled local connections, Diaz Parada would ensure law enforcement turned a blind eye to Colombian cocaine arriving by sea along the southern state's coastline. Diaz Parada was untouchable: he had once been sentenced to thirty-three years in prison for drug trafficking; upon hearing the sentence, he had turned to the judge: 'I will go free and you will die.'

Six days later, the capo was indeed free. The judge's body was found riddled with thirty-three bullets. A note had been left behind.

'A bullet for every year,' it read.

In Guerrero, a state with a long, unwatched coastline and an equally long history of drug production, Chapo would make the acquaintance of Rogaciano Alba Alvarez, an old-school cacique who ruled the impoverished people around him. Famous for the pistol in his belt and his sombrero, Alba Alvarez enjoyed the protection of the PRI; like Diaz Parada in neighbouring Oaxaca, he too was untouchable.

In three states heading up the west coast towards Sinaloa – Michoacan, Colima and Nayarit – Chapo also linked up with other caciques and local drug bosses to secure the smuggling route north. He connected with military men in those areas, too. He already owned Jalisco, which also bordered the Pacific, and, naturally, Sinaloa.

Whereas the Arellano Felix brothers controlled through violence and fear, and Carrillo Fuentes had his tendency towards diplomacy, Chapo was building alliances. He was building a network of corruption nationwide that was unrivalled. He, El Guero and El Mayo – essentially his most trusted No. 2, but a capo in his own right – were spreading their tentacles through the Mexican system, just as El Padrino had taught them. Chapo had visited El Padrino in prison at least once, where he had made the acquaintance of the deputy attorney general and a top federal police commander. They would become his main accomplices.

Anyone could be bought. On one occasion, Chapo was reputedly arrested in Mexico City. At the police station, he lifted up a suitcase and put it on the desk of the capital's chief of police. Inside was $50,000 in cash; within minutes, Chapo was out the door.

Another time, the Jalisco state police chief received a gift of one million dollars and five SUVs. Chapo's deal: the police chief and his men would allow a couple of planes filled with cocaine to land without saying a word.

Chapo's corruption network allowed him to remain discreet. The DEA was barely aware of his existence; he seemed to 'just creep in there', recalls agent Chavez. 'He was always in the background, operating with support from El Mayo.'

Chapo had first really appeared on the US radar in 1987, when testimony of criminals-turned-witnesses in an American court declared under oath that he was a 'kingpin' of their organization. One indictment, issued in Arizona, claimed that in the seven months between 19 October 1987 and 18 May 1990, Chapo had planned the delivery of 4,600 pounds of marijuana and 10,504 pounds of cocaine into Arizona and California. Chapo had later allegedly attempted to transport the proceeds – $1.5 million in cash – back to Sinaloa.

Another indictment claimed Chapo's group had imported 35 tons of cocaine and 'an unspecified amount of marijuana' into the United States during a three-year period, and earned profits of $100,000 – 'all returned to the organization's coffers in Mexico'. Their method of smuggling was simple: the cocaine was placed in the false bottoms of two trailers, which would deliver the drugs to a warehouse in Tucson, Arizona. From there, the goods would be distributed by US counterparts.

This was the first official mention that Chapo was in charge of anything. It was becoming clear to those DEA agents in charge of monitoring him that he was 'maturing'. He was proving to be innovative – and was definitely not to be underestimated.

Indeed, Chapo had taken charge of the smuggling corridor between Tecate and San Luis Colorado, just north of Sinaloa and in between Tijuana and Ciudad Juarez. Like the other capos, he was mainly utilizing land routes to get his drugs across the border, coupled with some light plane flights. This was the most common strategy: by keeping quantities of drugs relatively small, traffickers minimized the risk of arrest or losing the goods. It was what agents called a 'piecemeal strategy', but it worked.

It was slow and laborious, however. Cars would get stopped at checkpoints, and planes were always risky. The Caro-Quintero brothers were even resorting to horses and human backpackers (often, illegal migrants) to smuggle across the desert spanning from San Luis Rio Colorado to Agua Prieta.

Chapo was getting more creative, though. In Tecate 1,400 cans of jalapeno chilli peppers were seized; they were packed with 7.3 tons of cocaine. The drug lord had built up a network in Los Angeles through which he could conceal and traffic the drugs. The DEA arrested a Los Angeles grocer, Jose Reynoso Gonzalez. He and his brothers owned Cotija Cheese and Tia Anita foods, and distributed La Comadre canned goods – the perfect front for Chapo's cocaine deliveries.

Chapo was also smuggling drugs across the border in rail cars carrying cooking oil, and in rolls of chicken wire with hidden fibreglass compartments. His people set up warehouses from California to New Jersey to store the goods once they arrived. Chapo was also smuggling drugs inside oil tankers.

But that was just the tip of the iceberg. Wanting more, faster, Chapo began to build tunnels.

In early May 1990, US Customs agents near the Arizona–Sonora border received a tip about some suspicious activity at a warehouse in Douglas, Arizona. The agents followed a truck from the site to a cluster of farmhouses in Queen Creek, more than 100 miles away, where they set up surveillance. For the next two days, they didn't see much, except for 'flashes' inside one of the buildings. A welder, or torch-cutter, they thought. It was suspicious enough for them to get a warrant. On 11 May they searched the Queen Creek complex, and discovered a false compartment in the bed of the truck they had followed. They found 2,037 pounds of cocaine in boxes stored inside the farm's buildings.

Six days later, with a warrant secured for another search, they hit the warehouse in Douglas. They couldn't have anticipated what they would find when they lifted a steel drainage grate in the floor and then jack-hammered through a door disguised as a concrete plate. Beneath the rubble lay Cocaine Alley.

Lined with concrete walls, a 200-foot passageway led from the warehouse to the house of Chapo's attorney in Agua Prieta, Sonora. It featured an air-conditioning system, lighting and tubular piping in order to drain out water. To gain access to the tunnel from the house in Agua Prieta, one would simply turn on a water spigot located outside, which would then activate a hydraulics system and raise a false floor under a pool table inside. Once the drugs were lowered into the hole – via a pulley system, which effectively acted as an elevator – a worker down below would load them on to a cart on rails. Using a system that miners in the region had long employed, the workers would then move the drugs on to Arizona. It was wide enough to drive a small truck through, and had hidden rooms for weapons, cash, narcotics – you name it. It was one of the most creative and impressive narcotics-smuggling ploys the DEA had ever come across.

Chapo had employed an architect to design the subterranean complex, a man by the name of Felipe de Jesus Corona Verbera. According to testimony presented in US courts, Corona Verbera had quickly become a trusted employee. He referred to Chapo in the informal '*tu*' form, something one testifying witness had never heard before, from anyone.

Corona Verbera and Chapo were alike in some respects: when either had a job he wanted to be done, he oversaw it himself or made absolutely sure the right people were assigned to the task. He trusted the spadework to subordinates, but wanted to make sure the whole operation went smoothly.

Corona Verbera oversaw every stage of the construction of Cocaine Alley, according to testimony from Angel Martinez Martinez, named as a 'co-conspirator' by prosecutors. He and Chapo's lawyer, Francisco Camarena Macias, also allegedly spun well-constructed lies to supply the necessary hardware for the project as well as to those who were working on it.

William Woods, a contractor who helped fix up the warehouse in Douglas, where the drug shipments would arrive, was told that the site would be a holding point for trucks crossing the border – where they could be washed, for instance. They told another employee that a shipment of pistons and water pumps was for a petrol station in Guadalajara. Corona Verbera was at the site 'throughout the whole construction', recalled Woods.

This man, whom Chapo liked to call 'the Architect', had become a key player. After all, as the drug lord would put it, 'He built me a fucking cool tunnel.'

In spite of Chapo's creativity and the ingenuity of his architect, US and Mexican authorities did manage to seize some of his merchandise. But any major seizures only served to underscore the enormous quantities of narcotics that were actually getting through.

And with each bust came a reminder of just how clever Chapo was. Another tunnel was discovered leading from a Tijuana warehouse under the border into California. Dug some 65 feet below the surface, it then stretched 1,452 feet into America, towards a warehouse registered in the name of the very same brothers who had smuggled cocaine for Chapo in their chilli peppers. Authorities both in Mexico and the United States were stunned. Tunnels ranging from 15 to 30 feet in length had been found under the border before. Cocaine Alley had been most impressive, but this was something unimaginable. How could Chapo have got away with it?

Chapo may have been a stealthy operator, but he was greedy. It appeared that his thirst for dominance had spurred him to take risks beyond those of his predecessors and rivals, and to seek greater opportunities to satisfy his ambition.

'He thinks big,' said one DEA staffer of Chapo's hunger. 'When Chapo gets involved in a drug deal, we're talking about extremely large quantities. Tons.'

Cheap, disposable labour was one of his secrets: his people would seize groups of farm workers from Mexico's poorer regions (such 'recruitment', tantamount to kidnapping, was known as a *levanton*) and put them to work in the tunnels for weeks, even months, at a time. The tunnel-builders lived below ground or in warehouses near the tunnel entrance. When the job was done, Chapo had them killed.

This made it particularly difficult to detect the tunnels, recalls one DEA agent. The tunnels were so well concealed that the only way to find them was through informants – most of whom were dead by the time the DEA found out about them.

Being based in Guadalajara and eschewing the social circuit, Chapo still managed to remain a less prominent figure than the narcos in Tijuana and Ciudad Juarez. But his cutthroat nature and ambition caught the attention of his rivals, as did his desire for more control of the Mexican smuggling business.

The Tijuana crew, too, was getting 'selfish', as one DEA agent put it, and wanted to expand. Indeed, Tijuana had become the prized corridor for the Colombian cocaine suppliers, and the Arellano Felix brothers wanted to capitalize on their newfound clout. They also wanted to protect their turf from Chapo. He and El Mayo were highly regarded for their toughness, for being the only ones willing to stand up to the brothers from Tijuana.

Chapo was encroaching on their territory. He invested more than a million dollars in the massive tunnel in Tijuana; he also bought safe houses throughout the city, in which he kept guns, grenade launchers, night-vision goggles and bundles of cash.

The Arellano Felix brothers were 'not afraid to pull a trigger', as one Tijuana policeman put it. They placed a bounty on Chapo's head.

In early 1992 the hit men struck. A group of members of the San Diego-based Calle Treinta gang employed by the Arellano Felix brothers nabbed six of Chapo's lieutenants in Tijuana. They tortured them for information then shot them in the back of the head. The corpses, bound and gagged, were dumped along a highway outside the border city.

Shortly after, a car bomb exploded outside a house used by Chapo in Culiacan. No one was hurt; the narcos weren't at home. But the message was clear.

On 8 November 1992 Chapo struck back.

Two of the Arellano Felix brothers, Francisco Javier and Ramon, had headed for the resort city of Puerto Vallarta, Jalisco, for a little R & R. One night they went out to a popular discotheque, 'Christine'.

Fifteen of Chapo's men, wearing police uniforms, got out of their vehicles in front of the club. They brushed aside the doormen and walked in. They surveyed the scene; about 300 people were dancing and drinking under the disco lights. The music was blaring. They spotted the Arellano Felix brothers and their bodyguards and opened fire. The bodyguards shot back, as Francisco Javier and Ramon Arellano Felix fled out the back of the club and sped off in one of their vehicles. The shootout continued: six people died, some of them innocent revellers.

El Chapo had launched a war against the Tijuana cartel, the first war of the new era of Mexican drug trafficking.

Days later, another group of Arellano Felix hit men was deployed to Guadalajara. They spotted a vehicle they believed was carrying Chapo and opened fire with their AK-47s. Chapo escaped unharmed.

For the next six months, Chapo would be a wanted man in the eyes of the Arellano Felix brothers. But Chapo was both well connected and well protected in Guadalajara; their efforts to find him proved futile. Group after group of hit men was sent to kill him, with no luck.

In mid-May 1993, a team of top sicarios arrived in Guadalajara. Francisco Javier Arellano Felix came with them.

Chapo was playing it very safe, moving around Guadalajara frequently. He checked into various rooms at the Holiday Inn; then he moved to one of his safe houses. Then he moved to another hotel.

The Arellano Felix brothers had no success. After days of searching for Chapo, Francisco Javier and the hit men decided to head home, on 24 May.

Javier was checking in for his flight back to Tijuana when he heard the news: Chapo was in the airport car park, arriving to catch an afternoon flight to Puerto Vallarta.

The gunmen ran outside firing; a group of gunmen fired back. 'All hell breaks loose and there's a shootout all over the airport,' recalls one DEA agent of the scene. They spotted the vehicle they believed belonged to Chapo, a white Mercury Grand Marquis, a type of car commonly driven by narcos. They pulled open the door and opened fire.

But it wasn't Chapo in the car; he was in a dark green Buick Sedan near by. In the Mercury Grand Marquis was Cardinal Juan Jesus Posadas Ocampo, the archbishop of Guadalajara. Amid the chaos, Chapo rolled away from the scene, hopped in a taxi and sped off to a safe house. The cardinal was dead, his body riddled with fourteen bullets.

Francisco Javier Arellano Felix, meanwhile, took his seat in first class on the plane to Tijuana. In the seat next to him was Jorge Hank Rhon. The plane took off twenty minutes later; the authorities have never explained why it was allowed to leave.

At least, that's one version of what happened that fateful day in May. Some in the PGR believe that the Arellano Felix brothers knew Chapo was going to be there at the airport. They believe the brothers knew the colour of his car. They suggest that the Arellano Felix brothers hit men were actually going after the cardinal – but there is no firm evidence of this. Some witnesses have also testified that Benjamin Arellano Felix was also at the scene of the crime.

But these explanations are refuted by other investigators, who think the PGR claims and investigations are wrong – perhaps because of its complicity with Chapo. 'Lies! It's a fucking lie!' shouts one official, pointing to the PGR report on the airport shootout. 'You can't trust anyone here – not journalists, not secretaries, not cardinals, no one! It's fucked up – [the truth] will kill you here.

'If I say this, the PGR will fuck me, if I say that, the PGR will fuck me. They'll kill me,' he said, grabbing his neck as if he were being choked to death.

One former investigator also questions how anyone could come to the conclusion that the Arellano Felix hit men could have mistaken Chapo's car for that of Cardinal Posadas Ocampo – a white Grand Marquis. They had apparently known the colour of Chapo's car, after all. 'How could they have been aiming for Chapo if he was in a green car and . . . How could this happen?'

That Chapo had eluded his assassins wouldn't change the face of the drug war, but the accidental death of Cardinal Posadas Ocampo would. Outraged by the killing of such a high-ranking and respected religious figure, the government ordered a roundup of some of the nation's top drug traffickers; it offered a reward of nearly $5 million for information leading to the conviction of Chapo and several other major players in the illegal narcotics trade.

Chapo fled to Mexico City and stayed there for two days. He met with an employee, to whom he gave about $200 million to provide for his family if he were caught; he gave another employee about the same amount to make sure his organization continued to run smoothly in case of a short-term absence.

He was then driven down to southern Chiapas by another trusted employee. Chapo had established a network for his drug operations in Chiapas and Guatemala a few months before; so, upon his arrival, he got in touch with a lieutenant colonel in the Guatemalan Army.

Chapo paid the lieutenant colonel $1.2 million. In return, the drug lord and his cohorts – four men and a girlfriend of Chapo's – would be able to hide out in Guatemala. Chapo also had a fake passport – he was now travelling under the name of Jorge Ramos Perez.

On 31 May, just a week after the Guadalajara airport shooting, the PGR received intelligence that Chapo was indeed in Guatemala. Soldiers and federal agents were deployed there. At dawn on 9 June, Guatemalan troops surrounded the area where Chapo and his accomplices were hiding out. They arrested him, and handed him over to the Mexicans at noon that same day. Chapo had been betrayed.

It's unclear why catching Chapo in 1993 was so easy. At the time, however, US pressure and involvement in foreign anti-drug operations were at their height. American special forces and the Colombian military were closing in on Pablo Escobar in Medellin (he would be killed in December 1993). The sharing of intelligence between Central and South American nations, Mexico and the United States had reached unprecedented levels. This may explain why the Guatemalans were willing to ignore the deal struck with Chapo, and nab him. The Mexicans claimed that such co-operation had made the capture possible.

Once in the Mexican military's hands, Chapo opened up. His Colombian connections were from Cali – not Escobar's Medellin. He also revealed the extent of his network of corruption within Mexico: shortly after his arrest, one of the officials Chapo named in his confession would be found dead; another would be arrested.

Chapo also spilled the beans on the Arellano Felix brothers.

If the botched attempt on Chapo's life proved to be the defining moment of 1993, his revelations to the military about the Arellano Felix brothers broke a bond of secrecy between the cartels that would never be repaired.

The brothers also became Public Enemy No. 1. 'From this moment on, when the cardinal was killed, it was the [Arellano Felix brothers] against the world, against the other cartels, against the government of Mexico and against the United States government,' recalls one DEA agent who was based in San Diego at the time.

Francisco Rafael Arellano Felix, the eldest brother, was captured on 4 December 1993. He was locked up in a maximum-security prison. The remaining Arellano Felix brothers struck back, but this time without their guns. They sent a letter to the Pope, telling their version of what had happened in Guadalajara, claiming it was Chapo's gunmen who had mistaken the cardinal for Ramon Arellano Felix.

The fighting between Chapo and the Arellano Felix brothers sparked a war that since has spiralled into a nationwide version of the *Gunfight at the OK Corral*.

The Mexican drug trade would no longer be run by a tight-knit group of friends and family members originally from Sinaloa; it was now an anything-goes game. Disputes would no longer be dealt with at the talking table (although sometimes this would be attempted); they would be solved through bloodshed. Collusion by one cartel with the authorities in order to oust another cartel would become common. The main players – the Sinaloa, Tijuana, Juarez and Gulf cartels – would co-opt newer groups of enforcers to do their dirty work, only to find their own people turning on them in subsequent power struggles as they gained more clout.

Never again would the Mexican drug industry be a straight-forward criminal enterprise. From now on it would be a kill-or-be-killed, murky and messy world of mistrust, mythology and money – $40 billion a year, by some estimates.

By the new millennium, the Mexicans would be the ones in the global spotlight, not the Colombians. The DEA's Constantine would describe the Mexican narcos as 'a significant force in inter-national organized crime' and warn that they 'now dominate drug trafficking along the US/Mexico border and in many U.S. cities'.

The events of 1993 would also help propel Chapo to infamy and near-mythical status on a par with Malverde, the narco-saint. For the next two decades he would embellish his reputation. Even in prison his status would grow as tales of how he was living like a king behind bars spread far and wide. Along the south-western US border, more tunnels would keep being uncovered.

His escape would become the example cited whenever anyone – criminal or otherwise – wanted to shame the Mexican authorities. Whereas before 1993 he had been 'just another narco', according to veteran Sinaloa journalist Ismael Bojorquez, Chapo's escape from Puente Grande would transform him into the 'media-narco', every-one's favourite.

But Chapo, with his disdain for publicity, would still manage to outwit and outrun everyone.

'This guy is one of the cleverest we have ever come across,' said Jose Luis Santiago Vasconcelos, a top Mexican anti-organized crime prosecutor, prior to his death in a plane crash in 2008 that also killed the nation's interior secretary – an incident which many conspiracy theorists would attribute to Chapo. 'He is always in the most secret places. Always protected. He poses as a man of the people, who understands their problems, and gives them money, but he should not be treated as a hero. He is stained with the pain and blood of too many families.'

Those words were lost on millions of Mexicans, who would continue to regard Chapo as the modern-day Robin Hood who had managed to outwit a government they distrusted. But as more blood flowed, and more families felt the pain, the government's hunt for Chapo would grow more intense, as would his rivals' hunger for his head. The ring around him would close day by day.

6. 'Breaking the Neck of Destiny'

As the rain fell hard, the last of Badiraguato's revellers could be heard, singing, yelling profanities, stumbling or driving drunkenly home after the Independence Day festivities. They had just enjoyed a peaceful celebration – no violence at all, no shootings, *nada* – much to the delight of local government and residents.

Some local narcos, sporting gold chains, guns and fancy cowboy boots, had filed into the square at about 9 p.m. to listen to the live traditional banda tunes with the rest of Badiraguato, but they'd caused no trouble. Some were surely just wannabe narcos, too, dressing like those they aspire to become.

A group of mothers, lined up in a row along the side of the plaza, looked on as one young narco grabbed the hand of a beautiful brown-haired girl of about fourteen. She was decked out in stilettos, an open-backed top and a short skirt. Her long nails were neatly painted, specks of glitter on her cheek reflected in the lighting. He dragged her out in front of the band and they began to dance sloppily – like teenagers – as the brass banda group churned out another lively, upbeat tune.

Normally, the sight of an apparent drug trafficker and a dolled-up teen princess dancing to what can only be described as circus music would be sidesplitting. But in Badiraguato it's the norm – the narcos love their banda, and they love their princesses.

There was an air of calm to Badiraguato that Independence Day, 15 September 2009. The previous year had been a troubled one; homicides had dominated the talk of the town. 'Mochomo' – a nickname meaning 'fire ant' given to Alfredo Beltran Leyva – and Chapo had been at war, and no one really knew who was in charge any more. But now, with a pact between the feuding kingpins, there was control again and the violence was declining.

Soldiers in the shadowy barracks at the far end of Badiraguato peered out over the walls to catch a glimpse of the festivities – they had not been invited but they would enjoy as much of the moment as they could. Some residents glared at the soldiers; all opted for silence while walking by. Only when they were out of the soldiers' earshot did they resume their conversations.

The air of calm in Badiraguato felt precariously temporary. The Sierra of Sinaloa today is not what it once was. For several years now, the region has been what one resident calls a 'marked zone'. The military is ever-present, but so are the narcos. By and large, the military avoids conflict, but that doesn't mean the narcos aren't duking it out among themselves.

Homicide has become so common in Sinaloa that it costs a mere $35 to have a rival murdered.

The military's hands were covered in blood, too. One Friday night, a group of teachers and their children had been driving back to La Joya de los Martinez, in the Sinaloan hills, from a meeting in a nearby village. A unit of soldiers was returning from a long day of burning marijuana in the fields. As the car approached, the soldiers waved it down.

The driver was caught off guard. Were they really soldiers? In this part of the country, assaults on vehicles by bandits are all too common. He slowed the car, but kept it moving. The car got closer. The soldiers opened fire. A hail of bullets swept through the car.

Alicia Esparza Parra, nineteen, was dead. Griselda Martinez, twenty-five, was dead, too. So were her children. Edwin, age seven. Grisel, age four. Juana Diosminey, age two.

On another occasion, in Santiago de los Caballeros, Badiraguato, four youths in a car were heading to a party. The military stopped them as they rounded a bend on the country road. Tensions were high; an argument ensued. A shot was fired. The army peppered the car with bullets, killing everyone inside. Investigations would prove the soldiers were at fault – there was no gun inside the car, nor was there evidence of bullets having been fired from that direction. There was a tense atmosphere in Badiraguato. The people staged protests, at one point walking several hours to Culiacan in a large procession to demonstrate outside the governor's office.

Omar Meza and his friends remember that fateful day. 'El Comandante', as his friends call him, sang a traditional ballad known as a *corrido* at the funeral. As he sang, many locals wept.

> People of Badiraguato
> the blood flows again
> For the four lives
> who couldn't defend themselves
> Their families and friends
> couldn't believe it
>
> They were heading to a party
> when the soldiers came out of nowhere
> Without any motive
> they fired their rifles
> And how surprised were they
> the men were unarmed
>
> Sinaloa is in mourning
> for this situation
> La Joya de los Martinez
> already lived the same terror
> Reckless soldiers
> more dangerous than a lion
> Assassins through error
> there will be a simple repercussion
> These are published news stories
> on the radio and in print
> All we ask for is justice
> assassins without conscience
>
> This is your farewell
> goodbye Geovany my friend

Today God has called you
because that's how he wanted your destiny to be

Grandmother, mother and brothers
never forget that I love you
And that I'll protect you
when I find myself in heaven
I will continue on the path
of my father and my grandfather

'Tragedy in Santiago de los Caballeros' – narco-corrido sung
      by Omar 'El Comandante' Meza

Meza, like many other singers of corridos, considers himself a
social commentator. He sings of what's going on around him, on
TV and in newspapers. That includes the latest news in organized
crime – 'narco-corridos', as these particular songs are known. In
recent years these tunes have grown increasingly popular.

But for the likes of Los Canelos de Durango, Roberto Tapia, Los
Tigres del Norte, Los Tucanes de Tijuana and K-Paz de la Sierra, to
name just a few music groups who have recorded narco-corridos,
playing such music carries certain risks. The narcos themselves are
fans of the genre, and these groups often play at private parties for
them. Some of the musicians have chosen to embrace the life they
sing about, carrying gold-plated guns and sometimes acting like
narcos themselves.

Some have met narco-fates.

Sergio Gomez, the singer of the Grammy Award-winning
group K-Paz de la Sierra, was kidnapped after performing in his
home state of Michoacan. He was found the next day, beaten, tortured and strangled to death. Gomez and his band had tweaked the
nerves of a cartel. Supporting the wrong one in the wrong place
could get you killed.

One narco-corrido crooner, Valentin Elizalde, risked singing
the praises of Chapo at a festival in Reynosa, Tamaulipas – the

heart of Gulf cartel territory. He closed his set with 'A mis enemigos' ('To my enemies'), a song about Chapo sending a message to his Gulf cartel rivals.

Elizalde left the stage to rousing applause. He was followed by two vehicles. They opened fire, hitting the singer twenty-eight times.

More than a dozen musicians famous for recording narco-corridos have been murdered in recent years. All of the killings had the trappings of organized crime.

Chapo is a big fan of narco-corridos – unsurprisingly, when one considers there are at least half a dozen songs written in his honour. The narco has sometimes hired crooners to play at a private fiesta.

In one instance, a man approached the members of La Sombra Nortena in Badiraguato. He offered them $4,000 to play at an upcoming party; a private plane would be provided to take them there. They accepted, and were flown to a town in the mountains of Durango. They played their set and headed home. But when they got back to Badiraguato, they were arrested. They were carrying marijuana and a gun, but the authorities were more interested in the man they had just performed for – Chapo himself.

The members of La Sombra Nortena were lucky not to be charged with links to organized crime. In recent years, the government has taken to condemning narco-corridos, Malverde and other forms of narco-idolatry. Some politicians have sought to ban narco-corridos from the radio; some are even calling for prison sentences for composers of the tunes. One song, by Los Tucanes de Tijuana, was banned from the airwaves because it overtly ridiculed the government's efforts to fight the war on drugs.

The condemnation of narco-corridos is all part of a fight to kill off what many politicians and parents in Mexico call narco-culture. Yudit del Rincon, a congresswoman in Sinaloa's state legislature, has teenage children, and has witnessed the impact that narco-culture has had on them. She is distraught over the fact that her son listens to narco-corridos and wants to wear clothes and other paraphernalia (gold chains, for instance) that the narcos wear.

She is also adamant that the state's politicians lead by example.

On one occasion, during a congressional discussion about the drug trade in Sinaloa, Del Rincon suggested she and all her peers take drug tests to prove they are fit to be representatives of the public at large. Everyone applauded the idea. Then she hit them with her plan: let's all take drug tests right now. She had brought in two lab technicians to administer the tests.

The legislators nearly fell over each other trying to get out the door.

Fighting the culture of the narco is extremely challenging. There's a whole world connected to the narco, and it's not just the songs or the clothing. The narcos share a camaraderie of partnership in crime, as evidenced by their nicknames. These *apodos* are common in the Mexican underworld. Many are appearance-based – 'Chapo', for instance, or 'El Barbas'. Some shine light on the criminal's character – 'El Petardo', the Firecracker, is known for his explosive outbursts – while others are admiring. 'La Reina del Pacifico', the Queen of the Pacific, was highly regarded as a woman who had risen to the top levels of an underworld run by men, until she was brought down. El Padrino was another such name.

Some nicknames are quite humorous, masking the brutality of the person in question. 'El Chuck Norris', for instance, was suspected of being involved in executions and digging clandestine graves. A notorious human trafficker, David Avendano Vallina, was known as 'La Hamburguesa' (the Hamburger). A kidnapping gang in Mexico City took the irony one step further, calling itself 'Los Gotcha'.

Dead Men Walking

Just a few years ago – when Chapo was the only form of justice and before the Army came – there was more of a sense of discipline among Sinaloa's youth. 'When the cops pass Chapo on the road, they call him Boss,' explained one resident. There was less concern about narco-culture; Chapo actually kept the kids in line.

Several years back, a group of teenagers stole a number of gas tanks from a depot on the outskirts of town, residents recall. The local police were at a loss – they couldn't conduct a house-to-house search of the nearby mountains, it would prove fruitless and time-wasting, and possibly even put their lives in danger. So Chapo – or 'El Senor', as many locals call him out of respect – had his people ask around. They quickly rounded up the perpetrators, and dropped them off at the police station.

On several occasions, when violence in Culiacan or Badiraguato has got out of hand, Chapo has purportedly stepped in, talking to the offending parties. Calm down, he tells them. You're attracting too much attention. If you don't stop this, we will. He and El Mayo have reportedly visited homes in Culiacan, speaking to the parents of young offenders.

Stories of the discipline laid down by Chapo abound. Some appear true, some apocryphal. Once, a young man apparently robbed Chapo's niece's car, unknowingly. When Chapo found out, he sent his henchmen over to cut off the thief's hands.

But today, it's different, worried locals say. The feuding has taken its toll. The military's presence has only heightened tensions in the region. Gunfights have become routine, and the young narcos have no respect for the law; some even disobey Chapo's law.

A twelve-year-old boy walked over and pointed to a junction just in front of Badiraguato's church and opposite the mayor's office. 'They killed a boy over there the other day,' he said with a frown.

The police know they have no control over the situation. In 2006 Badiraguato's deputy police chief was shot dead, apparently for having arrested a young narco. A couple of months later, the local jail was raided by gunmen who had come looking for their man. The police force let them have him without a fuss. David Diaz Cruz, chief of police at the time, knew there was little he could do – he didn't even have the power to look into smaller fry.

'Even though I have my suspicions that they're selling drugs in the corner store, I can't investigate,' he said.

The narcos, particularly those like Chapo, are still admired by many, perhaps simply out of fear. In Culiacan there's an expression: 'Better to live five years like a *rey* [king] than to live a lifetime like a *buey* [castrated bull].'

The young people do indeed live and die by this code. Sinaloa consistently ranks No. 1 in Mexico for homicides of men between the ages of eighteen and twenty-nine.

The state police have taken note, but that's about all they've done. Much like the federal government, which often likens drug consumption to 'evil', Josefina de Jesus Garcia Ruiz, Sinaloa's police chief, has been pushing a moral line since taking up the post.

Garcia Ruiz stresses that kids need structure and family values in order to prevent them falling into the drug trade. She comes across as earnest, yet stern, much like a schoolteacher. 'Young Sinaloans want to be like people like Chapo. He has what they think is everything – money, power, women, weapons. But we need to change that. We need to love and cherish our kids, not abuse them [or] hit them, [not] love money, so [the kid is] not hating life.'

The death toll hasn't helped her plead her case: the majority of young people appear to be opting for the grave. Drugs are the only way to get ahead in Sinaloa. And with a government that largely doesn't care and a formal economy that takes pity on no one, the narco-elders remain the most respectable patrons of society. While politicians have stolen from the state coffers and failed to follow up on promises to provide education and medical care, Sinaloa's narcos have paid for schools and hospitals, and poured money into churches and homes. Locals are still indebted to them.

A group of teenagers in Badiraguato sat around in a shoe shop near the town square, considering whether to talk openly about this apparent irony. Sweat poured from their faces as they thought about what they should say. Reluctant to speak candidly, one asked, 'Will they kill me if I talk?'

Her friend, Jose de Jesus Landell Garcia, was willing to risk being open. 'The drug traffickers do good things here. They employ people. There's no corn, no beans here – the people here are all about drugs,' said the twenty-two-year-old, who co-owns the shoe shop with his father, adding that he was in two minds about narco-culture. Whereas he was lucky enough to have a job working with his father, most of his friends had taken up employment with the cartels because 'it was the only thing they could do'.

'On the one hand, I'm not against the narcos. But they also bring the violence. I'd like to see another form of employment here . . . The drug traffickers have money, create jobs and help people.'

His friend Gladys Elizabeth Lopez Villareal, aged seventeen, was even more supportive of the narcos. 'The people like Chapo are good people. We're their admirers. They help us and they respond how they have to,' she said, referring to the drug traffickers' ways of dealing with their business competitors and, often, the law.

The culture of illegality is not only entrenched in Sinaloa, it seems to have won out over any other options. 'What can a kid in Culiacan do?' asks Martin Amaral, the historian, raising his hands in despair. 'Work in a Wal-Mart? Study? Or be a narco? There's nothing he can do to rise up. Obviously for a boy, the better option is to break the neck of his destiny of poverty, and become a narco. I don't condemn it, I understand it.'

The average young Sinaloan narco today survives three and a half years in the business. He then ends up in jail, or is killed.

Among the Tombs

On the outskirts of Culiacan, the mausoleums of the Jardines del Humaya cemetery peek out through the trees. This is the most famous narco-resting place in the area; the mausoleums are resplendent, some boasting colourful domes and stained glass windows. Some have glass doors to keep unwanted visitors out; inside, balloons, candles and gifts have been left by relatives. Dozens of flowers are strewn atop one grave.

Off in the distance, two gravediggers prepare for the next arrival.

Some who rest in the Jardines del Humaya are well known. Years ago, 'El Guero' Palma Salazar's wife, Guadalupe Leija, ran off with a rival trafficker from Venezuela, who was believed to be working for the Arellano Felix clan. The Venezuelan purportedly then demanded Leija withdraw some $7 million of El Guero's money. Having served her purpose, she was murdered and decapitated. The Venezuelan sent back her head to El Guero in Culiacan in a cooler. He then took his rival's two young sons back to Venezuela, where he threw them off a bridge.

A fresco of Leija and the two boys adorns the ceiling of their mausoleum. Their serene faces look down on the spot where El Guero will one day rest alongside them.

Leija's beheading was the first that was linked to the drug trade in Mexico. Today, there are dozens of decapitated victims in the Jardines del Humaya.

The Velazquez Uriarte family was less well known than that of El Guero. Velazquez Uriarte and his young son died in a shootout. Inside the mausoleum, toys and balloons have been brought by well-wishers for the kid's birthday. The edifice is designed with a Batman theme in mind; its outer walls are painted black and grey, the symbol of the Dark Knight adorns the roof of the building.

On another grave, an unknown narco has left an inscription to his girlfriend: 'How difficult it is knowing you are no longer with us, how difficult it is not hearing your voice, your laugh, how difficult it is not to be able to touch you, hug you, how difficult it is to live without you.'

Hundreds of narcos are buried in the Jardines del Humaya. Thousands of others are buried in mass graves throughout Sinaloa, throughout Mexico.

Ivan Vazquez Benitez, aged thirty-six, was gunned down by a group of AK-47-wielding thugs as he drove home from work one Saturday morning.

The bodies of Omar Osuna, thirty-two, Victor Manuel Castillo Villela, twenty-six, and David Lopez Ruiz, twenty-four, were found in the Francisco I. Madero district of the Sinaloan port city of Mazatlan. Their heads had been chopped off and placed in a large cooler.

Ivan Toledo Lopez was kidnapped from a discotheque. Two days later, the police found a hand and forearm, accompanied by a pig's head. Later that day, they found a young man's legs with another pig's head. They believe they belonged to Lopez.

A young man wearing a road haulage company uniform was gunned down as he stood outside a car repair shop in the Lomas del Boulevard neighbourhood of Culiacan at 7.35 one Tuesday night. One of the four 9mm bullets that entered his body lodged in his head.

Many of the drug war's dead are never identified or claimed by relatives. They are known by forensics only as 'NNs' – *No Nombres*, or No Names.

7. The General

General Noe Sandoval Alcazar sat in his office in the military base on the outskirts of Culiacan, shuffling through a stack of papers. It was the summer of 2008. He had been fighting the drug war in Sinaloa for more than six months, since taking over as head of Operation Sierra Madre and Joint Operation Culiacan–Navolato on 14 December of the previous year. As head of the 9th Military Zone, he was in charge of anti-drug operations in the hills of Sinaloa – and the hunt for Chapo.

At this moment, Chapo wasn't really his priority. To be sure, General Sandoval and his men were working to catch the drug lord. But the violence in Sinaloa had reached such extreme levels that, for the general, quelling the homicide rate and instilling peace were the most immediate necessities.

In June alone there had been 143 murders.

'We're just trying to put them in jail. They're killing, decapitating each other. The other day, a [drug trafficker] was found decapitated, with a pig's head where his should have been.'

The general read off his list of successes in Sinaloa, but with little hint of pride. 'In the past eighteen months, Operation Sierra Madre has yielded the following results: 97,633 marijuana fields have been destroyed; 31,296 poppy fields have been destroyed; 418 landing strips have been shut down; more than 250 planes have been seized; 910 people have been arrested on drug trafficking charges; 1,099 weapons have been seized . . .'

The general looked up, as if wondering whether to continue. One of his lieutenants indicated that he should.

'The Army has seized more than $12 million in US dollar bills . . .'

The general was weary, practically on his last legs. Sixty-two years old, he had been fighting the drug war for forty-two years. During that time, he had ordered troops to clean up corrupt police forces, ordered raids on narco safe houses and overseen the destruction of hundreds of marijuana and opium plantations. He had seen them spring up again.

Mexico's military first became involved in the drug war in the 1930s, when soldiers were deployed to destroy marijuana and opium crops in Sinaloa and other parts of the country. Only 400 soldiers took part in that great effort. Further attempts were launched in subsequent decades, and in the 1960s the United States provided further support. The Mexicans were given aeroplanes, helicopters, jeeps and weapons.

The only real effect on the drug trade was that from then on, the gomeros would better conceal their marijuana and poppy plantations. At any given time for the rest of the twentieth century, the maximum number of soldiers deployed to eradicate drugs was about 10,000. And the Mexican drug trade simply grew.

There had been some big wins for the military; the bust at Rancho Bufalo in Chihuahua, for instance. But there had also been major losses.

In 1996 a general by the name of Jose Gutierrez Rebollo had taken over as the nation's drug czar. A former member of the presidential guard and a hard-hitting military commander, General Gutierrez had earned quite a reputation prior to his appointment. He had helped capture 'El Guero' Palma Salazar after the narco's plane crash-landed in the mountains outside Guadalajara. Gutierrez Rebollo had deftly – and quietly – deployed 200 soldiers to the house where El Guero was hiding and arrested him and thirty-three police officers (who were on El Guero's payroll) without a single shot being fired.

At sixty-two, he was made the top man in Mexico's war on drugs. Upon hearing the news, his American counterpart, General Barry R. McCaffrey, optimistically announced that Gutierrez Rebollo 'has a public reputation of absolute integrity. He is a strong leader. This is clearly a focused, high-energy man.'

Less than six months into his tenure General Gutierrez Rebollo was arrested in Mexico City. He would be sentenced to seventy-one years in prison for having links with the Juarez cartel.

The DEA and Washington officials were outraged: they had supplied Gutierrez Rebollo with key information leading to the arrest of certain traffickers, and yet all the while, under their noses, he had been in the pocket of the Juarez cartel.

Other military men would fall in Gutierrez Rebollo's wake, yet still the Mexican armed forces remained – and, to this day, remain – one of the country's most trusted institutions. They would always be called upon in times of dire need (during hurricanes and other natural disasters, for instance) and continue to wage a slow and grinding war against the drug cartels.

In the summer of 2008, that fight showed no signs of slowing. US–Mexican cooperation was at an 'all-time high', according to the DEA. Intelligence was being shared with the likes of General Sandoval in Sinaloa, and they were acting on it.

On the wall to the general's left, a map of the region was thickly covered with pins of various colours, like a voodoo doll. But this doll wasn't near dead. The red pins indicated major seizures – poppy and marijuana fields, clandestine airstrips and ranches – while blue, green and yellow pins denoted suspected targets that had yet to be hit. The reds were far outnumbered, and the general acknowledged it.

'We have a lot to do,' he muttered, sifting through another pile of paper before reeling off another set of numbers.

General Sandoval wasn't the first high-ranking military man to specifically target Chapo and the Sinaloa drug business.

In 2004 the Army had struck. It had received intelligence that Chapo and El Mayo had just thrown a huge bash in La Tuna, and were on their way by truck to Tamazula, in Durango. The journey would take hours, given the condition of the dirt tracks, and the Air Force would be able to corner them.

Having located their man, the helicopters swooped in on the ranch where Chapo and his compadres were believed to be resting en route. 'What's going on?' a shocked Chapo yelled at his bodyguards. They took off on foot.

The Air Force men got out of the helicopters and started rounding up the employees of the ranch. By the time they began a thorough search of the area, Chapo was long gone. According to police sources interviewed by local journalists at the time, the idea had been merely to scare the drug lord, not actually catch him.

Later that same year, in November, about 200 soldiers stormed another ranch in the mountains just north of La Tuna, after hearing his voice on a satellite phone that they had been tapping for months.

They missed him by a mere ten minutes. At the ranch, they found laptops with new photos of the drug boss – he was now sporting a moustache and was about twenty pounds heavier than he had been while in prison – and other evidence that he had been there. Furious that they had come so close, the soldiers torched two vehicles and trashed the ranch.

Officials blamed the network of informants in the area for Chapo's escape, but critics of the government saw the failed effort as evidence that no one was really making a serious effort to catch him. They were just going through the motions, the sceptics argued.

'The only explanation is [that] people told him; among the same people who are supposed to catch him are people helping him,' said Fernando Guzman Perez-Pelaez, a congressman who led a federal National Security Committee.

Eddy's Obsession

General Sandoval's predecessor, General Rolando Eugenio Hidalgo Eddy, took charge of the 9th Military Zone during the final days of the administration of President Vicente Fox, which had been humiliated by Chapo's prison escape. So when he arrived in Culiacan in January 2006, General Hidalgo Eddy – or simply 'Eddy', as locals would come endearingly to call him – vowed to take down the man responsible for this embarrassment.

Also a veteran, born in 1945, General Eddy had long been

regarded as a military man of action, who often took aggressive decisions. Some called him rash; one peer even described him as 'superfluous in his decisions, frivolous, [a man] who didn't analyse the consequences of his orders'.

Sometimes those decisions were the right ones. For instance, he had helped lead the military intelligence team that raided Rancho Bufalo in Chihuahua, cooperating with DEA agent 'Kiki' Camarena. Eddy's men had also discovered that members of the Mexican military had been guarding the 1,000-hectare marijuana plantation.

But like most generals in Mexico, Eddy had also suffered his share of negative, unproven allegations: while stationed in the northern state of Coahuila, Eddy had allegedly held meetings with Carrillo Fuentes. He denied this, but the sentencing of General Gutierrez Rebollo for the very same reason didn't exactly engender public trust.

So in Sinaloa, with the Puente Grande escape hanging over his government's head and his past loyalties in question, General Eddy would take on Chapo; he even pledged publicly that he would catch him.

Within the first months of his tenure, dozens of planes and vast quantities of opium and marijuana were seized. Eddy's soldiers also raided and seized properties belonging to Victor Emilio Cazares Gastelum and his sister, Blanca Margarita Cazares Salazar, a.k.a. 'The Empress', one of Chapo's alleged money launderers. This was the first substantial move that the Mexican government – working with its US Justice Department and DEA counterparts – had made against the financial operations of the Mexican cartels.

For the first time in several decades, the entire Sierra was a serious target, too. Eddy's troops conducted thorough searches of mountain pueblos and closed down airstrips, outraging locals who claimed they were being harassed. His troops stormed the towns throughout the county of Badiraguato. They raided the narco-havens of Santiago de los Caballeros and La Tuna, not to mention various towns in nearby Durango, where Chapo had more lairs.

The military base in Badiraguato, which had been abandoned

when soldiers were sent away to quell the Zapatista rebel uprising in southern Mexico in the mid-to-late-1990s, was reopened, and the soldiers' presence quickly drew local ire. Instead of support for development programmes and the economy, residents cried, the government has sent us soldiers.

Several hundred residents of Badiraguato and the Durango towns of Tamazula, Topia and Canelas – all part of Chapo's fiefdom – were more perturbed. They drew up and signed a petition, which they sent to both the president and the local human rights commission.

'With the promise of capturing Chapo Guzman,' read the letter, 'Hidalgo Eddy has unleashed complete terror on the families of the state of Sinaloa, violating the political constitution of Mexico, violating the human rights of all Sinaloans, openly ignoring the legitimately elected state government, the power of the judges, magistrates, and raiding each day and the next without orders of a competent judge, stealing jewels and vehicles under the pretext of finding . . . Chapo Guzman.'

It also accused Eddy of being in bed with Los Zetas, the hired guns of the Gulf cartel.

Authorities dismissed the letter as a propaganda ploy by Chapo. Locals in Badiraguato and Tamazula deny having been pressured or paid to sign the letter, but such tactics had been used in the past and would be used again in the future.

The complaints would do little to slow General Eddy. After only nine months on the job, he did what no other military man had ever done in Sinaloa: he went after a major narco's family. Eddy ordered an *operativo*, or raid, on the ranch of Maria Consuelo Loera Perez, Chapo's mother. They had been informed that Chapo was visiting her in La Tuna, but by the time they arrived he was nowhere to be found. They uncovered no evidence of illicit activity either, but, according to locals, completely trashed the ranch.

Shortly after, General Eddy's soldiers detained Luis Alberto Cano Zepeda, one of Chapo's cousins, as he was landing a light plane in one of the Sierra airstrips usually ignored by the authorities.

Chapo was furious. A group of his men drove by the 9th Military

Zone's headquarters in Culiacan and threw out a dead body – an informant who had been tipping off the military as to Chapo's whereabouts. His killers left a note, warning Eddy to back off. In spite of the threat – and several more in the ensuing weeks – the general would not be deterred.

In October Eddy received reliable intelligence that Chapo was in Sinaloa de Leyva, in the northern foothills of the Sierra. He sent a team of soldiers to storm the town. Three helicopters provided backup. But by the time the soldiers arrived, Chapo had fled. Someone in Eddy's own team had leaked news of the raid.

And so it would go on for the duration of General Eddy's tenure. On several occasions in the Sierra, his men would appear to have Chapo cornered. But every time, the drug lord would get away.

Chapo's resolve – or at least his network – proved stronger than Eddy's, and ultimately, the latter lost. Upon his departure, local newspapers played down General Sandoval's arrival and instead highlighted Eddy's failure to accomplish his goals. 'El Chapo wins, the war is over and General Hidalgo Eddy is gone,' read one headline.

Eddy would be haunted by his failure. One of his bodyguards was later arrested for having leaked information to Chapo. The bodyguard had known every single movement of Eddy's, almost every decision he made.

For General Sandoval, the struggle was only beginning. Although the general at times played down the turmoil consuming the region – 'Sinaloa is not at war,' he insisted to reporters – he wasn't about to roll over and play dead.

His strategy, however, was slightly different from Eddy's. For one thing, he sought to improve cooperation with the government, which in the past had been lacking, and attempted to circumvent bureaucracy. 'Every time we find or do something, a supervisor comes to supervise the supervisor who has been sent to supervise us,' he said as he collected evidence at one seized marijuana plantation. 'The drug traffickers . . . know right away when we find something.'

Like his predecessor, General Sandoval would go after those

members of Chapo's family who were implicated in illegal activities. But he would also go after his minions, his support structure, the roots of the narco-establishment. His men would seize hundreds of vehicles they thought might be used by narcos, and operate checkpoints throughout Culiacan in the hope of minimizing the amount of drugs and weapons able to circulate. They would patrol the streets day and night. The narco-network would be disrupted; in the Sierra, checkpoints and impromptu raids would tighten the noose around the narcos' necks.

This was President Felipe Calderon's initial, full-on approach to the narcos, to really shake things up, to fight a war that Chapo himself had begun. Anyone caught on a *plantillo*, or drug plantation, would be arrested in this war. Intelligence would be extracted from them whenever possible. Anyone caught driving with drugs would be arrested. Anyone driving through a checkpoint with false papers would be arrested.

General Sandoval's strategy had its share of opponents. On one occasion, a grenade was set off at the Army barracks in Navolato, about twenty miles from the state capital. No one was hurt, but the general was furious. He sent hundreds of his men into the streets and deployed several helicopters to search the city. He also paid a visit to Navolato's mayor, demanding a report on the grenade attack. It was the first of several times Sandoval would clash with local officials. The Army wasn't exactly welcome in these parts; the soldiers and their general didn't necessarily trust the locals.

'Little by Little'

The helicopter landed in a clearing in the foothills of the Sierra, and General Sandoval hopped off. Four soldiers had already cleared the area, and were standing guard on the perimeter, guns pointed towards the forest, eyes scanning the terrain for any sign of movement. The marijuana field had been found just hours earlier, that morning, by a helicopter unit.

The area was thought to be clear of narcos, but one never knew. Sometimes, when the soldiers arrived on the scene, any gomeros and narcos present would flee and never be seen again. Other times, when a big field or meth lab was spotted, they would run away – only to return heavily armed a few hours later. There was no room for error, particularly with the general arriving.

Sandoval wiped the sweat off his brow as the marijuana plants went up in flames behind him. The smoke billowed above the trees and through the small clearing. As he turned back to examine his soldiers' destruction of the 38,000-square-foot patch of marijuana, a song blared out from a stereo on the other side of the nearby lake. It was a narco-corrido hailing the exploits of Chapo. The near-inaudible lyrics were familiar to the general and his men.

'It's to let the others know to be on alert,' said the general with a chuckle. 'And to remind us that they know we're here.'

He and his men went back to work, burning the marijuana plantation to the ground and collecting evidence from the scene. Anything they found would be kept and handed over to federal investigators. Beer cans, cigarettes and packets of potato crisps had been left scattered by the marijuana growers who had fled when the Army first spotted them from a helicopter. A makeshift tent where they had spent their nights was still assembled; shirts and sweaters were piled up in the corner.

Walking past the tent, the general spotted a pair of shoes. Holding them up, he examined the soles. They had been recently repaired; a visit to cobblers in the nearby city of Culiacan might be in order for the investigators. Examining the beer cans that one of his soldiers had placed in a plastic bag, he smiled. 'See this beer? It's not from here. Most locals drink the local brew. It should be easy to find out if anyone's been buying this stuff in bulk.'

Maybe one of the leads would pay off. The goal was not to catch a bunch of small-time marijuana plantation workers. It was to beat a path towards their bosses and, eventually, to Chapo.

The general knew the road ahead would be a long one, and that this cat-and-mouse game was a slow, grinding process. But he was optimistic. 'Everyone is saying that we're losing the drug war. I don't think so. We're winning, little by little.'

The helicopter rose gradually over the outskirts of Culiacan. Below, wide streets lined by car repair shops and *tienditas* (little stores) gave way to a mass of single-storey concrete houses and alleyways. The new helicopters that General Sandoval's men had been given were helping in the battle against the narcos. We can spot them from above now, the general said, instead of having to go door-to-door in humvees or patrol cars – or worse, scramble men in the streets – in order to rattle them out of their cages. The helicopters, part of the Calderon administration's boost in the war on drugs, were invaluable. 'We can't win without them.'

Culiacan's mazes of alleys in which the 'rats' – as the soldiers call the lower-level narcos – operate are largely impenetrable without air support. The dusty, narrow streets, with back alleys leading to countless safe houses, provide perfect cover for any drug dealer or killer running from the law. On every street corner is an informant. Throughout the city, taxi drivers, petrol station attendants, car repair shop workers are paid off by the narcos to keep everything running smoothly. If anyone suspicious enters the area, the narcos know. If a foreigner lands at Culiacan's airport, the narcos know.

Across Mexico, in narco-infested areas, similar procedures apply. They know you are there.

The military has its camps throughout the Sierra, but most of these are still temporary; a group of a dozen soldiers sets up tents for two to three weeks at a time. Every morning, these young soldiers – usually accompanied by one or two ranking officers – hike up the steep slopes and search for poppy and marijuana fields. The soldiers almost always find a plantation, but the work is hardly rewarding. At night, the same group of soldiers sets up checkpoints on nearby roads to slow the transportation of drugs and stop anyone with weapons.

Most of the soldiers in these hills of Sinaloa are young, unaccustomed to real fighting, and on their own. General Sandoval has sympathy for his men. He knows how tough it is, to fight this war on one's home soil, with plenty of will but often, without any way.

On one occasion, he proudly declared that marijuana production had dipped significantly; minutes later he admitted that this was not due to his soldiers' efforts but because Sinaloa had just experienced a very dry winter. Thank God and the weather, he said.

Many of the soldiers doing the fighting in Sinaloa are from the state itself; some even hail from the Sierra. Often, this has led to leaks in information, and betrayals by the soldiers themselves. The Army has made an effort to reassign soldiers regularly, to avoid local conflicts of interest, but this has also caused difficulties: a soldier will be just getting to know the terrain to which he has been assigned when he'll be shipped off to another part of the country.

All the soldiers are suffering, Sandoval admitted. The dangers of fighting the narcos are taking their toll. At one point, everyone from foot soldiers to officers were wearing ski masks to hide their identities, and no one was allowed off the base. Forget about a little R & R at the weekend, a few beers and a strip club to unwind, or a trip to see the wife and kids. The risks of kidnapping were too great; the workload never-ending.

'We work 365 days a year. From the generals to the grunts, we all have a right to a vacation,' General Sandoval said, taking off his glasses and chuckling again.

8. The War

While Chapo was still locked up in Puente Grande, the heads of the nation's cartels had held a meeting in Puerto Vallarta.

Only the Arellano Felix brothers weren't present. They were the main issue on the agenda; their bloodlust was making such a hash of Tijuana that there was no way the Mexicans could ignore the situation. If they worked together, the heads of the other cartels concluded, they could find a way to control the Arellano Felix brothers, maybe even oust them from their plaza, and keep their own businesses flowing.

El Mayo was also having personal trouble with the boys from Tijuana. Ramon, apparently, claimed that El Mayo had dodged a $20-million debt.

The state of the Juarez cartel was another pressing issue.

First, General Gutierrez Rebollo, the drug czar with ties to Amado Carrillo Fuentes, had been arrested. But that was nothing compared to the events of 3 July 1997.

Carrillo Fuentes, the so-called Lord of the Skies who was famous for flying cocaine into the United States on jet planes, had always been careful not to attract too much attention. But he had an Achilles heel – this particular narco was extremely vain.

Undergoing plastic surgery is not unusual for a high-level narco. Chapo, El Mayo, El Azul and Garcia Abrego are all believed to have had work done to change their appearance. Sometimes a cheekbone lift or a nose job can alter one's face enough so that the authorities are left wondering.

Carrillo Fuentes, on the other hand, just wanted to improve his looks. He wanted to look a bit younger; he also wanted a little liposuction. He went under the knife at a Mexico City hospital. A team of his doctors would perform the operation. They gave him the necessary sedatives.

At some point during the operation, Carrillo Fuentes woke up. 'Give me a painkiller, I'm in pain!' he cried out. His primary doctor suggested it could be too dangerous; he was already heavily sedated, more painkillers could be lethal. But the other doctors caved in. 'Who's gonna tell this very violent drug lord that they're not gonna give him a painkiller?' recalls the DEA's Michael Vigil.

The extra medication did indeed prove too much; Carrillo Fuentes died of a heart attack on the operating table. 'It was basically vanity that killed him.'

The Arellano Felix brothers and the Gulf cartel had both been thirsty for Carrillo Fuentes' turf, and after his death, they encroached on the Ciudad Juarez plaza. This worried El Mayo and his Sinaloa counterparts, not to mention operatives in the Juarez cartel. None of this – neither the Tijuana situation, nor their hunger for Juarez – was any good for business; the government appeared to be making a greater effort to crack down on corruption, and the PRI's stranglehold of Mexico was looking weaker than ever. Change was in the air, and not necessarily for the good, from the narcos' perspective.

So El Mayo formed an alliance with Rodolfo Carrillo Fuentes, the Lord of the Skies' brother. They would be known as 'the Federation'.

They made their move into Tijuana. El Mayo ordered a series of high-profile assassinations, including the murder of Tijuana Police Chief Alfredo de la Torre.

The Arellano Felix brothers weren't keen on this encroachment. On a quiet, lazy Sunday in early February 2002, Ramon, the most hot-headed of the Arellano Felix clan, came to Mazatlan on a mission. He would kill El Mayo.

Ramon and his men cruised the streets of the humid Pacific coast town in a Volkswagen sedan for five days, asking around and working all the contacts they had to find their target. No luck. This was El Mayo's turf; finding him certainly wouldn't be easy.

On the fifth day, Ramon parked in the so-called 'Zona Dorada' (literally, the 'gold zone'), near a major hotel. A team of cops walked up to the vehicle; one of them asked for identification. Many of Mazatlan's cops were on El Mayo's payroll. Some were just corrupt, others were assassins.

Ramon and his men began to flee on foot, but the cops caught up. One of them, apparently a federal agent, presented his badge. Guns were drawn fast, and a shootout ensued. One of Ramon's men fled into the hotel; the cops caught up with him and hauled him off. They shot another of the men.

Ramon Arellano Felix received several bullets to the body. The head of the Tijuana cartel would die fifteen minutes later, on the way to the hospital. He had undergone various surgical procedures to alter his appearance, and had been travelling under the name of Jorge Perez Lopez, but DNA tests would prove he was Benjamin's brother.

El Mayo had lured Ramon Arellano Felix to his home turf and paid the cops to kill him, the US would say. The Mexican government, on the other hand, would continue to deny El Mayo's involvement. He would never be charged.

El Mayo and Chapo wouldn't take Tijuana, but thanks to the death of Ramon, the cartel would never again be as powerful. Just a month after Ramon's shooting, Benjamin would be captured in Puebla, without a single shot being fired.

The Tijuana cartel is 'totally broken up', the PGR declared triumphantly. The blows against El Mayo and Chapo's rivals would continue throughout the decade.

El Mayo, meanwhile, was attracting DEA attention.

Over Chapo's Shoulders

Ismael 'El Mayo' Zambada Garcia was born in El Alamo, Sinaloa, on 1 January 1948. Like El Padrino and, later, Chapo, he maintained a low profile during his rise through the ranks of the Sinaloa drug trade. A former farmer, he had also worked as a hit man in Ciudad Juarez during his youth.

El Mayo was always opportunistic. 'He learned early on how to hitch his wagon to other bigger organizations, and this has given him entry,' said one Mexican official. Highly calculating, he waited his turn for power.

When El Padrino gave him and Chapo their shot at running the Sinaloa cartel, he was already in his forties, mature and strategic. He knew corruption was a key to success in his business and he assigned the Beltran Leyva brothers the specific task of buying off the right people. (It was even alleged that El Mayo bought off then-President Ernesto Zedillo in the late 1990s, although that was never proven.)

Once in charge, El Mayo never killed for pleasure. According to DEA agents who tracked him, it was always business. He was ruthless, in a cold, calculating way; unlike the Arellano Felix brothers who let their emotions get the better of them, El Mayo planned the minutiae of his murders. Like Chapo, he employed a skilled security boss, Gustavo Inzunza Inzunza, a.k.a. 'El Macho Prieto' (the Dark-skinned Macho). Both calculating and fearless, he would become famous for clashing with federal forces. He fended them off using bazookas.

El Mayo learned from the best, as he was a liaison with the Colombians. Whereas many Mexican narcos – Chapo included – simply wanted to flood the American market with drugs, El Mayo understood the basic economics of supply and demand. He knew that if too much product turned up on US streets without controlled distribution, the price would go down and they would end up making less. It was this thinking that would eventually lead to the expansion of Mexican cartels within US borders.

Annually, Chapo and El Mayo were shuttling about 1,000 kilograms of cocaine with an estimated street value of $17 million to the New York area alone; $30 million dollars' worth of cocaine was being transported to the Chicago area. Even DEA agents admit that was just a small part of the payload.

Whereas Chapo was still hiding his cash throughout the country in homes and stash houses, El Mayo had figured out a way to launder it. Through front companies like Nueva Industria de Ganaderos de Culiacan S.A. de C.V., a Culiacan-based cattle and dairy company, and Jamaro Constructores S.A. de C.V., a construction company which operates in Sinaloa, Sonora and Nayarit, El Mayo would clean their money and make his and Chapo's lifestyles legitimate. He would allegedly bring in his former wife and their daughters to pose as owners of the companies. Dozens of businesses would be linked to him under the US Kingpin Act. El Mayo would also employ the services of Victor Emilio Cazares Gastelum and his wife, 'The Empress', a wealthy Culiacan socialite couple, to help him launder what Sinaloans like to call 'blood money'.

There are hundreds of businesses in Culiacan which are believed to be money-laundering fronts. On Avenida Juarez in the centre of the city, armoured vehicles arrive daily to deliver cash to bureaux de change, which then refilter it back into the system. Every so often, the federal police raid the currency bureaus, seize millions of dollars in cash, and close them down. But new offices and businesses simply pop up, and the money continues to flow.

Chapo's Independence

With the fall of Ramon and Benjamin Arellano Felix, Chapo and El Mayo also had an opportunity to improve their Colombian connections. There had been financial problems between the Arellano Felix brothers and the Colombians. Bills went unpaid, for instance, something the Colombians could not abide.

It was also rumoured that the Arellano Felix brothers were cutting into the Colombian supply to deal on their own turf – Mexican drug consumption was increasing at the time – instead of distributing directly to the United States, which risked both profit margins and the security of product delivery. The Colombians had been maintaining a hands-off approach, but now the Arellano Felix brothers were pushing their luck.

The Colombians sought other trafficking organizations they trusted more. They sought out El Mayo.

Of course, all this activity would put El Mayo firmly on the radar screen. US President George W. Bush designated him a 'Tier I drug kingpin', which meant that he would be targeted specifically. The DEA began to station more agents and informants in southern Arizona and Sonora to hunt El Mayo, and posted 'Wanted' billboards of the drug lord along the major highway between Tucson and Phoenix.

The DEA began receiving more information on the relationship between Chapo and El Mayo than they'd ever had before. They were tracking both closely, watching El Mayo's relatives in the United States and conducting raids on his homes in Hermosillo. They weren't sure exactly who was in charge, so focused more on El Mayo. (The authorities believed they were one step away from Chapo and two steps away from El Mayo; the thinking was that Chapo would be caught first.)

But the local DEA field office was also receiving calls claiming that El Mayo was not in fact the man they wanted; Chapo was the top guy, the informants claimed. Unlike many capos, El Mayo and Chapo had the same attitude, mainly because they shared a common interest – to keep the business strong and not undermine one another. Although they had their share of disputes over strategy, they had never broken rank. They were operating more and more independently, under what the Americans called 'a non-aggression pact'.

According to the DEA, the two narcos were 'very close'. They had, after all, helped each other become extremely successful. Chapo, for his part, had always looked up to El Mayo. Chapo was just a guerrilla of drugs, a man constantly on the move. Even if he was managing to outwit the authorities, he was in their crosshairs.

El Mayo, meanwhile, was always behind the scenes. One DEA agent likens him to a 'chairman of the board' who operated solely from the top floor and made the executive decisions. El Mayo knew what to do with the money, and he knew how to handle the

Colombians. He also knew what was good for business; he was 'the guy who wants to cooperate and bring people together', the DEA believed.

But Chapo was always seeking his independence, trying to assert himself. After he had escaped from Puente Grande and gone on the run, Chapo had been forced gradually to move back into the Sinaloa cartel's fold. El Mayo had arranged for him to take his place near the helm again, but he would have to prove that he was still as valuable to the enterprise.

During Chapo's meeting with El Mayo and the Beltran Leyva brothers in the central city of Toluca four months after his escape, it became clear that prison hadn't softened him up. His time on the run would make him even more accustomed to the hard life. He had spent the majority of 2001 travelling throughout Mexico, and had no qualms about continuing such a routine.

This was how he would operate from now on. Even as he ran – the authorities had certainly not given up on tracking him down – he would expand his operations and make new connections. It was always business.

Chapo's drive went beyond simply making millions; he wanted to be El Padrino, in charge of everything. His ambition appeared to come from deep within, from his pledge never to be poor again, from his defiance towards the government, from his determination never to set foot behind bars again.

He couldn't stay in one place for any length of time.

In 2002 Chapo roamed from Campeche in the south-east to Tamaulipas in the north-east to Sonora in the north-west to Mexico City with ease. The Army and federal police were still hunting him, but as always, turning up just a little too late.

On Friday 14 June 2002 they thought they had him pinned down in the Las Quintas neighbourhood of Culiacan. Acting on tip-offs, some 200 federal policemen surrounded four houses where both Chapo and El Mayo were believed to be hiding. They found El Mayo's ex-wife and a daughter, but no one else.

On Tuesday 2 July, less than a month later, the authorities received a reliable tip saying Chapo was in Atizapan, in the State of Mexico just outside the nation's capital. They raided the place; again, no Chapo.

The DEA's Chavez recalls just how frustrating Chapo was. Chavez would receive intelligence from the DEA's Mexico City offices regarding the kingpin's whereabouts. He would verify it as best he could, then feed it back to Mexican law enforcement, so they could conduct the raid. But they never could catch him. 'We'd have good intel on where he was. But [they] were always five minutes too late, always just missed him.'

Chapo was also getting even better connected. The Beltran Leyva brothers were corrupting their way into the Mexican system on his behalf, and he was thought to be getting tips from the highest echelons of power. They were buying off police commanders at all levels, assuming some of these men would soon reach the top. While the DEA and Mexican authorities had to rely on information that could turn out to be a hoax or, worse, a trap, Chapo was getting the best of intelligence. The Beltran Leyva brothers had even allegedly bought off President Fox's travel adviser.

By 2003 it was clear that Chapo didn't need to answer to anyone, apparently not even El Mayo. He still wanted to re-establish himself. The best way to do so would be the oldest: to go to war. He would go against El Mayo's wishes for stability, contradicting his closest colleague for the first time.

Trouble in Tamaulipas

The Gulf cartel would be Chapo's first target.

Juan Garcia Abrego, founder of the Gulf cartel, was born on 13 September 1944 on a ranch outside Matamoros, a sweltering city on the north-east coast of Mexico. Matamoros is just across the border from Brownsville, Texas, and four bridges link it to the US. The population of Matamoros has grown to about 500,000, drawn by jobs in factories and industrial plants. Crime has prospered.

Like Chapo, Garcia Abrego didn't finish primary school, and got a job as a milkman. Then he stole cars. But, also like his Sinaloa counterpart, Garcia Abrego had an uncle in the drug trade. He had to be taught everything – one informant recalls teaching him table manners and the proper way to show off his Rolex – but he was a quick learner. He would rise to the top of what became the Gulf cartel.

In the late 1980s, as 'El Padrino' Felix Gallardo's old empire was taking on a new shape under the command of Chapo, the Arellano Felix brothers and Carrillo Fuentes, Garcia Abrego came to be regarded as the nation's most powerful drug trafficker. His political connections were deep; it was his policeman, Calderoni, who arrested the founder of Mexican drug trafficking, El Padrino.

The United States wanted Garcia Abrego, and the authorities hatched a plan to bring him down.

An FBI man posing as a corrupt agent approached Garcia Abrego with an offer. For $100,000 he would feed Garcia Abrego tips on law enforcement activity. The two men communicated through letters and by phone, as well as by messenger. They became close, referring to each other as 'my friend' and 'my brother'. On one occasion Garcia Abrego sent the agent $39,880 in cash.

In early 1996 the Mexican authorities nabbed Garcia Abrego. Worse still for the drug lord, he held American citizenship, so he was deported to stand trial. In a Houston court the agent provided damning testimony. The Gulf boss was convicted on twenty-two counts of money laundering, drug possession and drug trafficking. His cartel had smuggled more than 15 tons of cocaine and 46,000 pounds of marijuana from Mexico into the US and laundered about $10.5 million, prosecutors estimated. Garcia Abrego, aged fifty-two, was sentenced to life in prison.

The fall of Garcia Abrego didn't exactly destroy the Gulf cartel, however; in fact, it made it stronger, at least in resolve.

A local by the name of Osiel Cardenas Guillen took over at the helm. Born in 1967 in Matamoros, Cardenas was humble in origin, much like Chapo. He had worked first as a mechanic, then as a waiter, and had even done a stint in a *maquiladora*, the Mexican manufacturing plants notorious for their poor working conditions and vast output of everything from computers to auto parts.

Unlike Chapo, however, Cardenas Guillen did finish secondary school. And unlike his West coast rival he was unable to avoid the authorities as a young man. By the time he was twenty-two, he had done two short stints in prison. On one occasion, he was detained in Brownsville, Texas with two kilos of cocaine. By the time he was returned to Mexico to serve out his term, he was a hardened criminal. He was so brutal that he had earned himself the nickname 'Mata-Amigos', or 'Friend-killer', when he had shot a key ally in the Gulf cartel.

In 1997 Cardenas Guillen formed Los Zetas, a paramilitary group of thirty-one former Mexican special forces soldiers who had deserted. Led by twenty-three-year-old defector Arturo Guzman Decena (no relation to Chapo), they were ruthless, and their reputation preceded them.

They had been groomed by the Mexican military to combat drug traffickers. They were also rumoured to have been trained by the US military (the government in Washington denies this). They operated in cells, and their goal was to assassinate high-level members of the nation's cartels, to create chaos within drug trafficking organizations. But Cardenas Guillen offered them better salaries than the military could. They became mercenaries. Los Zetas was born.

Their electronic intelligence and weapons were military-grade. They found a way to obtain grenade launchers, surface-to-air missiles and helicopters; they had training in explosives, espionage and sharpshooting.

Los Zetas rapidly set to training recruits in camps near the border with Texas, where they brought in fifteen–eighteen-year-olds and even some former Guatemalan soldiers known as 'Kabiles'. Because of their military histories, they were able to bring in more deserting soldiers.

By 2003 the Mexican Defence Secretariat had designated the 300-strong Los Zetas the most dangerous death squad in the country. Sporting military-syle buzz cuts and tattoos, they blackened their faces with charcoal and wore dark clothing into battle. They followed the orders of Z-1 – Guzman Decena. Some of the original Zetas had light-hearted names – 'El Winnie Pooh' and 'The Little Mother', for instance – but they were vicious. They took delight in torturing victims before finally killing them. They would decapitate, dismember, burn and dissolve victims, all with a military precision and detachment hitherto not seen in Mexico. On one occasion, the original Zetas placed four enemies inside barrels of gasoline and burned them to death.

Chapo wasn't to be outdone. He formed his own death squad, known as 'Los Negros'.

Los Negros would incorporate members of existing gangs like the Mexican mafia, and go on to execute members of Cardenas Guillen's gangs throughout Tamaulipas.

Chapo and the Beltran Leyva brothers placed one of their top new lieutenants, a Texan known as 'La Barbie', in charge of this squad. La Barbie (Edgar Valdez Villareal by birth) was different from Chapo in some respects: he was fond of designer clothes, luxury cars and drowning himself in booze and women in nightclubs. But like Chapo, he had proven himself to be vicious and willing to kill.

Trained as a bill collector by the Beltran Leyva brothers, La Barbie also appeared to be an expert in using his reputation, word-of-mouth and even the Internet to instil fear in rivals. La Barbie put online a video of his men torturing a group of Zetas. At the end of the clip, one of the Zetas was shot in the head. The idea was to instil fear in the enemy and all those who supported them.

The city of Nuevo Laredo turned into a war zone. For two years the cartels' gunmen would battle it out in this city, Reynosa and even Matamoros, where Garcia Abrego and Cardenas Guillen were born. The Army, too, was patrolling the streets and playing its part with some major arrests. Z-1, Guzman Decena, was killed, his No. 2 was captured. Heriberto Lazcano Lazcano, a.k.a. 'El Lazca', took over. The fighting continued.

Eventually, one of the two capos – Chapo or Cardenas Guillen – would have to fall.

The latter had a history with the Americans. Several years before, Cardenas Guillen and more than a dozen men armed with AK-47s and handguns had surrounded two US federal agents (one DEA and one FBI) in downtown Matamoros, where they were meeting a source. Cardenas Guillen had threatened to kill them, at one stage allegedly pointing a gun at one agent's head. The agents identified themselves yet the drug lord persisted; everybody drew guns and chaos ensued.

The agents reminded Cardenas Guillen of the DEA's heavy-handed reaction to the killing of 'Kiki' Camarena; it would be a fatal mistake to kill them.

'You fucking gringos. This is my town, so get the fuck out of here before I kill you,' Cardenas replied.

The agents had got away unharmed, but still, the DEA was out for revenge. It immediately launched an investigation, 'Operation Golden Grips'. Working with the Mexican government, the DEA, FBI and US Customs agents began to focus on taking down the Gulf cartel.

Chapo, perhaps not by coincidence, was doing the same.

In the early morning of Friday 14 March 2003, dozens of soldiers surrounded a house in a modest neighbourhood of Matamoros, where Cardenas Guillen was believed to be living. He and his men tried to shoot their way out, but the soldiers chased them to the airport. Three soldiers were injured in the fracas, but once the shooting had stopped, it became clear they'd prevailed. They had nabbed the head of the Gulf cartel.

Celebration was in the air. The blows against the Arellano Felix brothers a year earlier had been big news, but this was the first high-level narco to be caught on the Gulf coast during the Fox administration. The capture of Cardenas Guillen took some of the heat off the president for Chapo's escape, and signalled once again to his US counterparts that his administration was willing to go after the big narcos.

It also appeared that President Fox wasn't pandering to one particular cartel and leaning heavily on their rivals, which the

Institutional Revolutionary Party had been accused of. The secrecy of the raid that had brought down the Gulf capo was a source of pride, too: the only people who had known about it beforehand were the president, his defence secretary and the attorney general.

For the DEA, the bust was big not only because it was Cardenas Guillen, but because their own had been avenged. 'It is an important arrest because it sends a message to traffickers that violence and intimidation will not protect them from law enforcement,' the US agency declared.

Still, some officials were more cautious. Now they would simply have to investigate and gather new intelligence on who would fill Cardenas Guillen's place.

Just months after the fall of his foe, Chapo arrived in Nuevo Laredo. According to a witness now in protective custody, he had no fear of being there, even if the dust hadn't quite settled. That day, after a bloody shootout, soldiers approached a neighbourhood known as Santo Dellogado. Five thugs dressed in police uniforms and armed with AK-47s shouted their loyalty from the rooftop. 'We are Chapo's people, and he is here . . . in Nuevo Laredo!' They then fled. It was the first evidence that Chapo was operating openly in Gulf cartel territory.

Los Zetas weren't about to give up their turf easily. Within months of Cardenas Guillen's capture, they effectively merged his Gulf cartel with their organization. Via mobile phone, Cardenas Guillen was still giving orders from prison in the State of Mexico. Both Chapo and Los Zetas were intent on expanding throughout Mexico, and neither group would prove able to spare the resources to really solidify a hold on the Gulf coast. The war in the north-east simply intensified.

After Chapo's visit, hundreds more Sinaloa gunmen arrived in Nuevo Laredo that summer, and continued to lock horns with Los Zetas. Hundreds more people on either side would fall in the north-east. Nearly twenty police officers died in Nuevo Laredo alone.

Neither side wanted peace; neither side wanted law and order.

Those who did stood little chance. When a humble, fifty-six-year-old printing-shop owner and father-of-three, Alejandro Dominguez Coello, was sworn in as Nuevo Laredo's police chief, he admitted he wouldn't really be able to change much. But he vowed to at least represent the people. 'I'm not beholden to anyone. My commitment is to the citizenry,' he announced as he accepted the post.

Within six hours he had thirty bullets in him, courtesy of Los Zetas. Outrage over the incident prompted President Fox to send in the Army and the federal police again, but they were hardly welcome. From the moment they arrived at the airport, occasional gun battles would break out between the local police – who were bought off by Los Zetas and the Gulf cartel – and the feds. All 700 police officers in the city of about 35,000 inhabitants would be eventually removed from their posts and investigated.

In 2009 an eerie calm loomed over Reynosa, Matamoros and Nuevo Laredo. Soldiers were still stationed in the area, but there was no trust between them and the police. Matamoros is the kind of city where it's not hard to imagine being gunned down, kidnapped or tortured. The police ride around in their pickup trucks waving their weapons around and hollering like drunk college students on Rag Week. During the day, residents seem constantly on their guard; by dusk the streets are completely deserted. By contrast, just across the border, Brownsville appears idyllic, the epitome of stability.

Locals worried that at any moment the violence could erupt again. Los Zetas had branched out into extortion and all kinds of smuggling along the border. The federal government maintained that it was fighting a war against Los Zetas in Tamaulipas, but residents begged to differ.

'They've all been paid,' said Antonio, who has lived in Reynosa all his life. 'The soldiers, the government, everyone.'

Antonio owns a small store in Reynosa; he gets most of his profits from alcohol sales. He suffered extortion by a local government manager wearing his municipal government sash. The man, accompanied by armed guards who were possibly Zetas, demanded

Antonio pay him the equivalent of $50 every Friday for the 'right' to sell alcohol.

Antonio stood his ground. He went to the government to report the incident and prove that all his papers were in order. The official has not returned since, but Antonio was far from convinced by the reaction at the government office. They barely batted an eyelid over the allegation, and didn't even ask for the name.

'The biggest narcos are the politicians. What a shame, what's happened to Mexico.'

By early 2010, violence had again erupted in Tamaulipas.

9. Land Grab

Although he had walked away from the north-east, Chapo hadn't exactly been defeated at the hands of Los Zetas. The bloodshed of the conflict with the Gulf cartel hadn't damaged Chapo's operations at all; in mid-2005 his drugs were still flowing fast into the United States. The US law enforcement agencies were convinced that the manhunt targeting him would prevail: 'He's a very high-profile target, and eventually he'll make a mistake and get caught,' said one official. But Chapo clearly had other ideas.

Not only was he still outrunning the authorities, he was expanding his business to include methamphetamine. Also known as meth, ice, crank and speed, methamphetamine is a highly addictive stimulant. Users can snort it, smoke it or eat it. Meth can have serious effects on the central nervous system. In parts of the world, it's come to be known as 'crazy drug' (or local variations on the term) due to the paranoia and delusions it can instil in long-term users. A common side effect is the feeling (and belief) that bugs are crawling under one's skin.

Meth is easily produced in clandestine laboratories. All one needs are the right chemicals (the precursors), and 'cooking' equipment.

Jose de Jesus Amezcua Contreras is widely considered to have started the meth business in Mexico in the 1980s. He and his brothers, operating out of Guadalajara, made connections with organized crime counterparts in Thailand and India to obtain the chemicals (massive amounts of them), and then produced the drug in small, cheap labs in the Mexican states of Colima, Nayarit and Michoacan (where they partnered another crew, the Valencia brothers).

At their height, the Amezcuas were considered 'one of the world's largest smugglers' of ephedrine and clandestine producers of methamphetamine. They had networks through which they supplied meth to US users, and also sold the drug to the Arellano Felix brothers. According to the DEA, they moved their meth throughout the United States, where a scourge was taking hold. They were operating in California, Texas, Georgia, Oklahoma, Iowa, Arkansas and North Carolina, the DEA claimed; they were even sometimes producing it on US soil.

Lacking the political protection other major narcos enjoyed, the Amezcua brothers were arrested, but the US meth market was increasingly reliant on Mexico to satisfy a growing demand. In the absence of the elder Valencia brother, who was in custody, Mexican meth production was continuing, but it lacked a leader to coordinate shipments. Chapo seized on an opportunity. He moved in on the meth business.

Thanks to Chapo and El Mayo's contacts up and down Mexico's Pacific coast, arranging shipments of the meth precursors wasn't difficult. And distribution north would be easy; the Colombians would no longer have to be paid – they could simply put meth into their cocaine deliveries. They didn't have to pay millions of dollars for planes, pilots, boats and bribes. From $10,000 in chemicals, they could make $100,000 worth of meth.

Whereas the Sinaloa drug business had been a joint operation between Chapo and El Mayo, the meth business was Chapo's baby. He would cultivate his own ties with China, Thailand and India to import the chemicals, and build his large labs to produce meth throughout the mountains of Sinaloa and Durango, and in Jalisco, Michoacan, Nayarit and several other states where he had connections. With this new project, Chapo was particularly ambitious – 'not like a ruthless killer, but as a businessman', recalls the DEA's Chavez. 'He slipped away from El Mayo, into his own market.'

Chapo was expanding his organization rapidly. Moving from place to place had allowed him to nurture contacts throughout the country. He was now operating in seventeen states within Mexico. He was working under various aliases, including Max Aregon and Gilberto Osuna. He placed a trusted sidekick named Ignacio Nacho Coronel Villarreal in charge of meth production, so he could continue being the boss of bosses. Nacho Coronel had been working alongside El Mayo and Chapo for years. He would prove so reliable in the meth business that he would earn himself the nickname 'the Crystal King'.

Chapo was also thinking about war on another front. Since his escape from prison, he had been eyeing a move for the Ciudad Juarez plaza. He had convened a meeting in the northern city of Monterrey with El Mayo, El Azul the consiglieri/go-between, and one of the Beltran Leyva brothers. There, they discussed the possibility of killing Rodolfo Carrillo Fuentes, who had taken over operations after the death of his brother. They had an opportunity to end the Carrillo Fuentes' dominance of the lucrative Ciudad Juarez smuggling corridor.

Chapo took his time. After all, the alliance between the Sinaloa and Juarez cartels, arranged by El Mayo, still remained, even if mistrust between Chapo and his Juarez counterparts was high.

Chapo sent members of Los Negros to Ciudad Juarez to size up the turf. Chapo knew that Rodolfo Carrillo Fuentes always moved around with a police escort; it would be hard to get at him in his own city. But Chapo also knew that the family still regularly visited Culiacan and its environs, where relatives remained.

On 11 September 2004, at 4 p.m., Rodolfo, his wife and two of their young children were exiting one of the city's shopping malls. They entered the parking lot, escorted by police commander Pedro Perez Lopez.

He was a tough nut. During his tenure in Ciudad Juarez, he had taken down kidnapping rings and car thieves, and even survived two assassination attempts by the Arellano Felix brothers. Rodolfo and his wife were just getting into the car when the gunfire began from all sides. Perez Lopez fired back, keeping the gunmen at bay. But he could only do so for a few minutes; he took a bullet, and both Rodolfo and his wife went down, too. The policeman would survive; the narco and his wife would not. By the time backup arrived, the assassins had fled.

Chapo had successfully eliminated his main Juarez rival.

After Rodolfo's death, few gave Vicente Carrillo Fuentes, another brother, much chance of keeping control of the Ciudad Juarez plaza. 'Vicente Carrillo, since the death of his brother, cannot maintain leadership,' said then-Attorney General Daniel de la Vaca Hernandez in November. 'Vicente Carrillo must flee . . . he'll lose his operation to the "Chapo" organization out of fear.'

He stayed, but for the rest of the decade, Ciudad Juarez would never again be ruled by a Carrillo Fuentes. It would be ruled by violence.

Payback

Going into Ciudad Juarez and the Gulf of Mexico, Chapo must have figured there would be serious repercussions. But whether he could have expected the turn of events on 31 December 2004 will never be known.

That New Year's Eve, Arturo Guzman Loera, Chapo's wide-eyed, moustachioed younger brother, was sitting in a cubicle in the Cefereso No. 1. He had languished there for three years; there had been no attempts to spring him. He was talking to his lawyer. Another inmate, Jose Ramirez Villanueva, went to the bathroom near by, where a gun had been stashed. He then killed Chapo's beloved brother.

The hit could have been ordered by any number of Chapo's enemies; of that, but very little else, the PGR was sure. The principal suspect, however, was Rodolfo Carrillo Fuentes.

Another huge blow came less than two months later, in February 2005. This time the authorities were responsible.

One of Chapo's sons, Ivan Archivaldo Guzman Salazar, a.k.a. 'Chapito' (little Chapo), was arrested in Zapopan, Jalisco. The breakthrough came by chance: a team of agents had retrieved a mobile phone from the scene of a crime, and called the first number listed. Chapito arrived on the scene. He would be charged and sentenced for laundering money on behalf of his father.

Then in June, yet another blow. One of Chapo's brothers, Miguel Angel, and their mother had gone to a Chinese restaurant in Culia-can to celebrate the fifteenth birthday of the drug lord's niece. For a Mexican girl, the fifteenth birthday, or *quinceanera*, is traditionally a big do, and Miguel Angel was at least going to treat his daughter to a nice meal out, even if his brother was a wanted man.

Acting on intelligence provided by its informants, a group of around twenty Army special forces surrounded the restaurant, the Tai-Pei, at around 4 p.m. Dressed in black and wearing hoods, they filed in without a word, much to the astonishment of those who'd chosen to dine there that day.

Miguel Angel, known as 'El Mudo' or 'the Mute', was taken aback, and put up no resistance.

Although this brother had never been on any 'wanted' lists, the arresting forces were adamant that he was responsible for traffick-ing drugs to the US by plane and returning the cash proceeds back to Sinaloa on behalf of Chapo. He was buying properties in Culia-can to be used as stash houses, as well as vehicles and fake IDs for Chapo's employees.

Chapo's mother, Maria Consuelo Loera Perez, was outraged. 'They took him away without any arrest warrant. He makes an honest living,' she told reporters at the scene. 'I don't believe that he dedicates himself to illegal activities . . . They arrested him only because he's Chapo's brother.'

She sprang to Chapo's defence, too. 'He didn't force one door or threaten anyone to get out of jail, they opened [the doors] for him. It's as if one opens the cage for a bird, it flies away. It's been a long time since I've seen Joaquin; I'm not in contact with him. He only helps good people. How can I feel bad, if I am his mother? A mother has to bear all the problems that her children bring, for this I will plead to God on their behalf – he's my best lawyer.'

Deep down, the DEA had to know that none of this would really slow Chapo. It had posted a $5-million reward for informa-tion leading to his arrest and prosecution, due to charges of 'con-spiracy to import cocaine, possession of cocaine with intent to distribute, money laundering and criminal forfeiture'. The DEA's agents knew he was still intent on expanding his operation, and in spite of the loss of a few family members, Chapo would not be felled easily.

'He was at the top of his game before he went to prison, and it was only a matter of time before he'd get back up there if he stayed alive,' a US law enforcement officer told the *Los Angeles Times*. 'He's definitely back. He's strong. You can tell from the violence, he's more and more out there.'

The Mexican authorities, meanwhile, were in two minds about where they stood with Chapo. They could round up his family and harass his mother, but still couldn't find him. Accusations of corruption abounded – one Mexican journalist would later call Chapo the 'Capo of PANismo', a play on the acronym of the ruling party – and their efforts to stonewall an increasingly heel-biting Mexican press pack were falling well short.

'It's not that he's more intelligent and we're more stupid. He has better resources in the places he works, where he is protected . . . We won't find him in a city – this subject is in the depths of the Sierra, loyally protected by groups of locals who see him as a hero,' said Jose Luis Santiago Vasconcelos, who was deputy head of the special anti-organized crime unit known as the SIEDO. He admitted they had no real leads on Chapo.

They had nabbed some of Chapo's family members on minor charges, but the drug lord was still making a laughing stock out of the government. The recently formed SIEDO and the AFI – Mexico's equivalent to the FBI – were having no luck at all finding the man himself.

10. Law, Disorder

Top-ranking federal police commander Edgar Millan Gomez arrived home late on 8 May 2008. He had been working with his team to catch Marcos Arturo Beltran Leyva, a.k.a. 'El Barbas', operating on reliable intelligence that placed the Sinaloan narco near Cuernavaca, about an hour south of Mexico City.

They had come close, cornering him. But Beltran Leyva's team of bodyguards (some of whom were ex-military) had managed to outgun the police officers and make their escape.

Millan Gomez was coming home to one of several Mexico City residences he used due to safety concerns. His bodyguards dropped him off outside, and he made his way up the stairs. He opened the front door and was instantly met with gunfire. There were four assailants but the police commander wouldn't go down without a fight. He grabbed one of his attackers, and as they tussled, even as the bullets raked his body, he demanded answers: 'Who sent you? Who sent you to kill me?'

The assassins, a professional gang from Mexico City, had been assigned the job by the Beltran Leyva brothers. Millan Gomez died in the hospital hours later. His body had been riddled with nine bullets.

The loss of Millan Gomez was a huge blow to morale. After all, he was considered one of the good cops, deemed a hero by the government and a nuisance by Chapo and the Beltran Leyva brothers. He was a 'standup guy', said one veteran DEA man based in Mexico City. In charge of working with his Mexican counterparts and 'vetting' them, the DEA man had seen his share of good and bad cops during the drug war. The death of Millan Gomez was heartbreaking – he had lost a trustworthy counterpart.

President Calderon was distraught. His administration praised

Millan Gomez for playing a vital role in the country's battle against organized crime and denounced 'this cowardly killing of an exemplary official'. The week he died, six other federal policemen were killed.

Genaro's Crusade

Good cops are hard to come by in Mexico. Few cadets begin with an honest outlook towards their trade, knowing that bribery is a way of life, or, at least, a means of survival. Those who are honest are often lured into corruption either through sizeable offers of money or the threat of death.

When it was formed, the AFI was supposed to be a beacon of hope for Mexico's police forces – as trustworthy as the Army but less aggressive, far more honest than any local police force, and able to work in all quarters of the country. Led by Genaro Garcia Luna, a no-nonsense former spy agency and federal police director, the AFI sought assistance outside of Mexico. Groups of top AFI members were trained by the DEA and FBI in Quantico, Virginia, while others took part in binational exercises in order to ensure no lapse in standards.

While attorneys general and other police chiefs have come and gone, Garcia Luna has proven to be one of the central and more enduring players in Mexico's war on drugs and organized crime. He was trained as an engineer (and he was 'comfortable with new technology at a time when those skills were becoming valued in security circles', according to one journalist) and came to be known as a reformist as Mexico was undergoing expansive changes during its transition from one-party rule.

At only thirty-eight years of age, Garcia Luna was named federal police chief, and at the same time would retain command of the AFI.

As he had done at the AFI, Garcia Luna immediately pledged to vanquish corruption, even if that meant 'purging' the police corps.

He wouldn't hesitate to fire top members of the police force, and would later implement measures to improve police performance and confidence, introducing lie-detector tests, financial audits and psychological evaluations, for instance.

Throughout the Calderon presidency, Garcia Luna has vowed to keep up the hunt for Chapo. In interviews he comes across as earnest and honest. Those who have worked with him say he is 'affable' and 'sincere'. But there is another side to the man. He runs his tight inner circle like a personal fiefdom; any wrong decision could have fatal consequences. He is controlling, to the point that he won't tolerate disagreement even from his closest aides. His loyal few are totally paranoid, those who have worked with Garcia Luna say.

During the Calderon administration, Garcia Luna has sought to consolidate his power, according to observers. But he has his share of competitors.

Medina Mora, the attorney general from 2006 to 2009, couldn't have been more different from Garcia Luna. Both shared an unrelenting enthusiasm and dedication to their jobs, but Medina Mora was seen as a more compassionate boss. A prosecutor rather than a police chief, his interest lay in the law. He was known for being strategic, cautious with the lives of employees, and highly influential.

The Mexican press noted the differences between the two men in charge of the drug war, and pulled no punches. Whenever Garcia Luna and Medina Mora expressed a difference of opinion, the pundits jumped on it. Whenever the two laid out different strategies, or met with Calderon, the press buzzed about who would succeed in the battle for the place at Calderon's side.

Calderon finally decided Garcia Luna would be the man in charge of the drug war – his right-hand man.

Critics say putting Garcia Luna in total control was a fatal mistake – inter-agency cooperation is vital. Garcia Luna is reluctant to share intelligence and resources in the drug war because 'he would lose power in this game', said one academic who has worked with the police chief in an advisory capacity.

Garcia Luna has been accused of 'simulating a battle' against the drug traffickers, not actually waging a real one. It has also been said that he is fighting the war on drugs with one particular goal in mind: to consolidate power for Chapo's cartel.

Affidavits, signed by the police chief's employees, have alleged ties between Garcia Luna and the Beltran Leyva brothers. Nothing was proven. On another occasion, a member of the police chief's inner circle, Igor Labastida Calderon, was investigated for alleged links to Chapo. Again, nothing was proven.

But Garcia Luna has dismissed any talk of making any sort of deals or being linked in any way to the narcos. After rumours of a pact in Tijuana in order to quell the violence there, the sometimes-jittery police chief cut to the chase. 'Look, I'll tell you with all forcefulness, we are not going to make a pact with anyone,' he said. 'We are obligated to confront crime. That is our job, that is our duty, and we will not consider a pact.'

Dozens of 'narco-mantas' – banners attributed to the drug traffickers which are hung in public to denounce the authorities or enemies – have appeared in various cities throughout Mexico, accusing Garcia Luna of protecting Chapo. 'As citizens, we ask you [the authorities] to focus on the following people who we are 100 per cent sure are protecting the narco,' read one.

A federal witness even testified before the PGR that Garcia Luna and others had received gifts – including yachts and houses – from Chapo's people, in exchange for information. Again, nothing was proven.

The Honest Few

Still, many Mexicans believe the AFI was infiltrated early on. Erica Garza is one member of the AFI who believes leaks and corruption within the organization are rampant.

She and her husband, Antonio, met in training – he was her instructor. 'He was so honest, so right,' she recalled. Soon, they started dating, and within six months they were living together. She knew the attraction was for life. 'He had a different way of looking at the world. He wanted things to be the way they should be – not the way they were.'

During her first year of training – and her and Antonio's first year of courtship – Erica rarely saw him. First she was in Durango, then in Mexico City, then back on the road to other parts of the country for another three months. This would be the pattern for their eventual marriage. She was placed in intelligence, staking out the homes of big-time alleged drug traffickers. She would be holed up in a van with her cameras, wiretaps and radios in some far-flung part of the country, while Antonio moved into administration.

She was thrilled by her work – she was involved in the capture of Garcia Abrego of the Gulf cartel – but it took its toll. Even if she was in Mexico City, their home town, she often didn't share her whereabouts with Antonio, for safety reasons. Sometimes they would meet at weekends. When Amado Carrillo Fuentes was declared dead after his botched plastic surgery operation, she ran into her husband at the morgue. 'He was there by chance,' she recalled with a big smile. Even when they both got their break – a trip to Quantico, Virginia, to train with the DEA and FBI – they wouldn't be together. Erica went first, he followed later, after she had returned home.

But eventually their work allowed them to be together. They were sent to San Diego to work on a joint US–Mexican police programme, during which they developed strategies to clean up their own police corps. Their first child was born in the United States. It was the honeymoon they had waited so long for.

When they returned to Mexico, the hard work really began. The country had just experienced its transition from one-party rule, and an anti-corruption drive was in the offing. The war between the cartels was about to kick off. While Erica was having her second child, Antonio was placed in charge of auditing at a federal institution. But he couldn't stand the dirtiness of the place, the pressure to go along with the old way of doing things, Erica recalls. He had received countless bribery offers, which he had turned down. After about eight months, he left. 'I'm going to end up [corrupt], I'd better leave now,' he told his wife.

They both wound up working at the AFI. For the first time they were actually working together, crafting the AFI's ethics and training manuals. Redrafting Mexican police manuals may seem like a paper-pushing assignment, but it isn't. Mexico's police forces lack some of the basic necessities of a solid institution. Prior to the Calderon administration, there wasn't even a federal database of all Mexican cops; if a corrupt officer who had been arrested in Veracruz later went to work in Ciudad Juarez after his release, there was no way of knowing his history. Establishing ethical rules and writing up manuals was a high priority.

It was at the AFI that Erica and Antonio also first really encountered the power of the cartels to infiltrate institutions. In charge of deploying agents to various parts of the country, Antonio would find himself face to face (or on the phone) with a subordinate who simply didn't want to go. The agent had turned his local plaza (as posts were known, just like the smuggling corridors) into a comfortable gig, thanks to bribes from the local traffickers. The agent would offer Antonio money; he would refuse. His predecessor had been removed for corruption; he wouldn't let the same fate befall him.

Soon, Antonio's bosses took away his power to deploy personnel. The honest cop refused to give up. He ordered the implementation of a new system, one that his immediate bosses would not be able to refuse because their superiors would get suspicious: the deployments would be randomly selected by a computer program. 'That way we'll get rid of corruption,' he told his wife.

It appeared to work, and Antonio's rise through the ranks continued. Both he and Erica were now considered top cops, and worked closely with international agencies like the DEA. Only a privileged few colleagues knew they were working with the Americans – after all, a leak to the wrong person and they could be killed. They also switched departments within the AFI regularly, careful never to break nepotism laws in a country where, often, the only way to advancement is through family connections.

Antonio began directing investigations against the nation's top drug lords. The 'incorruptible', as Erica calls him, knew he was about to face the greatest challenge of his career. 'When he became a director, he said, "Things are going to be much more difficult now. The pressure is going to be worse."'

Antonio made enemies. Some were vocal, others were of the more behind-the-back variety. He would complain about the difficulties of trying to change colleagues' minds, their mentalities. He didn't drink or smoke, and his subordinates were used to bosses who allowed them to accept gifts from criminals. They didn't trust Antonio, they thought he was an oddball, and he often didn't trust them. When he spotted a bad cop he sent him to another post, in another part of the country. On one visit to Ciudad Juarez he was so wary of his colleagues that he didn't stay the night with them – it might put him in danger.

At times he did find himself in the gravest danger. On one occasion he was assigned to Monterrey, where the feds were pursuing Heriberto Lazcano Lazcano, a.k.a. 'El Lazca', the head of Los Zetas. Antonio and a colleague were cruising the streets and passed a children's party; El Lazca himself got out of a parked truck. The Zeta looked around, then got back in. Antonio and his colleague followed him, radioing for military and federal support. The backup arrived way too late. El Lazca had taken note of them and his men fired their AK-47s. Antonio fired back with his pistol. The narco escaped.

Antonio was convinced that he and his police colleague had been left to die. A colleague of Antonio's later said that his superiors had negotiated with the narcos to have him threatened or killed, because another police colleague wanted his job.

Antonio survived that round and continued to rise up within the corps. He once helped lead a raid on a mansion in the swanky Mexico City district of Lomas de Chapultepec. The property belonged to Zhenli Ye Gon, a Chinese-Mexican businessman who was allegedly importing methamphetamine precursors for Chapo.

Antonio and his crew found an enormous stash of cash in the mansion: 207 million in US dollars, 18 million Mexican pesos, 200,000 euros, 113,000 Hong Kong dollars and nearly a dozen gold bullion coins.

Antonio and Noe Ramirez, who at the time was heading the PGR's organized crime unit, wanted to make sure none of the cops walked off with any of the loot. So they ordered their men to empty their pockets and remove their clothes prior to leaving the scene. They did; no one had stolen anything. Ramirez and his men then began to leave, but Antonio blocked him. No, everyone, he told the ranking man. What my men do, I do. So the two of them stripped down to their underwear.

Ramirez and Antonio were both clean – that time. But Ramirez would later be charged with links to organized crime and, specifically, for receiving $450,000 a month from the Beltran Leyva brothers in exchange for information. (Former colleagues of his maintain that he is innocent; by the end of 2009, he had yet to be sentenced.)

Questions of Trust

For the US, knowing who to trust in Mexico has always been an extreme challenge. DEA agents say the major stumbling blocks are the finger-pointing between the two nations – Mexico, after all, is the supplier and the United States the consumer of drugs – and the endemic corruption in Mexican security forces, including the military.

Garcia Luna's monopoly on power in the drug war has not helped international cooperation. There is no system of checks and balances on intelligence shared. The DEA's Chief of Intelligence, Anthony Placido, said, 'I'm not naive enough to say it's impossible that Garcia Luna or anyone else is corrupt, but we don't have a smoking gun at DEA, and I'm sure Calderon would root it out. It's absolutely being investigated, but it's a dead end.'

In order to do its job, the DEA has to put its money on someone – and take some risks. On one occasion it picked Victor Gerardo Garay, an AFI agent with close ties to Garcia Luna. An immediate superior of Antonio Garza's, Garay had shown himself both willing and able to go after the narcos. The DEA supplied him with information. He would help them take down their mutual foes.

These included some of the biggest names in the business. The DEA sent him phone numbers it had been tracking and other useful information on Eduardo Arellano Felix; shortly after, the drug lord was nailed in Tijuana.

'He was a guy who got it done,' said one DEA agent of Garay. 'He was great.'

The two had come to know each other on a social level – they had barbecues at each other's homes and travelled together – and over time had built a rapport. The DEA man had his suspicions – he'd worked in the business for too long, seen more than his share of betrayal – but at his core, he trusted Garay.

On 19 October 2008, however, a few days after a raid on a party at a mansion in Mexico City that had led to the arrest of eleven Colombians, two Mexicans, an American and a Uruguayan, the red flags went up. Prior to their arrest, the narcos in question had been throwing an almighty bash at the mansion, which boasted swimming pools and private games rooms decorated in the height of kitsch. Faux stalactites hung from the ceiling in one room; a knight in armour stood watch in the corner of another. The narcos had a private zoo, too, with two lions, two tigers and two black jaguars, among other animals. Thirty prostitutes had been invited to join the party.

Garay, who had led the raid, took his DEA counterpart back to the site, to show off the spoils of war.

Except there were none, the DEA agent recalls. The house had been cleaned from top to bottom since the raid a few days before; there was no evidence that anyone had held a party that had been busted apart by the police. There wasn't one beer can or soda lying around. Someone – perhaps the cops? – had taken 'everything that wasn't nailed down'.

It had been the cops, and it turns out that wasn't all they'd done. Garay and his men had held their own little shindig at the house the night of the bust, after the narcos had been hauled off to jail. They had kept some of the hookers for their own entertainment, and snorted some of the seized cocaine. The so-called good cops had thrown themselves a roaring old narco-fiesta.

Garay was arrested and charged with more than just a slip-up; the PGR's investigations suggested he had deep ties to the narcos.

The DEA man was shaken by the news. 'Personally, it was a huge hit – a wake-up call.' He praised the fact that Garay was arrested – in the past, an offence like his might have resulted in a transfer to another state – but couldn't hide his dismay at having been duped. 'It's frustrating, aggravating, I lose my hair, I miss time with my kids,' he said. 'Everything I've done is in the shitter. [But] we get back on the horse.'

For international and Mexican law enforcement Garay's arrest was the first of several blows. A little over a week after the raid an employee of the Beltran Leyva brothers told the PGR that Garay had used his position working for Interpol and the US Embassy to leak information.

In November 2008 two former senior staff in Mexico's Interpol offices were arrested: one would be charged with accepting $10,000 a month from Chapo and his people in exchange for making sure officials sympathetic to the Sinaloans were in high-ranking positions; the other had been paid unspecified amounts for feeding them confidential information.

Around the same time, five men from the PGR's special organized crime unit, SIEDO, were arrested for being in the pockets of the Beltran Leyvas.

The Calderon administration was making a concerted push to combat corruption, having ordered Operation Cleanup. The results were both promising and disheartening. Dozens of high-ranking government and law enforcement officials, including the likes of Garay and Ramirez who worked on anti-drug operations, had been arrested, accused of being in the pay of the cartels.

The pundits didn't pull their punches. 'Garay is totally corrupt,' said Jose Reveles, co-founder of the hard-hitting Mexican news-magazine *Proceso*. 'But Garay was right underneath the top man for security for the whole government, who has not been arrested. The arrests only go to the neck, not to the head. It is not possible that the corruption ends at the neck. The whole body is corrupt. These cleanup operations are nothing but propaganda.'

Calderon was steadfast. This was just the first step, he argued. More discouraging truths would be uncovered, but the anti-corruption drive would continue. 'I'm convinced that to stop crime, we first have to get it out of our house.'

The Army vs. The Cops

President Calderon – a conservative who was only narrowly elected in July 2006 amid cries of electoral fraud – took office full of promises to create employment. But his agenda changed suddenly. Days into his tenure came the defining moment of his presidency: he ordered the deployment of several thousand soldiers to his home state of Michoacan to fight the drug war.

Cynics continue to argue that Calderon launched the war to divert attention away from the alleged fraud. The new administration, according to former Mexican foreign minister and renowned academic Jorge Castaneda, didn't even 'assume power' until after the president's inauguration, when Calderon 'donned a military jacket, declared an all-out war on organized crime and drug trafficking, and ordered the Mexican army out of its barracks and into the country's streets, highways, and towns'.

Other critics believe Calderon was simply acting at the behest of Washington; but the United States, it appears, wasn't all that influential in his decision-making. The DEA, for its part, has backed Calderon's decision 100 per cent. 'If somebody didn't take on these knuckleheads, Mexico could well have devolved into a narco-state,' said one former DEA man.

The president has staunchly defended his decision to go to war. He needed to consolidate his country's move towards full democracy; he has always maintained it will be a 'long' and 'costly' war.

For the first time in Mexican history, there would be a full-scale military campaign against the narcos. Within two years, 45,000 troops would be deployed. But the Army wouldn't only be fighting the narcos. It would enter into a war with the nation's own police.

Policing cities like Ciudad Juarez, Tijuana and Culiacan has always been a challenge. The police forces are small – in the low thousands – while the drug traffickers' armies number in the tens of thousands. The narcos have money and weapons, the police are shackled by their desire simply to survive and care for their families. Corrupting even the best policeman is not a difficult task.

The narcos are also smart. Most shootings take place on main thoroughfares; by the time the police arrive, the killers have fled in their vehicle via one of many routes out of the city.

Some argue that the police are paid too little. Indeed, with an annual salary of around $5,000, a cop in Ciudad Juarez or Culiacan can easily be bought.

There may be a more deeply rooted problem. 'There's a culture of corruption which we face in this country, which hurts our country, but is part of its soul,' said Ciudad Juarez government spokesman Jaime Alberto Torres Valadez. He used to be the police spokesman and saw the corruption first-hand. He believes that 80 to 90 per cent of people in Ciudad Juarez – 'if not 100 per cent of us' – are involved in some sort of corruption.

Sometimes the cops don't have a choice. In Ciudad Juarez, the narcos have been so bold as to put up posters with names of policemen who would be killed if they tried to do their jobs.

'For those who don't believe,' read one such message, listing more than a dozen names of policemen and their precincts. After several of those named were killed, a new message appeared.

'For those who still don't believe,' it read. The recently deceased had been crossed off.

Former Air Force Major Valentin Diaz Reyes was optimistic

when he took over policing operations in the Delicias precinct in Ciudad Juarez. 'When I arrived, I found a police corps without faith, without a soul, which was badly equipped and very corrupt,' he said after a month in charge. 'The challenge is to clean the corps, make it honest [and] give it dignity as a police corps that is recognized by citizens.'

Gaining public trust wouldn't be easy. The soldiers patrolled the city wearing masks. They set up checkpoints at random, and frantically waved down cars that approached too fast. Drivers quickly learned the new rules of the road – don't use a mobile phone in sight of a checkpoint, or you'd be shot; don't make unnecessary noise around the soldiers. Above all, don't drive too close to a military vehicle.

Some cops, however, took the Army's arrival as an affront to their integrity. In one neighbourhood a shootout between cops and soldiers broke out. Called to the scene of a reported crime, the soldiers claimed the police had started firing at them. The police claimed it was the Army that had fired first.

Around the back of one police precinct building in the southern part of Ciudad Juarez, seven officers shared their concerns about the military, as they gathered around a brand-new red Kawasaki motorbike.

Just days before, one officer said, a couple of colleagues had been detained by soldiers – allegedly on drug charges after a bag of marijuana was 'conveniently' found in the boot of their patrol car – and tortured. 'They broke their noses, and tortured them with electric shocks. They came, supposedly to support, but it doesn't appear that way. They don't want to work with us.'

The people of Ciudad Juarez, meanwhile, were largely happy the police weren't the only ones in charge any more. 'It's good that there's more security here – too many police agents are corrupt,' said Nadio Rivera, who lives in Ciudad Juarez's Plutarco Elias Calles district, which was subjected to numerous Army raids in the early days of the troops' arrival. 'I've paid bribes regularly. They stop you, search you, say you've been drinking, intimidate you.'

By early 2009 there appeared to be a semblance of cooperation between the Army and police. During an evening patrol in Tierra y Libertad, a downtrodden area near the centre of Ciudad Juarez, teamwork was in the air. A number of residents had phoned the Delicias precinct, reporting a gang of teenagers drinking in the square and causing a nuisance. Not big fish, to be sure, but the soldiers piled into the back of a patrol car and the cops drove them to the scene. There, they lined up a group of nine youths who had been drinking. The police searched them for drugs and weapons as the soldiers looked on, making sure correct procedure was adhered to.

With US support, more new police training programmes have been put in place across the country. Federal Police Chief Garcia Luna is seeking to attract college graduates to the force. Policemen already in the force have been told to reveal personal details like bank account numbers so they can be monitored for narco-links; they were also subjected to lie-detector tests.

Still, even if new recruits are brought in to the police, and the old bad elements cast out, Torres Valadez admits it will be difficult to keep criminals' bills from padding the policemen's pockets. 'We're trying to change the culture so that they don't fall into corruption. But even if we pay them $3,000 a day, the mafias will pay $6,000.'

'They've been trying to reform the police for fifteen years,' adds Gonzalez Ruiz, the former anti-organized-crime prosecutor. 'It's not a matter of making up rules, it's that [the policemen] don't follow them.'

Top federal cop Millan Gomez, it turns out, was killed, or at least set up, by some of his colleagues.

Just months after the raid on Zhenli's mansion in Lomas de Chapultepec, the bodies of two officers who had been involved in that bust were found in Guerrero, where they had been working on anti-drug operations. Zhenli was eventually arrested in the United States, but a judge declared that the evidence against him was insufficient. He denies all allegations and is currently fighting extradition to Mexico.

1. Chapo through the ages (*top, from left to right*): in the 1980s, in prison in 1993; (*bottom, from left to right*): after his arrest in 1993, shortly after his escape in 2001.

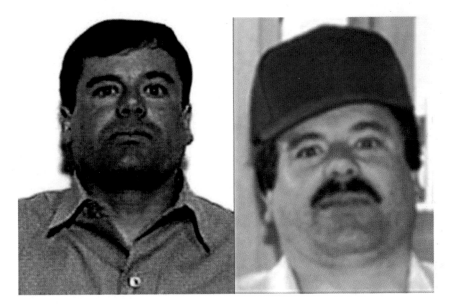

2. One of Chapo's infamous border tunnels: this one was dug from Nogales, Sonora, to an abandoned Methodist church in Nogales, Arizona. The exit, discovered in 1995, was within walking distance of a US customs office.

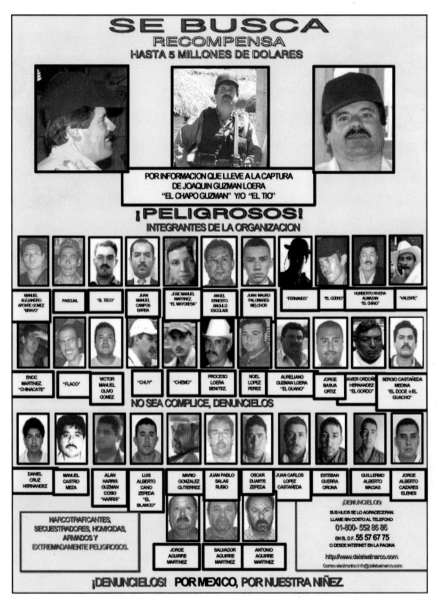

3. A 'wanted' poster of Chapo seen throughout Mexico in 2005. The Mexican authorities denied issuing the poster, prompting speculation that Chapo's rivals had created it to target the drug lord.

4. A bust of Jesus Malverde, the mythical patron saint of the narcos, at the shrine in his honour in Culiacan in 2008.

5. The church in Badiraguato, Sinaloa: locals say it was refurbished in 2008 with Chapo's money.

6. The second-largest cash seizure made by the Mexican army in its history, this $26.2 million had belonged to Chapo's people and was found in a house in Sinaloa on 14 September 2008.

7. The capos: (*top row, from left to right*) Ismael Zambada Garcia, aka 'El Mayo', Juan Jose Esparragosa-Moreno, aka 'El Azul', Ignacio Nacho Coronel Villarreal, Edgar Valdez Villareal, aka 'La Barbie', Heriberto Lazcano, aka 'El Lazca'; (*middle row, from left to right*) Arturo Guzman Loera, aka 'El Pollo', Miguel Angel Guzman Loera, aka 'El Mudo', Alfredo Beltran Leyva, aka 'Mochomo', Vicente Zambada Niebla, Vicente Carrillo Leyva, aka 'El Vicentillo'; (*bottom row, from left to right*): Amado Carrillo Fuentes, aka 'The Lord of the Skies', Ramon Arellano Felix, Benjamin Arellano Felix, Osiel Cardenas Guillen, Miguel Angel Felix Gallardo, aka 'El Padrino'.

8. Residents of Morelia, Michoacan, mourn after a twin grenade attack on 15 Sepember 2008 left eight dead and more than 100 injured.

9. The war cabinet of President Felipe Calderon (*centre*) meets on 24 November 2009. To Calderon's immediate right stands federal police chief Genaro Garcia Luna.

10. The beaten, naked and castrated corpse of an unidentified man hangs from an overpass in Tijuana in late 2009.

11. With more than 2,600 homicides in Ciudad Juarez in 2009, the city's morgues were on the brink.

12. Thousands of weapons seized in the drug war sit in a warehouse in Mexico City. By 2009 the military had seized more than 300,000 weapons.

13. President Felipe Calderon and his wife Margarita Zavala stand next to the coffin of his close friend and No. 2, Interior Secretary Juan Camilo Mourino. Mourino died in a plane crash on 4 November 2008; he was considered instrumental in the drug war.

14. Police officers stand next to seven bodies found in Ciudad Juarez on 25 November 2008. Accompanying the bodies were three banners, allegedly signed by members of Chapo's organization.

15. On a hill above Santiago de los Caballeros, Sinaloa, lies a cemetery reserved for local narcos. This grave is reserved for Ernesto 'Don Neto' Fonseca, who is in prison in Mexico.

16. A soldier stands in a poppy field high in the Mexican mountains in 2009.

17. Chapo stands in the courtyard of Almoloya de Juarez prison on 10 June 1993, shortly after his capture in Guatemala. He would be transferred to Puente Grande prison in 1995.

18. A masked policeman takes a cigarette break during a patrol in Ciudad Juarez in 2009.

19. A soldier on patrol in Ciudad Juarez in 2009.

20. The border area between Guatemala and Mexico, where Chapo was captured in 1993. Here, thousands of undocumented migrants and illicit goods cross the border every day.

21. Soldiers burn opium poppies in the mountains of Mexico in 2009.

22. The DEA's wanted poster for Chapo, issued in 2005.

Under Pressure

In Culiacan, things are even worse.

Thirty-five-year-old cop Hector Valenzuela is scared. Just over a year ago, he lost his friend – also a policeman. His buddy was driving alongside another patrol car, when two trucks carrying about fifteen men sped up on either side. They fired their AK-47s into his friend, a partner and the men in the other car. No one was spared.

Valenzuela lights up a cigarette outside Culiacan police station, as he describes how gunmen now come down from the Sierra and take potshots at policemen. Sometimes they dress in military uniforms and wield military-issue weapons. 'They rule up there.'

Culiacan's police force was once regarded as one of the best in Mexico. Today the police are vastly outnumbered and outgunned. Add to that the lack of decent pay, and they stand no chance; an estimated 70 per cent of Sinaloa's police force is, or has been, in the pockets of the narcos. At one point the Army temporarily took complete control of police operations in the city, and the entire force was investigated. Dozens of Culiacan cops are currently in prison. Dozens are dead.

It's hard to believe the city's police force can really change, given the level of corruption and the threat from the gatilleros. 'It'll never end,' said former law enforcement officer Miguel Angel Navarrete Cruz, of the violence and policing problems. 'Sinaloa is pure corruption. Eighty per cent of it is drugs. This is what makes Sinaloa.'

General Sandoval has issued an order that his men are not to wear masks; the narcos are walking around in military garb and wearing masks, posing a serious threat to security. Sandoval's men have seized dozens of vehicles that are reworked to resemble military humvees. They have also detained narcos in possession of military uniforms – both American and Mexican – who were travelling in vehicles painted green to match the colour of his own soldiers' jeeps.

Be on the lookout, General Sandoval has told the people of Culiacan. No one can be trusted.

Late one night, Antonio Garza, Erica's husband, was paid a visit by a group of narcos. They didn't come to kill him; they wanted to negotiate a deal to leave them alone. He refused. Thirteen days later, he was driving home from his office in Mexico City when another vehicle sped up from behind. As the assailants attempted to ram him off the road, he tried to outspeed them. They managed to block him into a corner so he couldn't drive any further. The assailants got out of the car and opened fire.

Antonio was killed.

No investigation followed his death; the AFI did nothing to honour him. The DEA, however, did lay on a ceremony for him and other fallen Mexican police officers in Washington.

'The moral of this story is . . . there are federal police in Mexico that are doing what they should be doing, that are working as hard as they can work. There are heroes in Mexico that have paid the ultimate sacrifice,' said then-DEA regional director David Gaddis of his Mexican counterpart's death.

Antonio's wife Erica remains troubled by the lack of institutional support from her own country. She still works in law enforcement, and goes to work every day in spite of the fact that she believes some in the police force may have been responsible for organizing the hit. 'Among them is the person who killed my husband,' she says, wiping tears from her eyes.

Also in the back of her mind is one, somewhat reluctant, request for a chance to do things over again. 'I'm proud that Antonio was an honest person. But sometimes I think, "Antonio, why weren't you corrupt?"'

If he had been, he might be alive today.

11. The End of the Alliance

My sons are my source of happiness as well as my sadness
Edgar I will miss you
You were my confidant, my right-hand man
you were a Chapito Guzman
Ivan Archivaldo I am truly proud
that you are a Guzman
You boys and your brother Alfredo you know I love you
God gave you to me to care for you . . .

I'm brave and I'm also a friend
that's how we Guzmans are
A greeting to my people of Badiraguato
and also of
Ranch in Jesus Maria I'll never forget you
I'll have to take you with me

'El Hijo de La Tuna', narco-corrido sung
    by Roberto Tapia

At 8.30 p.m. on 8 May 2008, one of Chapo's sons was walking to his vehicle through the car park at the City Club mall in Culiacan. Edgar Guzman Lopez, twenty-two, was accompanied by three people, one of whom was Arturo Cazares – the son of 'the Empress', Blanca Margarita Cazares Salazar – and a bodyguard. More than a dozen men in three cars approached.

Edgar and his boys rushed to their two trucks, one of which was armoured. The assailants opened fire. It was an onslaught of epic proportions. Investigators would find more than 500 shells at the scene; the attackers had even used a bazooka. At least twenty vehicles in the car park sustained serious damage. Edgar Guzman Lopez, son of Chapo, was dead. So was Arturo Cazares.

As with most incidents in Mexico pertaining to organized crime, there were few witnesses. Those who happened to be in the vicinity simply didn't see anything.

A cross rests at the site today, where locals pay their respects. 'We love you Edgar,' reads one note. 'Chapo will never fall,' reads another.

State sources initially laid blame for the killing on the Juarez cartel, but independent investigations revealed that those most likely responsible were the Beltran Leyva brothers, Chapo's long-time close allies. The brothers were indispensable to the Sinaloa cartel's operations; they were responsible for bribing from the lowest levels to the highest ranks of federal government. They also helped manage poppy and marijuana production in Guerrero, which was a key landing point for Colombian cocaine. They had helped Chapo escape from Puente Grande and re-enter the fold. And, like Chapo, they were *buchones* – narcos from the hills, not privileged rich boys from the city. Alfredo Beltran Leyva – known as 'Mochomo', or Fire Ant – and Chapo were even related; Mochomo had married his cousin.

But Mochomo and Chapo weren't alike. A big, bearded man, Mochomo was hot-headed; if an employee failed to fulfil a task, Mochomo would have a fit of rage – hence the nickname. Chapo, on the other hand, rarely shouted. He would kill, but wouldn't raise his voice doing so.

In late 2007 Mochomo was getting on Chapo's nerves. The heat was on – General Sandoval had made it clear that he would go after the cartel leaders, just like his predecessor General Eddy – and Chapo knew they could ill afford to be in the spotlight, or let anyone know where they were. Mochomo was being too conspicuous. He was throwing loud parties in Culiacan, going out to bars and generally drawing attention to himself. There were too many people coming and going from his home, too; neighbours were taking note.

So Chapo turned on his long-time ally. The story goes that the authorities were homing in on Chapo – they needed to land a big fish in Sinaloa to prove that they were going after that cartel too – and he gave up Mochomo. There is no evidence of this betrayal, but it has become the semi-official history in Sinaloa. There was also speculation that Chapo had turned in Mochomo in return for the release of his son, Ivan Archivaldo. (Again, this has not been proven.)

On 21 January 2008, operating on intelligence provided by General Sandoval's top team, a group of soldiers surrounded a BMW X3 driving through the streets of Culiacan. They pulled it over. Inside was Mochomo, eleven top-of-the-range watches, an AK-47, nine handguns and $900,000 in cash.

The government hailed the arrest of Mochomo as another major blow against organized crime. Like those capos caught before him, he was transferred to Mexico City in a cavalcade of dozens of military vehicles and masked soldiers, overflown by helicopters and all in the media's full spotlight.

For General Sandoval, the arrest of Mochomo would also prove to be a pyrrhic victory. He would discover that the Beltran Leyva brothers had made inroads into the 9th Military Zone. Four of Sandoval's men would be detained and sent to military prison to be interrogated.

As for the relationship between Chapo and the Beltran Leyva brothers, it would never be the same.

Close in Spirit

Like all Chapo's sons, Edgar was never supposed to die the way he did.

For Chapo, family had always been a priority. Although haunted by his own difficult childhood in La Tuna, Chapo maintained strong connections with his mother. Even while on the run after his breakout from Puente Grande, he had visited when he could. He had built her a splendid ranch near the home he had grown up in; he had supplied her with a plane whenever she needed to get to the city. Maria Consuelo Loera Perez would never want for anything.

His brothers, too, were near and dear to him. Drug trafficking in Sinaloa had always been a family business, and Chapo's organization was no different. Arturo, Miguel Angel, Emilio and Aureliano all occupied top posts in the Sinaloa cartel. They were in charge of logistics, money laundering and overseeing smuggling – according to the PGR – and had never had to murder their way up the greasy pole like their brother had.

Then there were Chapo's wives. Although his marriages had ended, they had always done so amicably. In Puente Grande, even as he was having relations with Zulema Hernandez and other prisoners, he received his third wife, Laura Alvarez Beltran, for conjugal visits. Shortly after he left Puente Grande, he was allegedly helped to flee by Griselda Lopez Perez, his second wife and Edgar's mother. She frequently dropped in to a house in the Guadalupe neighbourhood of Culiacan, where the PGR found stacks of documents being sent to Chapo by El Mayo while the former was on the run, to keep him abreast of the authorities' movements.

Chapo's wives, who lived in homes and on ranches provided by their drug lord husband, were always a part of his life, and remain so today. After all, they bore him his children. While Chapo was in prison, the psychologist who assessed him said he showed a great sense of responsibility when it came to his wives and offspring. According to some witnesses who have testified about his operation, Chapo even used his wives as envoys, deploying them to negotiate with rivals or make sure alliances were running smoothly.

At the time of his death, his son Edgar was studying business administration at the Autonomous University of Sinaloa. He had a common-law wife, Frida Munoz Roman. They had a child aged two, Chapo's granddaughter – Frida Sofia Guzman Munoz.

Edgar was one of a new generation of drug traffickers known in Mexico as 'narco-juniors'. Second-generation narcos have long existed in Mexico – nearly as long as the business, effectively – but since the 1970s the sons and daughters of kingpins have been taking a different route. Instead of simply following in their predecessors' footsteps right away, they've been increasingly attending top schools – sometimes foreign ones – in order to better learn business. In their twenties they rarely participate in any criminal activity.

Some who hail from Culiacan remember the narco-juniors of yesteryear. When they were in college there, Francisco Arellano Felix and his brother Eduardo were both working towards their degrees too. The former may have sold some ecstasy pills on occasion, but that was it, recalls one Sinaloan – although everyone knew who they were, 'it was believed they weren't working in the business'.

They would all go to the same parties, where drugs were available though 'very hidden'. But the Arellano Felix brothers were just part of the usual crowd – well connected, yes, and bound to go into the drug business; but narcos, they were not. Not yet.

According to Luis Astorga, one of Mexico's foremost experts on drug trafficking, the narco-juniors of today are highly regarded: 'The generational change within organized crime families has allowed a generation to reach a higher level of education . . . to have more knowledge of financial markets, an understanding of the technological environment, an understanding of the political environment and more sophisticated [knowledge] of weapons and power.' The narco-juniors, according to Astorga, have 'a better ability to [avoid] the mistakes of past generations'.

One alleged narco-junior, now in his mid-thirties and living in Mexico City, described a standard route for the son or daughter of a drug trafficker. The tall, handsome, dark-haired narco-junior grew up not knowing what his parents or relatives did for a living. His was a politically connected family. The children had parties on their ranches throughout Mexico, and flew around in private jets and helicopters. They enjoyed weekend trips abroad. They went to the best schools around.

'My father was – how do you say it – a businessman,' said the narco-junior, with a sheepish grin. In his twenties, through reading newspaper cuttings, he found out what his father actually did. Shortly afterwards he was offered a piece of the action, albeit more legitimately – leading some of the family businesses that are allegedly fronts for drug operations.

Chapo's son Edgar was of the same ilk. While his older brother Alfredo was actively working for his father, Edgar was studying. According to his wife, he had no involvement in the business itself – yet. But such claims of innocence, during the latter half of the Fox presidency and the first half of Calderon's, weren't enough for the authorities.

Chapo's son Ivan Archivaldo ('Chapito') had already been indoctrinated in the family business by the time of his arrest. When he was detained, his father sprang into action through one family lawyer, Jorge Bucio. '[Chapito] is a hostage of the state, with the goal of [forcing] his father to turn himself in,' Bucio declared; the government was trying 'to make him pay for the crimes of his father'.

Chapito was eventually convicted of depositing about $20,000 into one bank and about $50,000 into another – without proving that the money had been obtained through 'legitimate' means. Hardly a strong case; he would only serve a commuted sentence. Chapito was also investigated for the murder of Cesar Augusto Pulido Mendoza and a Canadian citizen, Kristen Paige, outside a bar called Balibar in Zapopan, but was never convicted.

So Chapito walked, but the government had made clear that it was not only going after the cartel leaders, it was also going after their heirs. They knew that most of the nation's drug organizations operated in close-knit fashion, with the capos surrounding themselves with brothers, training their sons to follow in their footsteps. Cousins, nephews, nieces would also be rounded up.

Often they were harder to track than the run-of-the-mill younger narcos employed by the cartels. They rarely wore the gold chains some of their fathers had worn; few were ever found carrying arms, let alone sporting gold-plated pistols.

'They're harder to identify because they don't look like typical drug traffickers,' explained Jorge Chabat, another top Mexican security expert. 'You can't detect them by saying, "Oh look, he has a big truck with wide tyres and automatic weapons, gold chains, snakeskin boots and a big belt buckle and dark glasses."'

That wouldn't stop the authorities from smoking them out.

One morning in the spring of 2009, Vicente Carrillo Leyva, the thirty-two-year-old son of the deceased Amado Carrillo Fuentes – the Lord of the Skies – went out for a jog in Bosques de las Lomas, Mexico City. The authorities had been looking for Carrillo Leyva for more than a decade; they had issued a $2-million reward for information leading to his capture.

The young narco had made a fatal mistake – or at least his wife had. Although he was living under an alias, she had neglected to change her name. So the AFI had been able to track him down, monitor his every move, and wait for him to be caught unawares and alone, without his bodyguards. When he went out jogging, they swooped in and grabbed him.

The sight of Carrillo Leyva in cuffs came as a surprise to many in Mexico. For two years the public had been flooded with media images of dark-skinned, tough-looking narcos. Paraded in front of the press, these culprits would nervously try to string together a couple of sentences. Most of them had glazed eyes; they were scruffy, unkempt.

Carrillo Leyva was anything but. Dressed in an Armani track-suit and sporting a pair of trendy glasses, he looked more like a male model. (It turns out he had a penchant for fashion, investing in high-end boutiques that specialized in Versace designs.)

Carrillo Leyva was the epitome of the new narco-junior: he had been educated in Europe, spoke French and English almost fluently and travelled frequently. In Mexico City he had kept his head down. 'No parties, no noise; these neighbours were very discreet. The young man went out running in the morning and his wife was very nice,' said one local resident after his arrest.

He was also second-in-command of the Juarez cartel.

Also that spring, the authorities made another dent in the family structures of the cartels, one that infuriated Chapo even more than the detention of Ivan Archivaldo.

The feds had received several anonymous calls from residents of Mexico City's swanky Lomas de Pedregal district. There had been complaints that some men were riding around in their cars with guns. One Thursday morning the authorities made their move. Backed up by soldiers, federal agents surrounded No. 269, Calle Lluvia. Without any shots being fired, they apprehended thirty-three-year-old Vicente Zambada Niebla, a.k.a. 'El Vicentillo' (Little Vicente).

They had caught El Mayo's son.

El Vicentillo, too, was paraded before the media. Wearing jeans, a neatly ironed dress shirt and a jacket, he looked like any other urban professional. He looked nothing like the pictures the DEA had of him, in which he was wearing a cowboy hat and sporting a moustache – Sinaloa style.

The arrests of El Vicentillo and Carrillo Leyva were successes, but also a wake-up call, drug war critics said. 'They are paying a lot of attention to developing their top brass,' said Mexican security expert Alberto Islas of the narcos. 'We are not outgunning them and we are not outsmarting them. I think that's why we are losing this war.'

Perhaps, but at the same time, their arrests were major blows. According to those who claim to have been with him at the time of El Vicentillo's detention, the normally cool-headed Chapo was outraged. How could this son of his partner be so stupid, so lazy, as to stroll around Mexico City with guns?

El Vicentillo should have known better. He and Alfredo Guzman Salazar, another son of Chapo's, were in charge of coordinating 'narcotics trafficking activities to import multi-ton quantities of cocaine from Central and South American countries, through Mexico and into the United States using various means of transportation, including Boeing 747 cargo aircraft; submarines and other submersible and semi-submersible vessels; container ships; go-fast boats; fishing vessels; buses; rail cars; tractor trailers; and automobiles', according to the US Department of Justice. El Vicentillo had risen to the upper echelons of Chapo's organization, replacing Mochomo since his split with the drug lord.

Chapo and El Mayo couldn't afford to lose any kin, at any cost; losing sons who were now crucial to running the business could be fatal.

Vengeance

Edgar Guzman Lopez would be avenged.

At the time of his son's death, Chapo was apparently hiding out in the hills separating Colima and Michoacan. According to some in Sinaloa, the drug lord spent the days following the killing drinking himself into oblivion, downing shot after shot of whiskey, which he is so fond of. Another story has it that Chapo – cool, calm and collected as ever, not to mention sober – immediately went into attack mode. Given his remarkable control in past high-stress occasions the latter is more likely.

The Sinaloa organization had undergone another transformation of sorts. Instead of Chapo and El Mayo reigning over it all, they had come to a power-sharing agreement with the Beltran Leyva brothers and other associates. They would be more loose-knit than ever.

With the authorities putting more pressure on the cartels, it would be safer to operate this way, with smaller 'cells' managing each stage of the operation. The cells would report to higher-ranking operatives, who would report to the lieutenants. They, in turn, would consult Chapo, the Beltran Leyva brothers and El Mayo for direction if needed. The structure of the network wasn't hugely different from in the past, but it allowed for layers of protection for the higher-ups, and would in theory allow the business to work more smoothly and safely.

However, bad blood had been brewing between the Beltran Leyva brothers and Chapo. It wasn't just Mochomo's antics. According to the DEA, they were fighting over the allegiance of a cell in Chicago, a lucrative part of the US market. The Mexican military, meanwhile, said that Chapo and the Beltran Leyva brothers were at odds over the former's relationship with the Valencia brothers in Michoacan, who were under increasing pressure.

Shortly before the killing of Edgar, the Culiacan plaza seriously heated up. Mochomo had been arrested – purportedly with Chapo's help – and trouble was brewing in the underworld. A formal 'war' was declared, and just hours later an attempt on El Vicentillo's life was made. Dozens of killings followed, apparently in retaliation for that attempt.

On 8 May 2008 it all erupted. That month alone, 116 people were murdered in Culiacan, 26 of them policemen. In June, 128 died; in July, 143. Culiacan had become a war zone. Residents stayed at home in fear; every night the streets were empty by nine. Those who dared go out did so only when absolutely necessary.

General Sandoval received a boost of more than 2,000 troops, and the streets were patrolled day and night, in a bid to instil some sense of calm. But the fear – not to mention the homicides – continued. The wave of violence swept over cities like Guamuchil, Guasave and Mazatlan, too. No one knew who was boss any more, not even in the Sierra, in Chapo country.

Banners began to appear, threatening supporters of Chapo. 'This is Beltran Leyva territory,' read one, found hanging on a fence in Culiacan. 'Chapo, you will fall,' warned another, pinned up on the wall of a home in central Culiacan. Other narco-mantas accused El Mayo and Chapo of being in cahoots with the federal government. Most were attributed to supporters of the Beltran Leyva brothers.

From prison, Mochomo apparently tried to put a stop to the bloodshed. According to the Mexican daily *El Universal*, Mochomo wrote a letter to his brother Marcos Arturo, saying that El Mayo and Chapo had had nothing to do with his arrest. He pleaded for calm. No one knows if the letter ever arrived.

The killings continued.

Chapo and El Mayo may not have had anything to do with Mochomo's arrest. But as it turns out, the Beltran Leyvas had been doing some double-dealing of their own. Marcos Arturo and Mochomo had met in Cuernavaca with top members of Los Zetas. They had agreed to form their own organization in order to fill the power vacuum nationwide. They wouldn't necessarily go after the main strongholds, like Sinaloa or the Gulf, but they would seek control of southern states like Guerrero (where the Beltran Leyva brothers already had a big stake), Oaxaca, Yucatan and Quintana Roo. They would also work their way into the centre of the country, where no single group had firm control.

At this meeting in Cuernavaca they had also decided to rupture the Federation.

In mid-May 2008, as violence spiralled out of control in Culiacan, the DEA unofficially confirmed the split between the Beltran Leyva brothers and Chapo. On 30 May the US government formally recognized the Beltran Leyva brothers as leaders of their own 'cartel': 'President Bush has designated . . . Marcos Arturo Beltran Leyva and the Beltran Leyva Organization . . . as subject to the sanctions under the Foreign Narcotics Kingpin Designation Act ("Kingpin Act"),' announced then-Ambassador Tony Garza.

Beltran Leyva and his organization comprise a major part of Mexico's Sinaloa drug cartel, with operations on both coasts of Mexico and along its southern and northern borders that move significant quantities of cocaine into the United States. His hit squads are responsible for scores of deaths and heinous violence. Marcos Arturo Beltran Leyva and members of his family have been indicted in both the United States and Mexico for cocaine smuggling . . . The decision to designate Marcos Arturo Beltran Leyva and his organization will provide the United States with additional tools to dismantle his operations, deprive him and his cohorts of resources, and prosecute them in the United States.

The Beltran Leyva brothers had made it to the big league as their own entity. They also continued to wage war against Chapo.

Amid the violence in Culiacan, the state reportedly tried to negotiate a pact, gathering Chapo and the brothers at a ranch in Durango. Another summit meeting also apparently took place, also in Durango. The head of every major cartel was said to be there, even representatives from Tijuana. A temporary peace deal of sorts would be agreed, but tempers would soon flare up again.

Culiacan remained a war zone. In 2008 Sinaloa registered 1,167 homicides; in 2009, 932 more people were murdered there.

By the time Los Zetas arrived, Chapo was still hiding out in the Sierra. But he appeared more isolated than ever before.

12. The Ghost

The seventeen-year-old brunette had a sad look in her eyes. She stared quizzically into the crowd of onlookers. Resplendent in her gold, flowing dress, she appeared every bit the beauty queen, but something seemed to be troubling her.

Emma Coronel Aispuro was born and raised in La Angostura, a small hamlet in Canelas. A niece of Ignacio Nacho Coronel Villareal, the 'Crystal King', she grew up in the narco-world. According to residents of Culiacan, Emma sometimes went to town to get her nails done, or fix up her abundant brown locks; sometimes she went shopping. But mostly, locals say, she stayed in the mountains.

The Durango mountains are some of the most drug-rich in the country. Poppy fields abound in this part of the Golden Triangle, as do meth labs. Between Canelas and Tamazula lies one poppy field of about 430,000 square feet. The authorities have been trying to eradicate it since the new millennium, with little luck. It keeps growing back too fast. Canelas is ranked twelfth among Mexico's more than 2,000 counties in terms of illicit growth of drugs.

On the night of 20 November 2006, Emma began her run for Queen of Canelas, an honour bestowed each year on the most beautiful young lady in the county of some 2,000 residents. The beauty queen tradition is strong in Sinaloa; throughout the state, even in the big cities, young girls look forward to the day they can enter the local contest, dress up in flowing dresses and compete against their friends. Everyone comes out to enjoy the event, as it's usually intertwined with a celebration of the local area's produce and agriculture. (In Canelas's case, guayaba and coffee are lauded.)

Emma faced some stiff competition from the other four ladies. But she would have some help in eventually winning the contest.

Although her competitors were equally beautiful, rumour already had it that she had 'someone very important' on her side.

Chapo had apparently taken a shine to young Emma the year before, when he had hidden out in La Angostura. That was when they had first met. It's unclear whether their relationship went anywhere immediately, but it's certain he was attracted to her.

For the contest, Emma set about organizing a big dance, a traditional part of the aspiring beauty queens' quest to garner votes; the people were buzzing about the fact that Chapo and his crew might show up.

On the day of the dance, 6 January, the residents of Canelas awoke to a winter mist. They began to prepare for the afternoon fiesta, which would likely last well into the night. Then they heard the roar.

Over the hill, on the road leading into town, some 200 all-terrain motorcycles appeared. The visitors were wearing black balaclavas and armed with handguns. They scattered around the town's entrances, and blocked off all the streets. A short time later, a plane carrying Los Canelos de Durango, a famous norteno group from near Tamazula who are thought to be one of Chapo's favourites, landed on the town's airstrip. Locals recall that they too were armed, wielding gold-plated pistols.

At about 4.30 in the afternoon, another six small planes touched down. A man descended from one of them. He was dressed casually in jeans, sweatshirt and black sneakers, and sported a cap. He was carrying a Kalashnikov AK-47, known in the narco-world as a *cuerno de chivo*, or goat's horn. In his belt was a pistol. Chapo had arrived.

Nacho Coronel followed his boss down the steps of the plane. Another three planes arrived, carrying men in green military-style uniforms. Another two planes arrived; they were carrying weapons and cases of whiskey.

Two helicopters circled above, keeping watch. Los Canelos de Durango kicked off the dance. It went without a hitch, well into the night. Chapo, an avid dancer according to those who have seen him frequent village fiestas, held sway on the floor.

The next morning, the men filed out just as efficiently as they had arrived. Locals throughout the area remember the event as if it were yesterday, even if they weren't even there.

On 2 July 2007, Emma's eighteenth birthday, in La Angostura, Chapo's fourth wedding took place. It was rumoured that several top Sinaloan officials were among the invited guests.

Emma Coronel Aispuro had become Emma Guzman Coronel, or, as one Mexican journalist likes to call her, Queen Emma I. On the night of her wedding, so witnesses told reporters, the fair-skinned beauty looked happy. In a photo of her dancing with Chapo, apparently from that night, she is seen flashing a coy smile at her new husband, who is wearing a baseball cap and still sporting a moustache. He too is seen smiling.

Emma's parents were proud of their daughter's nuptials; her father, after all, works for Chapo, according to those who claim to know him. He grows marijuana and poppy.

The revelations of Chapo's wedding were once again a slap in the face for the Mexican authorities. Just days after the big dance in Emma's honour, 150 soldiers had been deployed to the area, setting up checkpoints to – at least ostensibly – watch for Chapo. They remained in the area for forty-four days but left before the actual wedding. They had also left Canelas en masse for a few days in late February, with the result that Emma's coronation passed without interference. (And, in the opinion of locals, just in case Chapo showed up: they didn't want to be around and have to actually do something about it.)

A day after the wedding, the soldiers returned. As it turns out, Chapo had originally set the date for 3 July, and then pulled it back one day to outwit his foes. It had worked; by the time the military raided Canelas, Chapo and his new bride were already long gone. Some locals said they had gone to Colombia; others that they were shacked up in a new ranch further up in the Sierra.

Everywhere and Nowhere

For the authorities, hunting Chapo down has always been an experiment in frustration. They get hundreds of tips a year from people claiming to have spotted Chapo, but he's always one step ahead. Protected by his close circle – and layers and layers of other ordinary people who have a serious distrust of police and government – Chapo always gets away.

Journalists, too, hear of his whereabouts. 'Once, on a single day, I got tips of sightings in Nuevo Laredo, Mochicahui, Badiraguato, Mexicali, Caborca and Agua Prieta,' said now-deceased Tijuana-based journalist, author and narco expert Jesus Blancornelas in 2005. 'Everyone thinks they are seeing him.'

Deciphering which tips are accurate is a serious challenge. The Mexican military, PGR and federal police all claim to have their people working on the inside, trying to get close to the man himself, or at least gain good intelligence on him. But Chapo, too, has his circle of trust. He has had informants killed for their betrayal, and in recent years has opened up to newcomers less and less.

And in spite of the net appearing to close in on him, Chapo has remained bold.

One cool November evening, about thirty diners were enjoying their meals at Las Palmas, a restaurant in the Las Quintas neighbourhood of Culiacan. A group of armed men walked in the door.

'Gentlemen, please. Give me a moment of your time. A man is going to come in, the boss. We ask that you remain in your seats; the doors will close and nobody is allowed to leave. You will also not be allowed to use your mobile phones. Do not worry; if you do everything that is asked of you, nothing will happen. Continue eating and don't ask for your bill. The boss will pay. Thank you.'

Chapo walked in.

'The diners sat still, stupefied, embarrassed, frightened. The fear and the paralysis, an attack of the heart; here in this tiny space, amid the tables and wooden chairs, plates piled high with meat, bottles of cold beer, plates of squid and shrimp,' recounted local journalist Javier Valdez of *Rio Doce*, who initially reported the story.

Chapo, according to one witness, shook hands with each person, introducing himself and uttering the traditional Mexican greeting, '*A sus ordenes*' (At your service). He then retired to a back room for two hours, and feasted on beef and shrimp from the Sinaloan coast. The diners continued their meals; those who had already finished simply sat and waited until the drug lord was ready to let them leave.

Eventually, he did. Free to go, the diners found that their bills had been taken care of. Chapo had been true to his word.

It's always the same story: a dozen or so armed men walk into a restaurant full of diners; would everyone please hand over their mobile phones and remain seated while Chapo eats? And so it goes.

The authorities are forced to investigate these tales, or at least entertain their validity. On most occasions it's near impossible to prove anything happened; waiters and staff at the restaurants in question have largely denied everything.

When a tabloid in Nuevo Laredo – one of the war's main fronts – published an account of a Chapo appearance in a restaurant, the chef there vehemently denied it had happened. But the FBI did confirm witness accounts, and the *Los Angeles Times* ran with the story: 'The general had come to survey the battlefield,' wrote correspondent Richard Boudreaux of Chapo's brazen visit.

In one single month Chapo was supposedly spotted in the central city of Guanajuato, the south-eastern city of Villahermosa, the border region shared with Guatemala, and deep in Central America. The PGR investigated each sighting, each 'unconfirmed rumour'. No evidence of his presence was ever found.

In cities like Culiacan, Monterrey, Torreon and Mexicali, rumours of Chapo's impending arrival bring out a reaction in the masses. People in the Sierra, even in Badiraguato in the foothills, await his arrival at any given moment. Many call him 'Viejon' ('Old Man') or 'Tio' ('Uncle'), out of great deference.

'Everybody loves and respects him,' said one local who claimed to have worked with Chapo in the hills of Durango. There's good reason: after heavy rains devastated local agriculture one year, Chapo gave tens of thousands of dollars' worth of supplies to his gomeros. At Christmas, another gift arrived: 100 all-terrain vehicles for the locals.

Chapo is a 'seducer', the authorities say. He creates the appearance of being the people's 'protector', which creates loyalty and confidence among employees and even locals less closely connected to the drug trade. Because of his seductive style, everyone within his network identifies with him, trusts him, and the group structure remains permanent. It's an odd coexistence: at any one time, as the PGR put it, Chapo can instil both solidarity and 'reverential terror' in his organization.

The reverence infuriates the authorities. 'Why would you want to support a guy who's poisoning your society?' asks the Mexico City DEA agent, furious. The Mexican government, too, has repeatedly expressed outrage over media lauding of Chapo – in part because he continually reminds them of their failures in the drug war rather than their successes, but also because they fear he will remain on his pedestal.

When *Forbes* magazine included Chapo at No. 701 on its list of the richest people in the world, the Calderon administration was irate. The president condemned the publication and others, saying they are 'not only attacking and lying about the situation in Mexico but are also praising criminals'.

The then-Attorney General Eduardo Medina Mora declared that *Forbes*'s methodology was faulty, and lambasted the magazine for glorifying a criminal. Including Chapo on a list of honest businessmen was not in accordance with the magazine's prestige, Medina Mora said, adding that 'I cannot fail to mention that this money, in the case of my country, is associated with a wave of violence in the past few years, with confrontations between rival gangs and the deaths of many innocent people who have crossed into the gunfire of the assassins.

'Never will I accept that a criminal could or should be recognized as distinguished,' he went on, 'even if it's by a magazine like *Forbes*. This person will pay for the pain he has inflicted on Mexican society and the people of other nations [by going to] jail. That is his destiny.'

Medina Mora may have been right in his argument against Forbes, but perhaps for the wrong reasons. Some legal experts claim that even US indictments against Chapo wouldn't hold up in court.

Josue Felix, a son of 'El Padrino' Felix Gallardo, agrees; he thinks much of what people say about Chapo is hype – just like what they claim about his father. 'Look, it's obvious my father did some things that were illegal, there's no doubt. But they fabricated much of it, to make him [boss of] everything. There's no way he could have made such a fortune, and if he did, where is it? They've made him into some character, a symbol.'

But this has only served Chapo; he knows the audience he is playing to. He has become a leader of a people who have barely ever received anything from their government, people whose first priority is survival rather than worrying about whether they're on the right side of the law, people who look up to a man who rose from abject poverty to be a successful, free man, living as he desires in the mountains of Mexico. For the most part, the people of Sinaloa and Durango couldn't care less about his ranking on *Forbes*'s list – that is, if they've even heard of the magazine.

'Someone told me about that *Forbes* thing, but *Me vale madre* [I couldn't give a damn],' said one thirty-something Tamazula resident. 'Chapo is like a god; omnipotent, outside of the law, outside of Mexico. That's why I love him and always will.'

He's everywhere and nowhere at the same time. His name appears on narco-mantas, he has Facebook pages dedicated to him, and there's constant chatter on Internet forums about his exploits and whereabouts. Other legends add to Chapo's awa. It has been said that he has fathered more than twenty children, earning him much admiration as a true macho. According to one bishop, Chapo is a devoted religious man: these kids have all been baptized.

Chapo's mystique thrives not only among the people of Mexico, but also throughout its underworld. Few dare to cross him; it seems there is often little reason. If one does one's job, one is paid handsomely. If one fails to accomplish what the boss asked, there will be repercussions. It's business. In Culiacan, Tamazula and Badiraguato, those who claim to work for the man are beholden to him.

Chapo, according to the authorities, has shown himself a master of 'generating natural sentiments of dependence and loyalty'. This has enabled him to create an organization that does his bidding, one in which employees are often so loyal that they will 'sacrifice their own physical safety to save him or his family'.

He visits plantations from Guerrero to Chihuahua in order to make sure everything is operating smoothly. He's even said to have travelled under the protection of the military. The local gomeros are always happy to see him.

Carlos from Badiraguato helps oversee the transport of marijuana and poppy down from the Sierra. He has met Chapo, he claims, on several occasions. Once the boss came to check out a new marijuana plantation near Badiraguato itself. Chapo was concerned that it was too close to the town; the military would discover it and wipe it out. Carlos managed to convince Chapo he would bribe the soldiers to look the other way.

Carlos described how Chapo looked at him, serious as always: 'If I can count on you to continue to deliver the necessary amount of marijuana to the town of Pericos [where it would then head up north to the border], then there will be no problems.'

On 15 September 2009, Independence night in Badiraguato, some locals hoped to see him there. Carlos and his boys had conducted a thorough review of their operations to make sure the marijuana was growing and being delivered at the pace they had promised. When he arrived, Chapo would be pleased.

A helicopter circled overhead before the fireworks began. The next morning, the helicopter appeared again. General Sandoval's men were watching, waiting.

Chapo never came.

13. The New Wave

Congressman Felipe Diaz Garibay was standing just a few yards behind Michoacan Governor Leonel Godoy on 15 September 2008, when they heard a loud explosion from below the balcony, in the main square of the city of Morelia. Like the thousands of others in the plaza that night, they thought the bang was just another firework in celebration of Mexico's Independence Day. The governor's VIP guests continued with their idle chatter.

Moments later the state's chief of police came running in. A grenade had exploded. At least one person had been killed.

The guests quickly adjourned to a room in Godoy's offices, security detail and police chief in tow. Feverish discussions ensued, as they tried to make head or tail of what had happened, Garibay recalled during an interview several days later. Was it a political group? A mob of hired goons trying to put pressure on the left-wing Godoy? A botched assassination attempt? Drug traffickers? Was it a local outfit known as 'La Familia' ('the Family')?

'No one imagined such an attack,' Garibay said. 'It was narco-terrorism.'

Michoacan has long been a hotbed of drug production, with its share of violence. The gomeros of Badiraguato in Sinaloa had brought the first poppy to the region, and taught the local campesinos both how to grow and sap it for its precious gum. For decades, any opium produced in the region was then delivered to their Sinaloan counterparts in the north, who shipped it to the United States. The Amezcua brothers used Michoacan's main port, Lazaro Cardenas, to import the necessary ingredients to meet US meth demand. They also began to infiltrate Michoacan's political system, which was dominated by the left-wing Democratic Revolution Party (PRD).

On 6 September 2006 a group called La Familia had made itself known when a number of armed men had stormed into the popular Sol y Sombra nightclub in Uruapan, a town located about sixty miles from Morelia. They had fired their machine guns in the air, and proceeded to roll five human heads on to the dance floor.

As if that message wasn't enough, they had left a written note along with the heads. 'La Familia doesn't kill for money, doesn't kill women, doesn't kill innocent people. It only kills those who deserve to die. Everyone should know this: Divine justice.' It was a warning not to mess with the local mobsters.

The note was signed 'La Familia'.

Upon taking office a few months later, President Calderon sent in thousands of troops. The number of killings in the state immediately decreased, and major drug seizures were made, prompting the authorities to declare their Michoacan mission accomplished.

But residents remained wary. They spoke quietly of La Familia, and how fast it was growing. It was infiltrating the political sphere deeply. Turning one's back on the narcos had become a moral struggle each Michoacan politician had to face every day, said Francisco Morelos Borja, president of the National Action Party (PAN) in the state. 'If you don't open the door, no problem,' he said, looking nervously at the door of the small restaurant in Quiroga, a town just outside Morelia. 'The difficulty comes when you open the door.'

Morelos admitted it was impossible to fend off the narco-influence completely. 'They've come to our candidates in the past, I know that. [The candidates] came to me and asked for advice, for security. And I gave it to them . . . But then there are some that I don't know about.'

Another politician, Ignacio Murillo Campoverde of the PRD, was even more resigned. 'We'll never end the narcos' reign,' said the party man, as he sat outside his one-room office in San Juan Nuevo, a tiny town about five miles from Uruapan. His local office was adorned with photos of *mapaches* (literally, racoons) – the men who represent the narcos and come offering local politicians and officials money to look the other way. Campoverde had posted the pictures so that if the men came into town, members of his party would know to avoid them. He seemed determined. 'It's a problem if kids – the future – see drugs as the future.'

The other problem was that La Familia was pleading the same case. It had warned of the threat of methamphetamine to Michoacan society and its youth, and blamed Chapo's Sinaloa cartel for the rising addiction rates.

La Familia even claimed religiosity. Its leaders preached from the group's own bible, asking God for 'strength . . . to make me strong' and for 'wisdom'. Later passages used phrases similar to those of Mexican revolutionary times: 'It is better to be a master of one peso than a slave of two; it is better to die fighting head on than on your knees and humiliated; it is better to be a dead lion than a living dog.'

It was all well-orchestrated propaganda. While La Familia's leadership denounced drugs and preached their brand of wholesome goodness, they were producing and peddling methamphetamine far and wide.

This was a tactic long used by narcos in Mexico. Chapo and El Mayo had marketed themselves as social benefactors in Sinaloa; in Michoacan the Amezcua brothers and then the Valencia family had done the same. New outfits like La Familia sought to portray themselves as reputable organizations.

Jose Luis Espinosa Pina, a federal congressman from Morelia, agreed that the people in his state had suffered a serious blow on account of the violence and the rise of La Familia. 'There is a collective psychosis in Michoacan.'

On the eve of Independence Day 2008 it had all come to a head. It turns out that it was two grenades that had been set off just after 11 p.m., when Godoy had rung the independence bell and shouted 'Long live Mexico!' in accordance with tradition. Panic had swept over the square. Revellers whirled around, stunned and bewildered, and saw bleeding women and children, the staggering wounded. They fled the scene in terror. Paramedics arrived in the square, as police and soldiers cordoned off the area. Eight people died and more than 100 were injured.

Days later the stones of the square were still caked in blood; the police warning tape still marked the scene of the carnage. Flowers and wreaths, as well as cards written to the victims, served to remind the public that it had been ordinary people who had died that night, not drug-running thugs.

The authorities pointed the finger at La Familia, which had their own idea of who had done it. Propaganda banners were found hung on city overpasses in the area, pointing the finger back at Los Zetas. 'Coward is the word for those who attack the country's peace and tranquillity,' read one narco-manta posted in Morelia just days after the grenade attack. 'Mexico and Michoacan are not alone. Thanks for your cowardly acts, Zetas. Sincerely, La Familia Michoacana.'

'People of Mexico, don't let them fool you. La Familia Michoacana is with you and does not agree with acts of genocide. Sincerely, F.M.,' read another banner.

Chapo and his people spoke up, too. In an e-mail signed by Chapo and El Mayo, the Sinaloa cartel absolved itself of blame, saying that, 'Sinaloans have always defended the people . . . respected the families of capos and small drug couriers . . . respected the government . . . [and] respected women and children.' Chapo and El Mayo reputedly warned that the Sinaloan cartel would 'retake the Michoacan plaza and kill all who have offended Sinaloa family'.

The authorities took a different view. They focused on rounding up those responsible, regardless of their purported social standing. After all, the incident in Morelia was, in the words of congressman Espinosa Pina, 'the worst – the first – terrorist attack in the history of Mexico'. Within days dozens of arrests were made. Members of La Familia were smoked out of their safe houses in small towns all across Michoacan (often through anonymous tip-offs), and a federal crackdown on the group ensued. Several hundred members would eventually be arrested, as well as mayors and civil servants with alleged links to La Familia.

Sights were also set on Los Zetas, the new breed of narcos. They had been waging war with both La Familia and Chapo's people in Michoacan, according to the DEA, and were also hellbent on expanding nationwide.

Finally heeding commentary from critics of the drug war, the authorities were acknowledging that they had played a part in the power vacuum that had allowed groups like La Familia and Los Zetas to emerge. 'When we went in, we staked everything on taking on the heads of the criminal structure, going after the bosses,' explained Garcia Luna, the nation's police chief. 'The idea was that by taking off the head, the body would stop functioning. [Instead] the assassins took control.'

Originally the paramilitary wing of ex-Army elites in the pay of the Gulf cartel, Los Zetas were increasingly operating on their own – and with rising brutality. Many of the original thirty-one elite Army veterans had been captured or killed, but the organization was growing. It was divided into various subsections: groups of kids on bikes known as 'Las Ventanas' ('the Windows') would whistle to warn of any incoming police or suspicious strangers. Prostitutes who got useful information from clients (sometimes, cops) were known as 'Los Leopardos' ('the Leopards').

Nearer to the top were 'Los Halcones' ('the Hawks'), who supervised distribution zones, and 'Los Manosos' ('the Cunning Ones'), who would obtain the weaponry. Then there was 'La Direccion', a group of communications experts who would track phone calls, follow and identify suspicious vehicles, and order kidnappings and executions. At the very top was El Lazca and his close-knit crew.

As Los Zetas expanded out of their traditional territory – the north-east of the country, mainly along the border with Texas – beheadings became more common as far south as the state of Chiapas, which shares a border with Guatemala. Their method of taking over new turf – be it for drug trafficking, CD and DVD piracy, extortion or other forms of racketeering – was brutality. 'When a Zeta comes to town, he doesn't try to make a deal,' said one small business owner in the southern border city of Ciudad Hidalgo. 'He cuts off someone's head and says, "This [territory] is mine now." It's non-negotiable.'

Indeed, hostile (and brutal) takeovers were the only modus operandi these guys knew. In the words of one DEA official: 'They create terror, fear, gain a rep[utation], and people want to work with them.' Such an atmosphere spawned legions of wannabes, with thugs roaming around the whole country claiming to be Zetas. 'Just the name alone [is enough]. You get a military-style haircut and say you're a Zeta, and put fear in people.'

The Southern Front

As all-out war was consuming the northern Mexican border, citizens in the south were living in fear, too. Los Zetas were everywhere, infiltrating local businesses in both Chiapas and part of Guatemala.

When a narco-manta was posted on a Tapachula pedestrian bridge in December 2008, residents fretted over who had done it. Narco-mantas had been appearing throughout Mexico for some time, but this was the first in Chiapas. Most locals quickly jumped to the conclusion that it was Los Zetas.

At the Ciudad Hidalgo border crossing, a Mexican immigration guard was quick to point the finger. 'There are Zetas everywhere,' he said, asking that only his first name, Mario, be used. He confirmed reports that Los Zetas were now operating in Guatemala too. 'It's a mess over there.'

Mario pulled out a series of photos he had taken two days before at his post. A man lay slumped behind the wheel of his car, riddled with bullets. His wife clutched his arm, her face filled with anguish and smeared with blood. Blood had spilled on to her shirt, too, but she was unhurt. The next photo showed the windscreen of the car, shattered by a spray of bullets. In another, the Mexican side of the border crossing was in clear view.

Guatemala was indeed taking its own share of hits. With a weak federal government and even more corruption than in Mexico, the Central American nation had become a fertile ground for narcos seeking haven from the military.

On 25 March 2008 a shootout near Guatemala's border with El Salvador made headlines, in part because of its bloodiness – eleven people had died – but also because of the rumours that followed.

The local media began reporting that Chapo had been among the victims. Two of the bodies had been charred beyond recognition in a fire following the shootout, and investigators began testing blood samples. One Mexican was among the victims, that was for sure.

Was it Chapo? Mexico was on edge.

Then came the news: 'The information we have is that he was not among the dead and that neither of the burned bodies is his,' declared a spokesman for Guatemala's President Alvaro Colom. The president himself was even more assured: 'I was with the investigative team in the morning and we believe that Guzman is in Honduras.'

The methods of killing used by emerging groups like Los Zetas probably sent chills up the spines of even the old-school narcos. Chapo, some security experts said almost wistfully, had been a 'gentleman killer', or at least a respectful businessman. Unlike Los Zetas or La Familia, who would behead a man and leave him trouserless, Chapo had demonstrated decency and respect. When he wanted to kill someone who had betrayed him, he would speak with him, then take him out back and shoot him in the head. His men killed in the same way.

The game had clearly changed; Chapo would have to change too.

'El Avionazo'

The plane crashed into central Mexico City shortly after 7 p.m. on 4 November 2008. Within minutes everyone knew that the nation's interior secretary, thirty-seven-year-old Juan Camilo Mourino, had been on board. The consensus on the streets of the nation's capital was unanimous: Chapo did it.

Only Chapo had the power to blow someone out of the sky.

Chapo had killed Mourino, it was said, because the interior secretary was getting too close, putting on too much heat. 'Remember Escobar?' said one local journalist that night, raising an eyebrow.

On 27 November 1989 Colombian cocaine kingpin Pablo Escobar had ordered an Avianca airliner blown from the sky, in a bid to kill congressman Cesar Gaviria, a bold young politician who had dared oppose the Medellin cartel boss. For most Mexicans, 'El Avionazo', as the Mourino plane crash very rapidly became known, was no different.

Praised by the president as 'one of those Mexicans who cares about his country', Mourino had been at the forefront of the drug war, at least symbolically. As interior secretary, he was effectively Mexico's No. 2, a vice president of sorts. Since taking the post in early 2008, he had repeatedly vowed to take on the cartels with the unrelenting might of the state. Mourino had issued impassioned statements about the drug war, revealing more emotion than was customary for such a high-ranking Cabinet member. '*Ya basta!*' ('Enough!') he would cry in public, upon hearing that more policemen or innocent people had died in the drug war.

Organized crime specialist Jose Luis Santiago Vasconcelos also perished in the crash. Vasconcelos was in charge of the extradition programme at the time of his death. He had received threats from Chapo's people, who were conspiring to assassinate him. Shortly before the crash Vasconcelos had started to take precautions, sleeping in a number of different Mexico City apartments and travelling with extra security.

Investigations revealed no evidence that the plane had been blown up, or that there had been any sort of foul play. But that didn't prevent a sceptical public believing that Chapo had once again outwitted his pursuers and reminded them just how powerful he was. Even President Calderon appeared to have some scepticism. After the crash he told reporters that Mourino's death gave him 'a powerful motivation to fight without rest . . . for the ideals that we share'.

At the state funeral for those who died on the plane, Calderon turned his eulogy into a passionate affirmation of the justice of the war on drugs. 'Today, more than ever, is the moment to look to the future, the moment to persevere in the fight to overcome adversity and to build this country [into] a more just, prosperous and safe country that our countrymen dream of and that millions of Mexicans seek each day,' he pronounced.

Mourino and Vasconcellos were dead. More than 500 federal police had been killed in 2008. A bombing attempt near the federal police headquarters in Mexico City in February had been attributed to the Sinaloa cartel; Chapo was named the author of the plot. (Luckily, only the bomber was killed in the botched attempt.) The Morelia attacks of 15 September had proved that innocents, too, could be targets. In the minds of most Mexicans, the Avionazo was evidence that no one was out of reach. Everyone could – and quite possibly, would – be a target.

That included the military. Early on the morning of 21 December 2008, police found twelve heads bundled in a plastic bag just outside Chilpancingo, the capital of Guerrero. Across town, they found the bodies. Eight of them were identified as soldiers. 'For every one of mine you kill, I'm going to kill ten of yours,' read a note accompanying the heads.

It was the most brazen cartel attack on the military in Mexican history.

The Hell that is Juarez

'We're going to kill you like we killed the federales last night.'

Former Air Force Major Valentin Diaz Reyes was giving his men a briefing on the anti-gang raids planned for that night in Ciudad Juarez when the voices crackled over the police radio. He ran outside, sending his soldiers scrambling into position in front of the Delicias police station downtown. From behind the concrete blast walls, they set their sights on Avenida 16 de Septiembre. About sixty soldiers then scattered throughout the streets; the police followed them. Snipers aimed down from the roof of a nearby building.

When two vehicles appeared in the street behind the station, driving slowly, the soldiers yelled at the drivers to back away immediately. Advancing to secure a street corner a block away, one soldier ducked behind a car as he saw another vehicle approach. Crouching with his gun at the ready, he edged his way forward. His eyes were wide open, alert.

Eight minutes later, the all-clear given, the former major reassembled his soldiers and the police out in front of the station. He called his superiors on his mobile phone: 'It was . . . right when we were going to do the raid. I'm trying to figure out . . . We're closing off the streets, but most of my people are on the border – I don't have them all here. We've got to do a dynamic search . . . Tell me where we should meet and we'll meet. There were radio threats, and a vehicle passed in front of the station with weapons.

'This was a clear show of force,' Diaz Reyes explained.

It was March 2009, and the Army had taken complete control of security and policing operations in Ciudad Juarez, the Mexican city hardest hit by the drug war. Since Chapo had made his move for the Ciudad Juarez plaza, a horrific wave of bloodshed had engulfed the city. About 3,000 people died in Ciudad Juarez between 2003 and 2008. The presence of more than 5,000 soldiers and federal police in the border city had failed to quell the violence; more than 1,600 people died violent deaths in Ciudad Juarez in 2008; more than 2,600 would die in 2009.

The soldiers faced a powerful and unyielding enemy. The threat to Diaz Reyes' men – the eyewitness report of armed men in a vehicle turned out to be mistaken, but the radio threats were real – had become run-of-the-mill for the Army and federal police in Ciudad Juarez. The war on the streets, which had been waged for two years between gangs and rival narcos, now fully involved the Army and feds. Previously, they had simply come into troubled towns and quickly restored order; now, in cities like Ciudad Juarez, Culiacan and Tijuana, soldiers were on the front lines.

In Ciudad Juarez, the change was all too obvious. Outside several police stations in the city where the Army was now operating, impromptu blast walls had been set up – to defend against grenade and RPG attacks. Soldiers with heavy artillery kept watch over the streets outside, while snipers set up around the perimeter. Every patrol – routine or otherwise – was now conducted by soldiers. The fact that the war, and their role in it, had shifted course was not lost on any of the military men – many of whom were still just boys.

After the threat on the Delicias police station in Ciudad Juarez, nineteen-year-old soldier Pablo Antonio Maximus looked shaken. Clutching his gun tight to his chest, he laughed nervously with another soldier standing with him under the streetlights before asking for a cigarette. 'This is a normal Saturday night in Juarez,' he explained, lighting up. 'I don't smoke. But I'll have one every once in a while – for the adrenalin.'

Not only did the threats demonstrate a 'show of force', as Diaz Reyes put it, but they showed just how badly Army security had been breached. The anti-gang raids conducted by the soldiers were classified until the last minute – Diaz Reyes had been briefing his men the standard ten-to-fifteen minutes prior to go-time – but the drug traffickers knew the patterns. That's why they had radioed in the threat at that precise moment.

Another threat came across the radio the next day at lunchtime; Diaz Reyes expected more in the future. 'They know what we're doing.'

Residents of drug-producing regions like Sinaloa launched vigorous protests against the Army's presence. Following the killing of four apparently innocent people in Santiago de los Caballeros, hundreds of residents of Badiraguato walked down from the hills to Culiacan to demonstrate against the military – and in favour of Chapo. He's just a local businessman, our patron, unjustly persecuted, residents said at the time.

Similar protests were staged throughout the northern border region, from Ciudad Juarez to Matamoros and down to the industrial hub of Monterrey. The government claimed the protesters had been paid to march by the local criminal networks, whereas in truth the protesters had simply had enough of living with the oppressive presence of the Army.

Still, most Mexicans had to admit that living with the military, warts and all, was better than living with the constant stench of death over their communities. Ciudad Juarez and other blood-weary cities had come to resemble the Wild West – or in the opinion of some reporters, Baghdad – and the people had had enough.

Bodies were being dumped in full view of children walking to school; corpses were found headless, trousers pulled down for full shaming effect (their genitals or buttocks in full view), their feet trussed up. Sometimes limbs were left scattered near the site; sometimes they were found on the other side of town. On occasion, bodies were hung from overpasses, in full view of drivers on their way to work in the morning. Notes were left behind with the corpses, warning rivals or taking credit for the killings.

The blood and gore were impossible to ignore. The authorities hoped the people would voice their discontent, rather than succumb to the fear-induced peace of narco-rule. The same public outrage over violence had helped topple Escobar in Colombia; maybe it would work in Mexico. The attorney general called on the public to do its part and stand up to organized crime when it could, and denounce anyone involved. 'The hope is that the people will rise up and say, "No More!"' said one US counter-drug official.

Since its founding in the seventeenth century, Ciudad Juarez has had a reputation for being a smuggler's haven and a den of sleaze. Also home to Pancho Villa's revolutionary forces in the early twentieth century, the city has had its own love affair with lawlessness. During the American prohibition era it came to be viewed as one of those Mexican towns where Americans could visit and do everything that was forbidden on *el otro lado* (the other side).

But even when good news came to Ciudad Juarez, bad news followed. Shortly after the boom in *maquiladoras*, or manufacturing plants, in the 1980s and 1990s, women who worked in them started disappearing. Bodies were found in unmarked graves; many of the women had been raped. Promises to investigate proved empty. As many as 400 women are believed to have been killed during the period; mass graves outside the city are the only residue of the women's existence.

Around Ciudad Juarez, reminders of the murders haunt the conscience. The windows of city-centre shops selling bridal gowns and dresses are adorned with flyers for the missing.

'Help us find them,' reads the notice at the top: Lidia Abigail Herrera Delgado, 13. Last seen, 3 April 2007. Adriana Sarmiento Enrique, 15. Last seen, 18 January 2008. Carmen Adriana Pena Valenzuela, 15. Last seen, 4 April 2008 . . . Some date all the way back to 1994. Some are as recent as yesterday.

One Saturday night in 2009, a four-vehicle police convoy laden with soldiers rounded up sixteen people in the city's crime-ridden Rancho Anapra district – home to thousands of members of the city's most-feared gang, Los Aztecas, in the pay of the Juarez cartel. Just to add to the confusion, mayhem and propensity for bloodshed, some of Los Aztecas now work for Chapo instead.

Ciudad Juarez can be a haunted place – and Rancho Anapra is one of its darkest underbellies. Located on a hillside, its houses are largely one-storey, some of them simply constructed from whatever raw materials can be found easily in nearby scrapyards. There is no running water; here and there an illegally diverted electricity supply has been put in.

Life is brutal and virtually meaningless in Rancho Anapra. Most residents who have jobs work in the maquiladoras, but there is high unemployment. Dozens of women and girls were murdered in Rancho Anapra in the 1990s, and today homicide follows homicide. The dead sometimes lie there for days. No one wants to make a call to the authorities that could put their own lives in danger.

Most of Rancho Anapra's young men are gang members. They start young – kids act as lookouts on the corners – and few live beyond their twenties. Most of the gangs are small, neighbourhood affairs; they deal drugs locally. Then there are Los Aztecas. Often sporting tattoos of Aztec symbols such as pyramids or snakes, the young men of this gang have in recent years established links with organized crime in the area. They are an offshoot of the El Paso prison gang Barrio Azteca, which has long been on the US radar. Barrio Azteca controls cocaine, heroin and marijuana distribution in El Paso. Their connection with Los Aztecas in Ciudad Juarez has allowed for an easy thoroughfare for narcotics coming up from further south in Chihuahua.

The members of Los Aztecas work directly for Juan Pablo Ledesma, a.k.a. 'El JL', a top lieutenant of Vicente Carrillo's. They are no longer simply smuggling drugs, they are the hired killers. They also oversee meth production in the area. (During one raid on a lab where twenty-one gang members were arrested, soldiers found ten AK-47s, more than 13,000 doses of crack, two kilos of cocaine and more than 800 cartridges of ammunition.) Seventy-five per cent of inmates in the state prison, located outside Ciudad Juarez, are affiliated to Los Aztecas.

Organized crime in Ciudad Juarez doesn't only recruit young men with potential. It recruits those who are lost to drugs or despair, and have no other alternative. Drug gangs throughout Mexico have long trawled rehab centres for possible recruits. Addicts were easy to entice, they found, both because of their desperation and their addiction. They could be paid in drugs; they would sink to the lower depths of humanity for a fix or a paltry sum of money.

The DEA and Mexican authorities, too, found that addicts could be of use. After all, they had taken one step in the right direction by admitting they had a problem. If they could kick their habit and go back on the streets, law enforcement would have some pretty good informants. The recovered addicts could be paid meagre sums for what could amount to highly valuable information.

In September 2009 a group of armed men stormed into a drug rehab centre in Ciudad Juarez. They lined up seventeen recovering addicts against a wall and opened fire. It was the latest – and worst –

of several bloody attacks on rehab centres in the city that year. The word on the streets was that gang members working for Chapo were responsible for the murders.

Sinaloa Status Quo?

Back in Sinaloa, the conventional wisdom was that the Army had simply settled in. With the rise of La Familia and the expansion of Los Zetas, not to mention the out-of-control bloodletting in Ciudad Juarez, Chapo appeared to have fallen off the priority list. Soldiers were still conducting raids in the Sierra, seizing landing strips, vehicles, meth labs and marijuana plantations, but by and large, the status quo had returned, as the military muscle dealt with problems elsewhere.

Chapo was still in his homeland, hiding out – locals were convinced of that. He had still not been caught, and the feds appeared to be losing interest in catching the boss of bosses. Attorney General Eduardo Medina Mora had gone so far as to dismiss Chapo as a 'washed-up football star', much as President George W. Bush had spoken of Osama bin Laden when he continued to slip through the net time and time again in Afghanistan.

One PGR insider even likened Chapo to Bin Laden, but offered up certain caveats. 'Look,' recalls the former adviser to Medina Mora, 'he's hiding, probably in the mountains of Durango. He's good at running, he has money. Rumour is that the government hasn't captured him because the government has a pact with him. [The United States] has the most highly advanced military in the world, but can't catch Bin Laden. [Does the US] have a pact?'

In April 2009, however, it took a religious man openly to show his disgust over the fact that Chapo was still free. 'He lives in the hills of Durango,' stormed Archbishop Hector Martinez Gonzalez, specifying that Chapo was now calling the mountain town of Guanacevi home. 'Everyone knows it, except the authorities.'

In fact the authorities did know it, and some were still trying to hunt him down. Members of Mexico's National Security Council were meeting several times a week to find ways to take down Chapo. They discussed these strategies – a massive frontal assault on Chapo's ranch was one option – under conditions of complete secrecy and tight security.

Military presence had been beefed up in the Sinaloan and Durango hills, too; there were even rumours that the authorities were using female intelligence officers to seduce information out of top narcos. (One senior official denied this: 'I don't know of any of my agents who has fallen in love with a *capo guapo* [handsome capo].')

Just days after the archbishop's comments, two military intelligence officers were found dead by the side of a Durango country road. They had been working undercover in the Sierra, posing as campesinos tending the marijuana plantations. Their killers had left a note by the side of their bodies.

Its message left no room for misinterpretation: 'You'll never get Chapo.'

14. United States of Fear

'*The growing assault by the drug cartels and their thugs on the Mexican government over the past several years reminds one that an unstable Mexico could represent a homeland security problem of immense proportions to the United States . . . In terms of worst-case scenarios for the Joint Force and indeed the world, two large and important states bear consideration for a rapid and sudden collapse: Pakistan and Mexico . . . Any descent by Mexico into chaos would demand an American response based on the serious implications for homeland security alone.*'

– US Forces Joint Command, 25 November 2008

Almost immediately after the election of President Barack Obama on 4 November 2008, Washington insiders with an eye on Mexico, not to mention the military brass and DEA, began pushing Mexico as a priority for the incoming administration.

The Bush White House had set out to make the war on drugs and US–Mexican relations a priority, but the terrorist attacks of 11 September 2001 had shifted its focus elsewhere. After 2001, efforts had been made to connect drug traffickers with Al-Qaeda and other terrorist groups, but no link was ever proven with respect to the Mexican cartels. So, for much of the Bush administration, Mexico was effectively ignored. Colombian President Alvaro Uribe Velez's crackdown on his cartels was deemed the priority in the region; Iraq, Afghanistan and Pakistan were the focus elsewhere.

But with the rising tide of violence, particularly in the border cities, Washington could no longer brush aside the trouble on its doorstep. The Bush administration pushed through the Merida Initiative, a $1.4-billion aid package that would provide Mexico and its Central American and Caribbean neighbours with planes, helicopters, intelligence and safety equipment and much-needed police and military training.

Then came the dire warnings. The Justice Department in Washington stated that Mexican gangs were the 'biggest organized crime threat to the United States'. Retired US Army General Barry R. McCaffrey, a former drug czar, said that the Mexican government 'is not confronting dangerous criminality – it is fighting for its survival against narco-terrorism'. Outgoing CIA chief Michael Hayden warned that Mexico – along with Iran – would likely pose the biggest challenge for the new administration.

Mexican drug traffickers have long operated on American soil. They have acted as couriers, distributors, dealers, growers and even enforcers. Ever since the Colombians had restructured the system of delivery of their cocaine, the Mexicans had stepped up their presence in the United States.

Sometimes, they were caught. In December 2000, for instance, the US announced the arrest of 155 people connected to Mexico's drug cartels in ten American cities, marking the end of a year-long investigation that also resulted in the seizure of 5,490 kilograms of cocaine, 9,526 pounds of marijuana and 11 million dollars in US currency. It was a big bust, and all Mexican.

Still, the Mexicans had never been so prominent throughout the United States. The drug distribution trade in the south-east, for instance, used to be controlled by various groups – mainly Dominicans, Cubans and Colombians. By 2008 the Mexicans had taken complete control of local cell operations.

They were also handling things their way – more than 700 kidnapping-for-ransom reports in Phoenix between 2006 and 2008 prompted a slew of American newspaper headlines about infiltration by Mexican cartels there. All of them had the same gist: 'Mexican cartels make Phoenix the US kidnap capital.'

Some in the DEA sought to put the worries into context. 'Certain isolated incidents in the United States, such as the torture by a Mexican trafficker of a Dominican drug customer in Atlanta, are frightening, but do not represent a dramatic departure from the violence that has always been associated with the drug trade,' said El Paso Special Agent Joseph M. Arabit in March 2009. 'Recent news reports concerning drug-related kidnappings in Phoenix also rarely, if ever, qualify as "spillover" incidents as defined by the interagency.' But, he added, 'We are by no means trying to downplay our concern.'

Indeed, the Mexican cartels were spreading their tentacles into small towns and clearly moving into what the DEA man in Mexico City calls 'non-traditional places'. Places like Shelby County, Alabama.

Chris Curry, the sheriff of Shelby County, was called to the scene of a multiple homicide at an apartment complex located just off an interstate highway on 20 August 2008. Five Hispanic men had been beaten, tortured with electric shocks, and their throats slashed. 'It was very clear to me that I was not fishing in a Shelby County pond,' he recalled.

Reaching out to the Hispanic community in the area and to the feds, Curry learned that right under his nose, his quiet little county in Alabama had become a major thoroughfare for cocaine, meth and marijuana being trafficked in from Mexico. He had already seen signs of drug-related activity – nearby counties had had their share of drug trafficking difficulties, and Curry had noticed a rise in armed robberies and thefts with a 'definite drug connection' in his county of nearly 200,000 inhabitants.

Subsequent investigations, and Curry's cooperation with the feds, led to new revelations. In Atlanta, forty-three people were arrested for connections to the Mexican cartels. Atlanta was identified as a 'regional hub' for the Gulf cartel. Sheriff Curry, meanwhile, was learning through his new law enforcement connections that Shelby might actually be a hub for the Juarez cartel. A search of one home in the county yielded fourteen guns, most of them assault weapons. 'The criminal element is definitely organized. [It] is in place . . . sophisticated. It's serious, and it's home – in our backyard.'

Curry, like many of his southern law enforcement counterparts, was looking further south towards cities like Ciudad Juarez and worrying what might happen if such violence spilled over. 'That's frightening,' he said of the homicide rate in Ciudad Juarez. 'What we don't want to see is that level of behaviour, that level of violence, being brought into our area.'

In Columbus, New Mexico, they were watching the fallout from Ciudad Juarez closely. A tranquil desert town of 1,800 people, Columbus had witnessed Mexican invasion first-hand before: in 1916 the Mexican revolutionary 'Pancho' Villa led a raid into Columbus during which eighteen Americans died. The US military was sent in to capture Villa. (It failed.)

Now, residents feared another, more worrying invasion. Across the border in dusty Puerto Palomas, Chihuahua, dozens of people had been gunned down in battles stemming from drug gangs moving out of Ciudad Juarez. Kidnappings had become rife. After a threat in 2008, the entire ten-man police force had quit; the police chief then fled across the border seeking asylum. Residents of Palomas were starting to trickle over the border too, in search of a safer life in the United States.

Columbus and its surrounding county, Luna, were well aware of the problem. With a major interstate highway linking El Paso with Tucson, Arizona, Luna County had long been a transit route for drug shipments. They sympathized with their neighbours in Puerto Palomas. 'Mexico's problem is Sheriff Cobos's problem,' said Raymond Cobos, the sheriff of Luna County. 'No doubt about it.' Still, it was difficult for the cartels to operate out in the open – 'they have to go way, way underground'.

Conventional wisdom has long had it that corruption along the border is a Mexican problem, not an American one. Mexico has the dirty, undisciplined cops, while in US border towns, only the most upstanding citizens sport badges.

The case of Rey Guerra, a sheriff in Starr County, Texas, proves otherwise. In 2009 Guerra was charged and sentenced for working with counterparts on the Mexican side of the border in Miguel Aleman, Tamaulipas. He admitted to leaking intelligence and hampering investigations in exchange for thousands of dollars and other gifts.

Residents of Starr County were shocked – their sheriff had lived in a splendid home decorated much like a Mexican narco-mansion but for some reason it hadn't really dawned on them that he might be so corrupt – but law enforcement officers in the area weren't. Ralph G. Diaz, an FBI special agent based in San Antonio, Texas, said Guerra's involvement was pretty much par for the course. 'It's almost cultural. Throughout their entire lives, folks have watched this kind of activity pass through their communities, basically unimpeded. They come to accept it.'

The drug traffickers 'feel they can buy law enforcement', added Tim Johnson, the US attorney for southern Texas, confirming what many had suspected but could rarely prove. 'And sometimes they can.'

Further embarrassment would come during the first year of the Obama administration. In September 2009, for instance, Richard Padilla Cramer, a former agent for Immigrations and Customs Enforcement (ICE), was arrested for allegedly leaking information from confidential law enforcement databases to the Mexican drug cartels. At one point stationed in Guadalajara, Padilla Cramer had also allegedly helped an unidentified cartel smuggle 660 pounds of cocaine into the United States en route to Spain.

When news broke of Padilla Cramer's alleged offences, several former colleagues sprang to his defence. 'Of the people I worked with in my career, he's one of a group of four or five who I would trust with my life,' Terry Kirkpatrick, a former ICE supervisor, told the *Los Angeles Times*. 'Unless somebody says, "Here's a videotape", I am not going to believe it.'

Rumours surfaced that there was a contract out for Padilla Cramer's life. His colleagues considered him top-notch. 'He and I got death threats because of work we did,' Kirkpatrick recalled. 'If it turns out to be true, I'll never believe anybody ever again.'

Padilla Cramer eventually cut a plea bargain; he would be charged with obstruction of justice, not drug trafficking.

More cases of alleged corruption would emerge in the first year of the Obama administration, and the influence of the cartels north of the border was impossible for Washington to ignore. According to the Department of Justice's National Drug Intelligence Center, by early 2009 the drug trade in 230 US cities – in forty-five states – was controlled by Mexican cartels and their affiliates. The Mexican cartels, warned Senator Dick Durbin, are 'the new face of crime'.

The Calderon administration went on the defensive. It spent the early part of 2009 refuting allegations that Mexico was a failed state. 'To say that Mexico is a failed state is absolutely false,' the Mexican president said. 'I have not lost any part – any single part – of Mexican territory.'

Some US state sources jumped to Mexico's defence, saying that Calderon was in fact destroying what had been a failed state under the Institutional Revolutionary Party – a system in which organized crime thrived. But perhaps the state's role in drug trafficking during the PRI era had been crucial to maintaining peace. The state had been 'the referee', said one expert on Mexican governance, and once that crumbled the traffickers had to sort out their problems themselves. Unfortunately they were more prone to shooting it out than talking it through.

President Obama was taking it all into consideration. In April 2009, during a visit to Guadalajara, the new president made his position clear. 'You can't fight this war with just one hand. You can't have Mexico making an effort and the United States not making an effort . . . We are going to be dealing not only with drug interdiction coming north, but also working on helping to curb the flow of cash and guns going south.'

During his election campaign, Obama had pledged to try to reinstate a federal assault weapons ban in the United States, but in Guadalajara effectively admitted he had given up on that ambition. He would, however, increase enforcement of laws against hauling such weapons across the border. He admitted openly that the flow of illegal guns into Mexico was a US problem; Mexico breathed a sigh of relief.

The US drug market has always been the most insatiable in the world. According to United Nations estimates, 12.3 per cent of

American citizens aged 15–64 used marijuana or cannabis in the past year. In England and Wales, by comparison, it was 7.4 per cent; Germany was lower at 4.7 per cent, as was the Netherlands, at 5.4 per cent. With regard to cocaine, heroin and methamphetamine, American citizens once again ranked at the top or very near.

The DEA estimates that $65 billion is spent on illegal drugs annually in the United States, with the RAND Corporation estimating the distribution of this spending as follows: $36 billion on cocaine, $11 billion on heroin, $10 billion on marijuana, $5.8 billion on methamphetamine and $2.6 billion on all other illegal drugs combined.

The US estimates that Mexican drug cartels earn between $18 billion and $40 billion a year from US drug sales, which they then smuggle back to their country and launder.

Guns from the North

In recent years Mexico has come to view America's role in its drug war as even more insidious, due to the flow of illegal weapons into the country. Some 90 per cent of the arms used by Mexico's cartels and traced by US and Mexican authorities come from the United States. This figure is debatable, but there is no doubt that much of the cartels' arsenal is purchased north of the border.

It's a huge arsenal. Since the launch of Calderon's drug war, the Army has seized more than 40,000 weapons from cartel members. (The PGR and federal police have not published their own data.) Among those weapons were AK-47 and AK-15 assault rifles, shotguns, handguns, grenades, grenade launchers and armour-piercing munitions known as *mata policias*, or cop killers.

In a single raid on a house in Reynosa, Tamaulipas, the Army discovered a cache of 540 rifles, 165 grenades, 500,000 rounds of ammunition and 14 sticks of TNT. Officials drily noted that the cartels were expanding their arsenal.

'The cartels are using basic infantry weaponry to counter government forces,' a US operative in Mexico said in early 2009.

'Encountering criminals with this kind of weaponry is a horse of a different colour. This has all the makings of an infantry squad, or guerrilla fighting.'

US authorities, knowing full well that their Mexican counterparts were outgunned by the cartels, launched Project Gunrunner in a bid to stem the southward flow of weapons. The Bureau of Arms, Tobacco and Firearms, or ATF, deployed about a hundred special agents and twenty-five investigators to the south-west US border and stepped up firearms tracing capabilities, looking into the origin of guns used in crimes in Mexico. The results were impressive: in 2008, for instance, 656 weapons used in Mexican crimes were traced back to McAllen, Texas, just across the border from Reynosa.

Knowing that the majority of Mexican crime weapons traced back to the United States were being bought in Texas, the ATF beefed up its operations in the southern state. There was more cooperation internationally, too: in 2008 Mexico asked the United States to trace about 12,000 weapons, compared to roughly 3,000 the year before.

Others warned of American complicity in another matter – its gangs. The Sinaloa cartel operated through cells located in cities like Chicago and New York. These were Americans, members of local gangs, dealing their drugs. One day they might explode. Attorney General Medina Mora referred to the estimated one million gang members who deal drugs in the United States as the 'sleeping monster in the US basement'.

If the US agencies were seriously to go after these gang members – as Mexico has done within its own borders – they would turn the United States into a 'living hell', predicted Medina Mora's former adviser. 'They [the gangs] will shoot back with American weapons that they can buy like pancakes.'

There had already been evidence of the potential of the 'sleeping monster'. Chapo and the Beltran Leyva brothers had gone to war in part because of disputes over a cell allegedly run by Pedro and Margarito Flores, two brothers based in Chicago. According to US indictments, they helped run a network that ran from Los Angeles to cities throughout the midwest; they allegedly transported two tons of cocaine a month in tractor-trailers to Chicago warehouses, from where it would be distributed. Cash was sent back to the Sinaloa cartel. The Flores brothers' father had allegedly run drugs in Sinaloa; they later moved to Chicago, where they blended into predominantly Mexican neighbourhoods like Pilsen.

But being Mexican in Chicago isn't enough to have it easy in the drug trade; the city is the home of various gangs, all of whom compete for rival turf. All the major Mexican cartels operate in Chicago, according to US law enforcement. This makes the city a potential flashpoint.

The Flores brothers, according to the US Department of Justice, had already caused some trouble of their own because of their Chicago operation. They had been working with both Chapo and the Beltran Leyva brothers, rather than the Sinaloa organization as a whole. One of the main reasons Chapo and the Beltran Leyva brothers went to war, it was claimed, was over the loyalty of the Flores brothers.

DEA Chief of Intelligence Anthony Placido told the *Washington Post* that due to law enforcement pressure, the Mexican cartels were now using inexperienced operators like the Flores brothers, posing a risk of violence. There had long been US operatives working for the Mexican cartels, but they 'used to be gods, and they would control an area for years. Now they often last months before they are arrested or assassinated. What that creates is opportunities for a 28-year-old who . . . isn't worried about dying.'

Under Obama the DEA also began working to expand its operations within Mexico. The DEA has long had its largest international presence in Mexico, with offices in the capital, Tijuana, Hermosillo, Ciudad Juarez, Guadalajara, Mazatlan, Merida, Monterrey, Matamoros and Nuevo Laredo. It authorized the deployment of 1,203 special agents – 23 per cent of its worldwide total of agents of that rank – to head to the south-west US border.

Chapo was watching. In March 2009, he and his associates met for three days in Sonoita, Sonora. There, he addressed his cohorts about the increased domestic US crackdowns. Chapo wasn't going to go down without a fight, ordering his US-bound smugglers to 'use their weapons to defend their loads at all costs'. Chapo and his crew even discussed the possibility of orchestrating attacks against US or Mexican government buildings, according to the US Department of Justice. They were also thought to be plotting attacks in Mexico City – Beltran Leyva turf – in order to shift the authorities' attention to their allies-turned-rivals.

15. Sinaloa Inc.

US officials believed, and hoped, that Chapo was acting out of desperation.

The month before the Sonoita meeting, the drug lord had suffered a severe blow. Operation Xcellerator, a DEA-led multinational investigation, had caused the arrest of 750 suspected members of the Sinaloa cartel in the United States. It was a 'crushing blow' to Chapo, DEA chief Michele M. Leonhart claimed. 'Rest assured that, while this is DEA's biggest operation against the Sinaloa Cartel and their networks to date, it won't be our last.'

Operation Xcellerator had indeed been a noteworthy success. It had begun in Imperial County, California. Starting with a drug seizure, the DEA had managed to track seventy cells pertaining to the Sinaloa cartel to towns and cities in twenty-six US states, from the east coast to the west coast. Some of the operatives were distributors in metropolitan areas like New York and Los Angeles. Others were working in little-known Brockton, Massachusetts, or Stow, Ohio.

Stow is a small, midwestern town of about 35,000, which in recent years had been transformed by Chapo and his people. According to the DEA, they had been flying dozens of kilos of cocaine through Stow's tiny airport from California. It was then distributed to major Ohio cities like Cleveland and Columbus. It was also sold on college campuses in the local area. The residents of Stow had no idea of what was going on right under their noses.

Although the DEA was proud of Operation Xcellerator – it had deprived Chapo of nearly $1 billion in revenue, after all – the initiative had uncovered an ugly truth about Chapo's reach. 'The spread of the Sinaloa Cartel is a direct threat to the safety and security of law-abiding citizens everywhere,' the DEA's Leonhart said. Operation Xcellerator had also uncovered a 'super meth lab' in Canada, which belonged to the Sinaloa cartel and was capable of producing 12,000 ecstasy pills in an hour.

So it wasn't clear that Chapo was acting out of desperation. In fact evidence was being uncovered that showed his cartel had expanded globally, developing a web of supply lines, operatives and management more suited to a multinational corporation.

Mexican authorities had long warned that, for Chapo, control of Mexican drug trafficking wouldn't satisfy his appetite. His mission, according to the PGR, 'is to attain an omnipotent status that will allow him to form international alliances'.

By 2009 he was achieving that goal. Chapo's organization was now operating in nearly every nation in Central America, from Guatemala down to Panama. In the key cocaine-producing countries of Peru and Bolivia, a series of Sinaloan arrests was evidence that Chapo's people were moving in on what had formerly been Colombian turf. Chapo's people were also more violent than even the Colombians; drug-related executions were spiking. Even in Colombia itself, Chapo and his Mexican counterparts were powerful enough to set up camp. They were now operating as bosses deep in Colombian territory.

In July 2009 more than seventy properties throughout Colombia were seized, all linked to Chapo. Valued at $50 million, the properties comprised ranches, urban residences, hotels and offices in both remote parts of the country and its biggest cities, like Cali. Seven members of the Sinaloa cartel were arrested during the bust. 'We have evidence of Mexicans sitting in Medellin, sitting in Cali, sitting in Pereira, in Barranquilla,' said Colombian police Director General Oscar Naranjo.

The Sinaloa cartel wasn't stopping at Colombia. A Mexican ban on the importing of ephedrine and pseudoephedrine – the necessary precursors for methamphetamine – had made it more difficult to produce the drug that was in such demand throughout the United States. Increased US Coast Guard presence in the Pacific, the Gulf of Mexico and the Caribbean, which had hampered the

Colombians, was now proving bothersome to the Mexicans. So the Sinaloa cartel had begun to use Argentina as a primary transit point.

The Argentines weren't keen to admit the presence of Mexican organized crime inside their borders. But it wasn't easy to deny. On one occasion, two Mexican men who had recently entered the country were arrested with 750 kilos of cocaine. A judge investigating their case believed they were working for the Sinaloa cartel. With Colombian counterparts, they were planning to smuggle the cocaine to Spain, where it would have a street value of $27 million.

Ephedrine imports to Argentina had also risen from 5.5 tons in 2006 to 28.5 tons the following year, according to the DEA. Fifty per cent of the 1.2 tons of ephedrine that Argentina seized in 2008 had been bound for Mexico, concealed in crates of sugar.

Another raid outside Buenos Aires had netted twenty-three Sinaloa-linked Mexicans and a meth lab: the cartels were thinking of production in Argentina as a future option for quicker and easier distribution to Europe.

And where there were Mexican drug traffickers, there was also violence. In one instance, three Argentines were found in a ditch outside the capital, their corpses riddled with bullets, their hands bound. The killing had all the hallmarks of a Mexican gangland execution. According to a retired DEA agent working in Argentina, the young men had tried to rip off their Mexican counterparts.

By late 2009 it was clear that Argentine dismissals of cartel activity were empty. There was now no doubt that the Sinaloans had arrived in the Southern Cone.

The Sinaloa cartel had long ties to Asian nations like China, India, Thailand and Vietnam, where they obtained the chemicals needed to make methamphetamine. (Chapo, at one time, allegedly imported heroin directly from Thailand in order to distribute the product in the United States, suggesting that Mexico alone couldn't keep up with US demand.) These connections were usually through businesses and at high levels; rarely did Mexican operatives set foot in Asia to distribute drugs or launder money themselves.

In Europe and Africa, however, the Sinaloans were certainly on the ground. The cartel was using its key European centres of operation – Portugal, Spain, Germany, Italy, Poland, Slovakia and the Czech Republic – to establish what one expert calls a 'patrimonial base' for its resources. The reasoning was simple: the Sinaloa cartel wanted to stabilize its assets and safeguard its billions for the future.

Through special financial intelligence units, the French and Spanish managed to seize some assets, but they couldn't get them all.

Throughout Europe, Mexican operatives were distributing cocaine and heroin. They were recruiting Central American gang members to represent them in Europe, according to the UN International Narcotics Control Board. A report in the newspaper *El Universal*, claiming that Chapo was sending his gunmen to Iran to train, was dismissed by the US. But in some instances the Mexicans were definitely communicating directly with organized crime outfits on other continents.

Africa was particularly attractive to the Sinaloa cartel because of its failed states and rebel movements. Some experts warned that the Mexican cartels now had a presence in as many as forty-seven African nations. It was easy for Mexican drug traffickers to obtain local passports and travel throughout Africa with guns and drugs – all they needed was a contact in local government and some cash. South American narcos were also setting up fake companies – fisheries in Senegal, for instance – through which they could launder money. According to experts on the ground who study cartel activity, even some governments in West Africa were suspect – the influx of foreign cash into their coffers was considered highly suspect.

Former DEA Chief of Operations Michael Braun, meanwhile, argued before the US Congress that an increased demand for cocaine in Europe – about 500 tons of cocaine from Latin America and Mexico was destined for Europe in 2009, he estimated – was making West Africa, in particular, more and more attractive to

Mexican cartels. Think of it this way, he said: what the Caribbean and Mexico are to the United States, West Africa is to Europe.

There was more. With the euro strengthening against the dollar, Braun warned, Europe 'has naturally emerged as the perfect, latest playground for these ruthless cartels . . . I see Europe today teetering on the brink of a drug trafficking and abuse catastrophe similar to the one our nation faced about thirty years ago. If you need a visual on what I predict Europe is facing in the years to come, just picture Miami in the late 1970s, followed by the "crack" cocaine epidemic that exploded across the US in the 1980s.'

In early 2010, police in Egypt dismantled a cocaine processing lab run by Mexicans; *conejos* (literally, 'rabbits', as cartel scouts are known) had been spotted throughout North Africa and in Asian nations such as Japan. As for the possibility that Mexican cartels were now working with terrorist cells in destabilized parts of the world, Braun said, 'I am still losing sleep over something that haunts me like nothing else.'

The relationships between Mexican cartels and terrorists were strengthening by the day, Braun warned. 'They're staying in the same shady bars, sharing the same prostitutes,' he said, and 'developing relationships today that will soon evolve from personal to strategic.' In the foreseeable future, he cautioned, 'corporate al-Qaeda will be able to pick up the phone and call corporate Sinaloa . . . It's going to bite us in the ass.'

Making Waves

The cartels were not only expanding; they were getting more and more creative in their methods of smuggling.

In July 2008 a Mexican Navy plane spotted its target off the coast of the southern state of Oaxaca. It looked like a boat, heading north fast. But it didn't appear on the radar as a normal ship. About 140 miles south of the tourist resort of Huatulco, a 32-foot-long semi-submersible submarine was skimming the surface.

For three hours, the Navy plane and Coast Guard pursued the vessel. Finally, they managed to force it to come to a halt. It was carrying 5.8 tons of cocaine, wrapped in 257 packages.

Still, the seizure itself wasn't all that impressive. In the Mexican port of Manzanillo, the authorities, acting on DEA intelligence, had previously hauled in 23.5 tons of Chapo's cocaine. But the method of smuggling used off the coast of Oaxaca appeared to be novel. The green submarine had been built or at least modified without authorization, probably in the jungles of Colombia.

Colombian police had discovered such vessels in their ports and heading away from their coastlines as early as the 1990s; the US first spotted one about 100 miles off the coast of Costa Rica in November 2006. They nicknamed it Bigfoot. It was carrying three tons of cocaine. These first makeshift semi-submersibles were between 40 and 80 feet in length, constructed from fibreglass, steel or wood. Only about 18 inches of the craft was visible above the water. They operated on single or twin diesel engines, with about a 1,500-gallon capacity. They cost around $2 million to build.

Because most of the hull is submerged these subs were extremely hard to spot. Once approached they were also easy to flood: the drugs would wash away into the ocean. Often the crew would abandon ship, putting the Coast Guard in a position whereby they had to rescue them and bring them safely to land.

The incident off the coast of Oaxaca was the first time Mexicans had ever come across their own makeshift submarine. They had tracked it from Colombia's west coast thanks to US intelligence.

US Admiral Jim Stavridis warned that cocaine was not the main concern, terrorism was. 'What worries me [about the submarines] is if you can move that much cocaine, what else can you put in that semi-submersible. Can you put a weapon of mass destruction in it?' said the head of the US Southern Command. Taking note, Senator Joseph Biden introduced the Drug Trafficking Interdiction Act to make it a 'felony for those who knowingly or intentionally operate or embark in a [self-propelled semi-submersible] that is or has navigated in international waters, with the intent to evade detection'.

With the spotlight now on their subs, Mexico's narcos were adopting other techniques, too.

The narcos had long moved drugs over the American border hidden inside tinned goods and dolls; for instance, two Mexican men suspected of helping smuggle 110 kilos of cocaine to New York from Mexico inside five three-foot-tall statues of the Virgin Mary were once arrested in Brooklyn. The narcos also smuggled smaller loads of drugs inside toys, furniture, shoes and candles.

If devotional statues weren't outlandish enough, the narcos are now using . . . sharks. In a raid on a port in south-east Mexico, using sniffer dogs, guards found more than twenty shark carcasses filled with a ton of cocaine.

Women and Children First

The cartels are also now more frequently using women and children to convey their cargos.

A forty-year-old Mexican woman was detained at London's Heathrow airport after customs found fifteen kilos of cocaine strapped to the legs of her two children, aged thirteen and eleven. They had flown in on a British Airways flight from Mexico City.

A woman travelling across the border in Nuevo Laredo was stopped by guards. She told them she had been approached by a man who said he had too much baggage, and would pay her $80 if she would take a Jesus statue across the border for him. The US border agents checked out the statue, which was made entirely out of cocaine. It was valued at roughly $30,000.

At the border crossing in Nogales, Sonora, a 94-year-old lady was arrested trying to enter the United States with more than four kilos of marijuana – presumably belonging to Chapo's people, since Nogales is his turf – strapped to her torso and legs.

Women have long held a special place in narco-culture – but usually as the brides, girlfriends or mothers of the narcos, nothing more. In Culiacan, long-nailed, makeup-caked princesses accompany their narco-boyfriends to nightclubs. When they get older, they ride around in their SUVs with no licence plates, take their kids shopping to the mall and dine at the best restaurants in the city. On Sundays, they have long brunches at the Hotel Lucerna, the five-star establishment favoured by travelling businessmen and politicians, and other restaurants around town.

Everyone knows who they are, and no one dares criticize them. They pretty much own Culiacan. If they commit a traffic violation, no one gives them a ticket. If they commit a petty crime, no one dares report it. If they want the best seat in the restaurant or hair salon, they get it.

Rarely do they get deep into the business itself. But culturally, they're a part of it.

In late December 2008, one particular Sinaloa beauty queen caught the world's attention when she was arrested with a group of seven alleged Juarez cartel members at a military checkpoint outside of Guadalajara. Twenty-three-year-old Laura Elena Zuniga Huizar had been riding in a car with assault rifles, handguns, cartridges, more than a dozen mobile phones and 53,300 dollars in US currency – the standard narco haul.

The media couldn't get enough of it. A former preschool teacher, Zuniga had won the Miss Sinaloa contest just six months before; TV news programmes interchanged images of her accepting the winner's bouquet with the newer ones of her being paraded by the authorities, head bowed, dishevelled.

While the story was a sensational one, at its heart was a sadness that haunts mothers and fathers throughout Mexico. Zuniga wasn't involved in trafficking, it turned out, but she was dating Angel Orlando Garcia, a high-ranking member of the Juarez cartel. Parents throughout Mexico are asking themselves the same thing: what prompts a young woman with a future to hang around such types? There's no doubt young women everywhere love the bad boys, but what is attractive about men who traffic drugs and kill for a living?

Some say it's the riches, others say it's the freedom. Narcos live outside a system of law that, in the minds of most Mexicans, doesn't look out for them. That sort of life can be attractive, particularly to a young woman with beauty and brains but not necessarily a clear future.

And in some quarters the shadowy, higher-up narcos aren't even considered to be doing anything particularly illegal. They're normal citizens who attend political gatherings and support their candidates of choice, help fund schools and churches, sponsor local events and spur regional economies. Like others their age, they also date, go out to nightclubs and get married.

That's where the risks lie. The drug traffickers pose yet another problem. After all, if you're a woman, it's hard to reject, let alone break up with, a narco who propositions you. 'If a woman turns down a proposal [from a drug trafficker], her punishment could be death,' said Magdalena Garcia Hernandez, head of a women's activist group known as Milenio Feminista.

It's still unclear why Zuñiga Huizar, who was born and raised in Culiacan, chose to associate with the men with whom she was arrested. It's unclear whether she had a choice. She was released without being charged, and has stayed largely out of the spotlight in Culiacan since.

In Ciudad Juarez's state correctional facility, a group of women were locked up for trafficking on behalf of Chapo's organization; they claimed not to have known what they were carrying (marijuana) and were sentenced to several years. Carmen Elizalde was arrested trafficking 220 pounds of cocaine from Panama to Mexico, and sent to the Culiacan prison. She claimed her husband had tricked her, pretending they had simply been going on vacation.

To some young women, the allure remains. Sitting in the bright yard at Santa Martha Acatitla, a women's penitentiary on the outskirts of Mexico City, a group of prisoners huddled around, talking about their crimes. One of them was in for car theft, another for commandeering a city bus with a machine gun.

A leggy inmate strutted down the stairs and into the yard. Sporting Jackie O-style sunglasses and heels and walking with a supermodel swagger, she headed over to the payphone in the shaded corner.

'Look,' said one inmate, her eyes lighting up and jaw dropping: 'La Reina.'

Sandra Avila Beltran, a.k.a. 'La Reina del Pacifico' ('the Queen of the Pacific'), was taken into custody in late 2007. She now spends her days here in Santa Martha Acatitla. She is still awaiting sentencing. When she was arrested in Mexico City – she had changed her name and was living a low-key life but had been tracked down because she had not given up her taste for the best restaurants in town – La Reina became an instant celebrity. She pouted at the cops, saying she was just a housewife who sold clothes and homes to make a little extra on the side.

The forty-six-year-old brunette, originally from Baja California, had also been indicted in the United States for conspiring to import cocaine. She had allegedly risen through the narco-world via family connections (as a niece of 'El Padrino' Felix Gallardo). Over time, and thanks to her Colombian narco boyfriend Juan Diego Espinosa, 'El Tigre' ('the Tiger'), she became a vital go-between for the Mexicans and the Colombians.

She had seduced her way to the highest levels of the Sinaloa cartel: her list of past paramours included El Mayo and Ignacio Nacho Coronel. (She had also been married to a corrupt federal police commander, Rodolfo Lopez Amvizca, with whom she had a son. Her husband was murdered.)

'It's unheard of in the sense that we haven't seen a woman inside the organized crime cartels reach such an exalted position in decades,' a Mexican official told a reporter at the time of her arrest. 'Sandra's rise has to do with two circumstances: her ties to a family that has been involved in drug trafficking over three generations, and a physical beauty that made her stand out as a woman.' But the DEA's Michael Vigil was more condemning in his assessment. 'Sandra was very ruthless. She used the typical intimidation tactics of Mexican organizations.'

For weeks after her arrest, while the papers pored over every detail of her story, Mexican radio stations repeatedly played a narco-corrido in which she is hailed as 'a top lady who is a key part of the business'. Once in prison, however, the sheen appeared to wear off. She filed a complaint with human rights groups, saying there were cockroaches in her cell; the food was not to her liking.

'She's so cool,' one of the inmates in the yard at Santa Martha Acatitla said as she spotted La Reina making her entrance. Another called her a 'hero' who had worked her way up through the macho system. At this, another convict frowned. 'She's just one more here in the prison.'

16. The End Game

The archbishop had said Chapo was in the hills of Durango; the authorities were taking no chances. They had spotted him once before in the area, in 2006, driving through in an SUV. Urban surveillance cameras had captured him; the police and Army didn't arrive in time. Patrols throughout the area would now be routine.

Attorney General Eduardo Medina Mora looked tired as he fielded question after question about the drug lord. He'd repeatedly told the media that catching Chapo wasn't the be-all-and-end-all: the war on drugs was a long and complex process. Medina Mora may have been a hero in the eyes of his American counterparts, who admired his integrity and determination, but to an increasingly rabid press pack, he sometimes appeared on the verge of giving up. At one point he had even said that the goal of the drug war 'cannot be destroying narcotrafficking or drug-related crime'.

Garcia Luna, too, at times appeared to be running out of steam. 'Given the temptation . . . there are people who are always going to play the game [of drug trafficking] whether by airplane or helicopter, by land, by sea, because there is a real market. There is no product like it in the world.'

But in May 2009 the two had renewed resolve. 'Criminal organizations have evolved . . . the functions and circumstances of [Chapo's] role were taken over by other members of his organization,' Medina Mora said. 'He continues to be an emblematic figure . . . [but] he's less visible, less relevant in terms of the day-to-day operations of the group's criminal activity. The capture of Mr Joaquin Guzman Loera remains a priority for the government.'

There had been more close-but-no-cigar raids. In Sinaloa, members of the military admitted there was a possibility that Chapo's people were receiving advance warnings of raids from inside their camp. More of General Sandoval's soldiers were suspended and investigated for allegedly filtering information to Chapo and his people. Nine soldiers in the southern state of Guerrero were detained for the same reason.

Guerrero had always been Chapo territory, but it had long been run by the Beltran Leyva brothers on his behalf. Although Chapo owned a home in Las Brisas – a wealthy neighbourhood in the Pacific resort city – the brothers had recruited top police commanders, local kidnapping gangs and other criminal outfits to work for them there. With a major port and endless virgin coastline, Guerrero was ideal for cocaine arrivals; with mountain stretches rivalled only by the Sierra of Sinaloa, the state was ideal for poppy and marijuana production.

When the Beltran Leyva brothers split from Chapo, war had broken out in Guerrero. Gunfights between rival gangs erupted all over the state. Bodies began appearing at a rate akin to that of Ciudad Juarez and Culiacan. Some corpses were accompanied by messages signed by 'El Jefe de jefes' ('the Boss of bosses').

Marcos Arturo Beltran Leyva, a.k.a. 'El Barbas', was apparently now the only boss in town.

The Beltran Leyva brothers had the corruption network nationwide; they pretty much owned Guerrero. They had serious clout in Culiacan, and had worked on alliances with rivals in Ciudad Juarez before. Some authorities – not to mention average Mexicans – wondered whether Chapo could be overthrown.

Chapo was taking some serious hits. Federal police captured one of his top lieutenants in the central state of Jalisco. The man had been in charge of Jalisco operations, and was one of Chapo's most trusted allies.

In Culiacan, Roberto Beltran Burgos, a.k.a. 'the Doctor', was caught. A close confidant of Chapo's, the Doctor had been doing El Vicentillo's job since his arrest; he was a right-hand man. He had also become Chapo's mouthpiece, in charge of relaying the boss's orders to subordinates nationwide.

The military and federal police received an anonymous tip that a group of armed men were riding around the city of Durango. About 200 agents and soldiers encircled the area where they had been spotted and cornered them. A shootout ensued. Among the dead was Israel Sanchez Corral, a.k.a. 'El Paisa'. He had been in charge of the Culiacan plaza for Chapo, overseeing teams of dealers, distributors and killers. He had also been in charge of making sure no one moved in on Chapo's turf, particularly Los Zetas.

Antonio Mendoza Cruz, a.k.a. 'Cousin Tony', one of Chapo's close confidants, was arrested in Zapopan, Jalisco. Purportedly in charge of pseudoephedrine and cocaine purchases for Chapo in the states of Quintana Roo, Jalisco and Sinaloa, Cousin Tony worked directly with the Colombians. He had been a member of the drug lord's inner circle since the early days, and had allegedly helped coordinate Chapo's escape from Puente Grande.

By punching holes in Chapo's network, in the hierarchical structure of the cartel, the authorities aimed seriously to disrupt his operations. Every time they caught or killed one of his high-ranking men, Chapo had to replace him immediately. If they kept catching the next guy in line, the thinking went, Chapo wouldn't be able to adapt in time. He would also run out of people he could trust.

A group of Chapo operatives were planning an assassination attempt against President Calderon. No details of the conspiracy were revealed, but the president admitted it wasn't the first time the government had received intelligence of such plans. It won't be the last, either, Calderon said. 'The criminals are basically looking for the authorities to stop ... because we are forcing them to retreat ... In this fight, they will neither intimidate us nor stop us.'

The military was also coming across meth labs in the hills of Durango and Sinaloa, some of the biggest they had ever seen. (One such lab, outside Culiacan, had the capacity to produce about 20 tons of meth – US street value, $700 million – in only a month.) Earlier in 2009 Attorney General Medina Mora had declared that La Familia was now the major producer of meth in the country; the Culiacan lab appeared to contradict that.

As the feds and military closed in, residents of Sinaloa knew something was amiss in their neck of the woods. 'They're going to catch him,' said one Culiacan resident in early August. 'It's only a matter of time,' predicted the young man, who said he moved drugs on behalf of Chapo's people. He didn't know the big boss and had never met him, but he feared him.

General Sandoval and his men were maintaining the pressure throughout Sinaloa. One day they received a tip that Chapo was about to pay his respects to his dead son Edgar at his tomb, which had been erected in Jesus Maria, the town outside Culiacan where the boy was born.

Since Edgar's death the year before, residents of Jesus Maria had been left alone, both out of respect for the dead and on account that no one prominent would likely risk a visit. But on 8 August General Sandoval had deployed his men to the area around the tomb, which was still under construction. They guarded it for twenty-four hours, determined that Chapo wouldn't get away this time. He never showed.

Undeterred – and trusting of his information – Sandoval sent in two helicopters to survey the area, and scrambled his men throughout the tiny town. They searched from house to house, but found no one.

From the helicopters, Sandoval's men spotted two suspicious vehicles. The cars were driving around the town; around and around. As they were leaving Jesus Maria, the helicopters blocked the road, and soldiers surrounded the vehicles. They yanked out three young men, and began to question them. Was Chapo in town? Had he come? What did they know? According to local media reports, the soldiers repeatedly beat the suspects, accusing them of being Chapo's gunmen.

Frustrated, and still without answers, the soldiers left the scene; the three young men lay there, bruised and bleeding. When a group of local reporters turned up, the soldiers returned to haul the suspects off to an undisclosed location.

On 7 August 2009 the soldiers got a break. They stumbled on something in the mountain town of Las Trancas, Durango, near where

Chapo had married Emma Coronel, and about 100 miles from both Badiraguato and Culiacan. On a 240-hectare piece of property, the soldiers found twenty-two meth labs. According to one witness, there were more synthetics drugs there 'than you could ever imagine'. On the compound, they came across dormitory-style living quarters fit for about 100 people, with three kitchens and two washrooms. The entire property had been evacuated.

But there was more: several rooms were decked out with full bathrooms, high-speed Internet, satellite and plasma screen TVs, kingsize beds, minibars and air-conditioning. Clearly, the residents of the compound weren't all lowly workers.

From a lookout point above the compound, where gunmen had stood, one could see for about fifteen miles in every direction. Then the soldiers found a huge stash of cash – tens of thousands of US dollars. Whoever had been living there was high-ranking. There were several of them. They had just left, in a hurry, leaving the money behind.

Speculation quickly followed: had Chapo been there? Had he been hiding out, watching over the valuable property? Locals from the surrounding hills believed so, as did some soldiers stationed in the area. Chapo had apparently been living at the compound, along with El Mayo and Nacho Coronel.

'We're going to get him.' The DEA agent took a long sip of his beer. He was convinced that Chapo would one day be caught in the Sinaloan or Durango hills, his own homeland. He would never leave the place he loved, and this was one advantage the Mexicans had over past counter-drug operations in countries like Colombia. With the exception of Pablo Escobar, the old-school South American drug lords had never been reluctant to flee to the Amazon or mountainous rebel-held regions outside their own borders, if it meant their survival.

Every time Chapo was nearly caught in Sinaloa or just across the state line in Durango, the DEA man was certain they were getting closer. It was only a matter of time before they got him, he said with a smile, taking another sip of beer.

While the Mexican Army's efforts pleased him no end, the DEA man was most optimistic about the fact that Chapo no longer had his closest friends around him and instead had amassed a slew of enemies. Since the split with the Beltran Leyva brothers, Chapo had become increasingly isolated. The brothers had been crucial to his operations, and not only because he had known them all his life. When the Beltran Leyva brothers split, the DEA agent said, Chapo lost his safety net.

To be sure, he was still safe in his hills and in nearby cities like Culiacan, but not elsewhere – and neither was his drug operation. His people were turning on him all the time. A middle-ranking employee of Chapo's, a Californian man, had been responsible for routing money from Chicago drug sales to Los Angeles, and on to the Sinaloa kingpin. The DEA had caught him channelling $4 million to Chapo in one go. 'He works for us now,' the counter-drug player said.

There were also signs that Chapo was losing his grip on Sonora. Without control of that smuggling corridor, the Sinaloans could produce as much meth, marijuana and heroin and import as much cocaine as they wanted, but they wouldn't be able to get it to the US market.

As the DEA man went on, explaining how Chapo was now thought to be using multiple mobile phones for just a day or even mere hours (for fear they might be traced), he could barely contain his glee. Chapo can't trust anyone any more. His closest allies had either turned on him or been arrested; the Mexican military was doing a highly efficient and determined job of cornering him in the Sierra.

'He's up in the hills in Durango. It's gotta be brutal, living like that, holed up [or] moving all the time.'

Chapo had also lost relatives – his most trusted allies:

- Arturo Guzman Loera, brother. Killed 31 December 2004.

- Edgar Guzman Lopez, son. Killed 8 May 2008.

- Miguel Angel Guzman Loera, a.k.a. 'El Mudo' ('the Mute'), brother. Sentenced to thirteen years for money laundering and carrying military-grade firearms.

- Esteban Quintero Mariscal, cousin. Sentenced to fifteen years in prison for involvement in organized crime and carrying military-grade firearms.

- Isai Martinez Zepeda, cousin. Arrested in Culiacan for carrying military-grade firearms.

- Alfonso Gutierrez Loera, cousin. Arrested at a house in Culiacan with guns, grenades and thousands of rounds of ammunition.

More was to come. On 18 December 2008 a woman was found dead in the boot of a car outside Mexico City. She had been covered in a green blanket, held together by a belt. The dismembered corpse of a man, assumed to be her lover, rested at her side.

They had each been killed with a single bullet to the head. On various parts of the woman's body – her buttocks, her breasts, her back, her stomach – the killers had carved the letter 'Z', the calling card used by Los Zetas.

Zulema Hernandez, the inmate with whom Chapo had fallen in love at Puente Grande, was dead.

Chapo still had his 'onion ring' – the layer upon layer of informants and protectors within a specified radius of wherever he was at that given moment. After all, that's how he kept getting away, just in the nick of time. But during the last raid in Durango, he'd lost a meth lab worth millions of dollars. He had lost relatives and lovers. He stood to lose a lot more.

It's only a matter of time, the DEA agent promised. Only a matter of time.

The Failed War?

Throughout 2009, calls for the war to end were mounting. A trio of Latin American ex-presidents – including Mexico's Zedillo – had denounced the US strategy against drugs as 'a failed war' earlier in the year. Former foreign minister Jorge Castaneda condemned the Calderon administration for launching its war in a bid to win public support.

'There is a paradoxical situation,' he argued. 'In Los Angeles, there are a thousand legal and public places to buy marijuana – for medical reasons – but in reality it is available anywhere. There are more dispensaries of marijuana than public schools; 150 kilometres to the south, from Tijuana onwards, hundreds die every month, police, soldiers, assassins and civilians, in the war against the narco. This is a double standard on the part of the government and I think it will be hard for the US to sustain.

'The United States is not to blame for Mexico's drug war,' Castaneda went on, 'Mexico is not to blame for Mexico's drug war. President Felipe Calderon is to blame for Mexico's drug war, a war of choice that he should not have declared, that cannot be won, and is doing enormous damage to Mexico.'

Some Mexican experts suggested that a return to the old status quo – where the government effectively turned a blind eye towards certain major drug trafficking operations – might be the best way forward. The Institutional Revolutionary Party was the favourite to win the presidential elections in 2012, which some said would facilitate such an agreement.

Even President Calderon appeared to be pushing the war on drugs on to the back burner. Creating jobs and eradicating poverty would now be his top two goals; the war on drugs was named a distant third.

Residents of Culiacan, meanwhile, were slowly trying to rebuild their cities, their communities. On one occasion, a small group of residents in Culiacan met in a backroom to discuss ways to restore wholesome pride in their city. They planned fiestas, book-donation drives, and made a list of respectable citizens they could invite to events. But their meeting resembled that of a war-time resistance. At the end, they quietly shuffled out, wishing each other good luck.

Everyone in Culiacan feared the young narcos more and more each day, because they appeared to have no respect for anything.

In one instance, the girlfriend of a young narco tripped on her heels outside a nightclub. Another man in the vicinity dared to laugh at her misfortune. The narco shot him dead.

The bishop of Culiacan, Benjamin Jimenez Hernandez, made calls for society to rise up and combat the tide of violence. In a packed and sweltering church, he called for action, as his flock sweated it out. 'We must fight for our faith, we must fight for our future . . . This heat we're living in today, we must use our faith to conquer it.'

But November 2009 was Sinaloa's bloodiest month in sixteen years. And worse was yet to come. Even inside prisons themselves.

Mexico's jails were increasingly problematic. By the end of 2009 more than 121,000 people had been arrested in the current war on drugs. Many had been released, but jails were nonetheless filled with many tens of thousands of alleged and convicted traffickers.

Many were Chapo's people: nearly 30,000 members of the Sinaloa cartel had been detained, most of them foot soldiers who had never met the man himself but had done dirty work for him. There were dealers, gang members, cell operatives, hired killers and even high-ranking lieutenants:

- Roberto Beltran Burgos, a.k.a. 'The Doctor', lieutenant. Arrested for alleged involvement in organized crime.

- Israel Sanchez Corral, a.k.a. 'El Paisa', lieutenant. Arrested for alleged involvement in organized crime.

- Jose Ramon Laija Serrano, a lieutenant who helped run the business while Chapo was in Puente Grande. Sentenced to 27½ years for kidnapping.

- Diego Laija Serrano, a.k.a. 'El Vivo', lieutenant. Sentenced to 41 years in prison for drug-related crimes and possession of military-grade firearms.

- Carlos Norberto Felix Teran, a lieutenant in charge of drug production in Tamazula and of warning Chapo of any military movements in the area. Arrested for alleged involvement in organized crime.

But the arrests weren't only hitting Chapo hard; they were pushing Mexico's penitentiaries to the brink. Riots broke out in facilities in Matamoros, Ciudad Juarez, Culiacan and Tijuana, among others, as Sinaloans clashed with their rivals from Juarez and Los Zetas.

Matamoros prison holds both the Sinaloa cartel and Los Zetas. Prison warden Jaime Cano Gallardo witnessed a riot, watching helplessly as inmates from rival gangs attacked each other in one of the prison's courtyards. His guards couldn't handle it; he called for backup. By the time the Army and federal police arrived, two inmates were dead and more than thirty injured.

At the state prison in Durango, rival gang members used smuggled guns and other weapons to attack one another, leaving twenty inmates dead and twenty-six injured. And in the most brazen prison break since Chapo snuck out of Puente Grande, fifty-three alleged drug traffickers were escorted out of a penitentiary in Cieneguillas, Zacatecas, by a group of men masquerading as federal agents.

The Mexican government didn't ignore the problem, pledging to build a dozen more maximum-security prisons. Tello Peon, the man who had been so humiliated by Chapo's escape in 2001, was now back in the fold, as a national security adviser. He demanded a 'brutal' reform of the prison system.

Ciudad Juarez and Culiacan's prisons were particularly bad. Because of the war between Chapo and the Juarez cartel, the city had become a melting pot of criminals from all over the country. On the streets they shot each other up and wore their allegiance on their sleeves; once locked up they sought to do the same.

The Ciudad Juarez penitentiary is vast; concrete buildings sprawl out across the desert towards the mountains in the distance. Many of the walkways are secured only by chain-link fencing and barbed wire. A riot broke out between members of Los Aztecas and a rival group. Four guards were taken hostage. By the time the Army arrived to quell the violence, twenty inmates were dead and dozens more injured. Prison officers built a huge wall separating the gangs' cell blocks and hired soldiers to patrol the grounds round the clock. But Los Aztecas remained effectively in charge. Guards are regularly denied access to Los Aztecas' cell block by the inmates themselves.

In another prison courtyard in the Ciudad Juarez facility, a band performed a narco-corrido, as inmates received visitors. The narco-corrido being performed in what should have been the heart of enemy territory was an ode to Chapo. As the band played on, a guard indicated members of Los Aztecas, staring through a chain-link fence. 'Be careful. It barely takes anything to set them off.'

And all those years since Chapo's escape, inmates were still walking free. During a party organized for prisoners and their visiting kin, an alleged associate of Chapo's made his way out of the gates within the facility, past the guards armed with AK-47s and handguns at the outer perimeter, and through the parking lot to freedom.

'This happened because of human failure,' said Pedro Cardenas Palazuelos, who was installed as Culiacan's prison warden immediately after the escape. 'We have cameras, electronic doors; if no one opens the door, no one gets out. It's corruption.'

Cardenas Palazuelos's stint in Culiacan was brief; two months after he took over, Lieutenant Colonel Carlos Suarez Martinez replaced him. 'We will increase security, discipline and control,' insisted the ex-military man. Less than two weeks later, another prisoner escaped. He, too, waltzed out under the nose of the authorities. He, too, reputedly worked for Chapo.

The Last Narco

'El Padrino' Felix Gallardo sits in a maximum-security facility in the State of Mexico. His health is failing. Writing from his cell, he sets out the defence he claims he never was allowed to make. 'When we, the old capos, we who were detained, we were few . . . We didn't kill or rob nor impoverish Mexicans like many politicians did.' El Padrino claims he doesn't want to be released, but adds that blaming him for the current violence is not only unfair but ridiculous. 'One can fight violence with jobs . . . schools, sports fields, communications, medical services, security and a fight against poverty . . . We must remember that Mexican territory in [the Sierra] is forgotten, there are no good schools, roads . . . only repression.'

Construction of 'Don Neto' Fonseca's mausoleum, a vast Graeco-Roman structure built overlooking the tiny Sinaloan pueblo of Santiago de los Caballeros, is complete. Dozens of other narco-graves are scattered on the hillside cemetery plot, which looks out towards the Sierra's peaks. Don Neto's mausoleum towers over the others majestically. It's a resting place fit for a king.

Imprisoned in the same facility as El Padrino, Don Neto knows his days are numbered.

Rafael Caro Quintero, the other accomplice in the 'Kiki' Camarena affair, is also serving a forty-year prison sentence in Mexico; his brother, Miguel, is serving a seventeen-year sentence in the United States. 'El Guero' Palma Salazar is in prison, too.

The Arellano Felix brothers have all fallen. Ramon is dead; Benjamin in a maximum-security facility in Mexico. On 14 August 2006 Francisco Javier was arrested by the US Coast Guard in international waters just off the coast of Mexico; he later pleaded guilty in a San Diego court and was sentenced to life imprisonment.

On 25 October 2008, after a prolonged gun battle with Mexican special forces in Tijuana acting on DEA information, brother Eduardo was captured. 'The arrest of Eduardo Arellano Felix closes the book on this once powerful and brutally violent criminal band of brothers,' declared DEA Acting Administrator Michele M. Leonhart. Rumour has it that Chapo helped the authorities take them down.

After the fall of the Arellano Felix brothers, Tijuana once again descended into conflict at the hands of an Arellano Felix sister and her son, Luis Fernando Sanchez Arellano, a.k.a. 'the Engineer'. Chapo moved in; policemen were killed and violence rose.

Chapo allied with a local Tijuana drug boss named 'El Teo' Garcia Simental, a former member of the Arellano Felix organization. Formerly in charge of extortion and kidnapping rackets, El Teo was particularly brutal, even by Tijuana standards. One subordinate, Santiago Meza, confessed to having dissolved more than 300 bodies in caustic soda on El Teo's behalf. He was nicknamed 'El Pozolero' ('the Stewmaker').

Juan Garcia Abrego is in prison. The DEA says that the Gulf cartel and Los Zetas have splintered due to the killing of a high-level Zeta over a dispute; the DEA also says that Chapo has made a temporary alliance with the Gulf cartel leadership to put Los Zetas out of business.

In February 2010, Cardenas Guillen bowed his head before a judge in a Houston court. 'I apologize to my country, Mexico, to the United States of America, my family, to my wife especially, my children, for all the mistakes I made. I feel this time that I have spent in jail, I have reflected and I've realized the so-ill behaviour that I was maintaining, and truthfully, I am remorseful. I also apologize to all of the people that I hurt directly and indirectly. That's all, your honour.'

Cardenas Guillen pleaded guilty. He was sentenced to twenty-five years.

Amado and Rodolfo Carrillo Fuentes are dead; Amado's son Vicente Carrillo Leyva is in prison.

La Familia has struck up an alliance with Chapo; they now work for him.

El Mayo's brother and son are locked up. (The latter was extradited to the United States to face trial.) In late 2009 El Mayo's nephew, Jesus Zambada Reyes, committed suicide in Mexico City. He had been cooperating since his arrest, providing good information on El Mayo's operations and whereabouts. Shortly after another protected witness linked to El Mayo was gunned down at Starbucks in Mexico City; he too was giving valuable intelligence.

El Mayo was the only one of his inner family circle still free. 'The Zambada dynasty is extinct,' proclaimed the daily newspaper *Reforma*. El Mayo would counter such claims. In February 2010 he said that, in fact, it was the drug war that had failed. (He also refuted reports of Chapo's extravagant wedding in the mountains of Durango.)

On 11 December 2009 the federal agencies received a valuable nugget of information. Marcos Arturo Beltran Leyva, a.k.a. 'El Barbas', was going to be attending a party in Ahuatepec, in the central state of Morelos. A team of Mexican marines raided the site, but arrived too late to catch El Barbas. They arrested dozens of people, including singer Ramon Ayala and his group, Bravos del Norte.

The DEA kept feeding them intelligence, and the marines kept on his tail. Six days later, in the afternoon of 16 December, 200 marines swooped in on a residential neighbourhood in the Morelos city of Cuernavaca. They cordoned off parts of the city, and quickly moved in on a luxury high-rise apartment block. Helicopters buzzed overhead; the marines discreetly moved residents of the building downstairs to the gymnasium. They homed in on one particular apartment. A shootout ensued. Bullets spattered. Grenades were thrown. Five narcos inside were shot and killed; one jumped to his death. Inside the apartment lay El Barbas. Chapo's biggest rival was dead.

Within hours of his death, eight narco-corridos were written and uploaded to the Internet. In Nogales, Sonora – Chapo country – locals fired their guns into the air in celebration. 'A stray bullet injured a little girl, but it's all about the celebration,' said one witness. 'It's a *posada* [holiday party].'

El Barbas had posthumously suffered the ultimate narco-humiliation. His trousers had been partially pulled down to reveal his underwear; his stomach and chest were covered in dollar and peso notes. All those involved in the raid denied having tampered with the corpse; members of the forensic squad were hauled in for investigation.

Immediately following the raid that left El Barbas dead, four relatives of one of the marines who took part were murdered. El Barbas was buried in the Jardines del Humaya in Culiacan under close watch by the military. Days later a decapitated head was dumped in front of his grave.

Less than two weeks after that, another Beltran Leyva brother, Carlos, was arrested. Chapo was believed to be feeding information once again, in an act of self-preservation.

Chapo was winning. He had always shown an astounding ability to bounce back after any defeat. He never walked away; he came back with a vengeance.

As Los Zetas, by then allies of the remnants of the Beltran Leyva organization, made their move into Durango, Chihuahua and Sinaloa, more bloodshed ensued. Three heads were found in a cooler in Parral, where the revolutionary Pancho Villa met his fate. They were Zetas; Chapo's people claimed responsibility. But the surge continued. Los Zetas made their move into Culiacan, Mazatlan, Guasave and Tamazula.

By the end of 2009, both Culiacan and Ciudad Juarez had become free-for-alls. Narco-mantas threatening Chapo's people were strewn about in both cities, while the word was that Chapo couldn't even move around on his own turf in parts of Sinaloa. But it still looked like he had the advantage. Just as his resilience had kept him strong throughout his career, so had his ability to forge alliances – effectively to let sleeping dogs lie. Always at the right time, in the right place, he would strike the right deal.

Chapo, it was claimed, had made a deal with the military and federal government in Ciudad Juarez; he would take over the border city once the authorities had got rid of the remnants of the Juarez cartel. This was staunchly denied. Bloodshed continued between Chapo and Carrillo Fuentes' gangs in what one newspaper called the 'never ending war'.

But Chapo was doing his best to end it. 'We're witnessing the extermination of the Juarez cartel,' said Alfredo Quijano, editor of the *Norte de Ciudad Juarez* newspaper. The Juarez cartel 'is down to its last line of defence' because Chapo's men are 'killing people at will, hitting them like sitting ducks'. Shortly after, US officials said that Chapo had effectively won the battle for Ciudad Juarez; a Mexican federal agent supported these 'valid theories'. 'If you control the city, you control the drugs,' he told the Associated Press. 'And it appears to be Chapo.' The Sinaloa cartel was now held to be the most powerful drug trafficking organization in the world.

Chapo was also getting even more violent.

In Caborca, Sonora, a gang of his and El Mayo's killers had kidnapped a group of rivals. Limb by limb, they were sawn to bits. The remains looked like dismantled mannequins.

Thirty-year-old Carlos Ricardo Romo Briceno from Culiacan was gunned down in the Sinaloan city of Los Mochis. A group of more than a dozen armed men travelling in three vehicles had cornered him; they fired more than 200 rounds from their AK-47s and AR-15s until his body was in tatters.

The headless bodies of two men were thrown out of a small plane flying over Sonora. Stunned farmers discovered them shortly after the plane landed near by.

A thirty-six-year-old man was found dead in Sinaloa. His body had been cut into seven pieces. His face had been carved off, delicately. It was later found, stitched on to a football. A note was left with the ball: 'Happy New Year, because this will be your last.'

The spree of killings was attributed to Chapo's people. He clearly wasn't letting up.

One former DEA agent, watching the action from Washington, believed that Chapo's days were numbered. The other major players in the Mexican drug trade had fallen; Chapo would too. The drug lord was beginning to believe he was invincible, the DEA man said. Far from empowering Chapo, this would make him more vulnerable, prone to stupid mistakes. 'He'll be in handcuffs or on a slab in ninety days. It's only a matter of time.'

Back in Culiacan, General Sandoval was showing no signs of

quitting, either. 'In the past, external interests came to snatch our territory; today, crime wants to strip us of our valour, our youth. Narcos are permanently kidnapped and alienated, just like the victims of this ferocious criminality. For them, for the criminals, there are only two roads – death or jail.' Sandoval candidly admitted that they had never been close to nabbing him. 'We don't know where he is,' he conceded.

One of Sandoval's immediate subordinates, General Federico Eduardo Solorzano Barragan, was frustrated – and equally candid. His men had searched Culiacan thoroughly for drugs and guns; he was convinced Chapo was not hiding out in the capital. 'We've gone house to house. If he were here, we'd know.' He didn't even think Chapo was still in Sinaloa. 'If everyone were looking for you, would you stay where they're looking or go somewhere else? It's logical. You'd go.' The narco may have undergone plastic surgery again. 'Or maybe he's just a farmer.'

Chapo, however, *was* still in the area and running the operation. He had issued a warning: no one was to move around in the Sierra in groups of more than five or six. The helicopters could spot them too easily and would arrest them on sight. Even under the cover of darkness, his people were not to be conspicuous. The helicopters had heat-seeking capabilities, he warned.

Chapo was aware of the military's new equipment. He was also said to be increasingly paranoid, hiding up in the hills of Durango or Sinaloa, depending on the day. He was moving more frequently than ever, driving around with only one bodyguard to avoid detection or suspicion. Sometimes he would even take the wheel himself – no one would ever suspect a man who looks like a farmer in a pickup truck of being a drug lord.

By early 2010 Chapo hadn't been seen in public for more than two years. There were rumours – denied by the DEA – that he had prostate cancer. 'He can't spend too long in one place. He might spend the morning in one place but by the afternoon he has to move because word will have got out,' said a Mexican soldier in Culiacan. 'That's his life, trying to keep from being killed.'

Chapo trusted no one. The only person he was listening to now was El Mayo.

There were three real capos left in Sinaloa: Chapo, El Mayo and El Azul, the ever-discreet adviser who had always remained well in the shadows. Bets were being placed on which of these three capos would fall first – and which would be the last narco standing.

In Badiraguato the locals insisted that Chapo, the real boss of bosses, would never be caught.

In Mexico City the DEA man finally admitted that catching Chapo might well prove impossible.

'I doubt he will ever fall.'

Postscript

I first became interested in Mexico's drug war in 2004, when I interviewed Jorge Hank Rhon in Tijuana. But at the time, it was a purely Mexican story – the war was nothing compared to what it would become two years later when Calderon took office. Since then it has developed into a major global news story.

Increased international interest has allowed many Mexicans to be more open about drug trafficking than in the past, but it has also brought out of the woodwork all sorts of characters who want to talk about the drug war to curious journalists. Some of them you can believe; some, most definitely not.

I have simply done the best I can as a journalist, working with the most trustworthy sources available to me, to try to tell a version of what is happening in Mexico.

Even working with newspaper clips and official statements has posed its challenges. Often, *Reforma, El Universal, Milenio* and *La Jornada* (Mexico's leading newspapers, each with its own political agenda and sources) contradict each other on even the most basic of stories. Throughout the book, I have tried to rely on *El Universal* and *Reforma* for historical accounts (cross-referencing most stories for accuracy), and turned to *Milenio* and *La Jornada* when those papers provided unique coverage. I have also used countless articles from local newspapers throughout Mexico. I cannot be convinced of their complete accuracy, and have not been able to check the veracity of each and every reported item, so have tried to use their facts only when they carry an obvious semblance of truth. (For instance, I've dismissed as bogus countless 'Chapo sightings' printed in local papers, because they give no details and fail to provide at least one witness; many just seem to be pulled from thin air.)

Statements from the PGR, federal police and military often contradict each other too. I can now understand General Sandoval's frustration over intelligence sharing.

I have used a selection of books, particularly those by Mexican crime authority Ricardo Ravelo, primarily as background. I haven't used them as much to recount specific incidents because I preferred the straight-facts accounts provided by the newspapers. I do highly recommend his books to anyone more interested in organized crime in Mexico.

Foreign journalists often encounter a wall when trying to access real narcos or even official sources in Mexico. Even the PGR, military and federal police – who have been quite open to my approaches at times in the past – quickly decided that my requests for information about Chapo weren't to be entertained. It could have been for their own safety: one former PGR official who I interviewed was ultra-cautious to the point that we had to sit behind a pillar in an empty coffee shop while we talked. His fears were understandable – just a few months before a protected witness had been gunned down in broad daylight at a Starbucks in Mexico City.

To report in Badiraguato, I spent several days there at a time; even then, everyone was wary of talking about Chapo, and accounts from those who did must be taken with a healthy dose of scepticism. The big narcos in Mexico, the higher-ups like Chapo, rarely talk to anyone. There is very little way of cross-checking what one lower-ranking narco tells you. (One can ask, for instance, for details about a crime they claim to have committed, and then check with the authorities or local papers to see if it happened, but it is virtually impossible to prove they did what they claim to have done.) Josue Felix, El Padrino's son, was open to my talking to his father in prison, but the authorities ignored my formal request for that interview. As a result, most of the information about El Padrino (his quotes, for instance) comes from a selection of writings he has posted on a website run by his son.

Throughout my research for this book and for stories on the drug war for various publications, I've always maintained that my life and the lives of those people I interview are more important than any great scoop I might get. The best journalism requires risks, but those risks have to be calculated.

One journalist friend, who reports on Al-Qaeda and global terrorism, regards the Mexican narcos as the most dangerous and 'scary' of the world's criminal elite; from what I've seen and read over the past three years, I would have to agree. Mexican soldiers do not wear masks twenty-four hours a day because they like to look tough; they know that if they are spotted and identified by the narcos, they could easily become the next statistic.

Every minute one spends reporting on organized crime, one feels a little less secure. (Admittedly, during one stay in Badiraguato, I realized that I felt extremely comfortable, and slept like a baby; but this was only because I knew full well that Chapo's people knew I was there and, as they had not yet killed me, were not likely to do so.) When one speaks to locals in Sinaloa about organized crime, the blood pressure rises. People whisper, tremble and cry when they talk about their experiences and their knowledge – even rumours.

Many won't even speak Chapo's name; they have a handful of other nicknames by which to call him – some respectful, some less so. Some ordinary people and officials will simply turn and walk away when you mention Chapo. The people of Mexico who live under the shadow of organized crime do not enjoy what most of us know as freedom of expression. I've written this book with them in mind, changing names where appropriate and bending my normal rules about anonymous sources due to their understandable fears.

I have also taken precautions – lying to some sources about my true assignment, for instance – for my own safety and theirs. There are parts of Mexico where speaking to an official can be as dangerous as speaking to a criminal – after all, there is little way of knowing if your source is closely linked to the narcos. As I wrote earlier, when you are in Sinaloa reporting on organized crime, everyone knows it, and assumes you are DEA or CIA. You rarely know who's

on whose side. Sometimes, it's safer to just pretend you're research-
ing some other aspect of Sinaloa's culture; if a local then chooses to
open up about the drug trade, great. If not, you go on your way.

I am no 'Kiki' Camarena, the DEA agent who so daringly infiltrated the narcos back in the 1980s; as a result, this book is not
really meant to be an investigation, per se. I have no desire to wind
up dead, my decapitated corpse dumped on a roadside in north-
western Mexico.

Every night while I was reporting in Sinaloa, I realized that this
could be my fate. On one occasion, after a group of gun-toting
young men pulled up to my motel and checked into the room next
to mine, I opted to sleep in the bath. Perhaps I was being overly
cautious, but I didn't want to become another innocent victim of
a shootout, the kind that occurs almost daily in Mexico and barely
even makes the evening news.

There are reporters who are far braver than me, who have tried
to make real headway into the mystery and atrocity that is organized crime.

On 2 April 2005 Alfredo Jimenez Mota went to meet a source,
who had sounded 'very nervous'. His colleagues at *El Imparcial*, a
newspaper in the Sonoran city of Hermosillo, were not particularly concerned, given Jimenez Mota's penchant for digging up
stories on crime and all kinds of sleaze that others wouldn't touch.
An honest, hardworking kid, Jimenez Mota was said to have had a
keen sense of justice. Ever since joining *El Imparcial*, he had dedicated himself to writing about crime and drug trafficking. He had
written about Chapo's operations in nearby Nogales; he had investigated police corruption in his home town.

He never joined his colleagues for drinks that night after going
to meet his source. He was never seen again.

Alejandro Fonseca, a thirty-three-year-old radio host from
Villahermosa in the south-eastern part of the country, was just
another ordinary Mexican fed up with the violence who wanted
to spur change and see justice. In September 2008 he became particularly concerned about the drug violence consuming his city.

One Tuesday night, he and colleague Angel Morales began putting up banners in the streets, publicizing their cause.

'No to kidnapping' and 'Kidnapping thrives as long as citizens let it,' read the banners.

A group of armed men drove by, and told them to stop what they were doing. Fonseca refused; they fired. Fonseca died the next morning.

On 13 November 2008 forty-year-old Armando Rodriguez was leaving his home in Ciudad Juarez to drive his eight-year-old daughter to school when an unidentified gunman sprang from the bushes and shot him at point-blank range. Rodriguez had reported on crime in the violence-racked city; he had received a call earlier in the year from someone telling him to 'tone it down'. In spite of the threats, he had insisted on continuing his work without body-guards; just the day before his death he had reported on a story of the killing of two local police officers.

In July 2009 the body of Juan Daniel Martinez was found in a shallow grave in Acapulco. He had been beaten and gagged. He had covered crime for W Radio.

In Reynosa, Tamaulipas, one local journalist who covers the crime beat said that the situation has returned to 2005 levels. There is a new arrangement – a so-called peace, since Chapo's departure – but it's not for the better. The local police, 'possibly the most corrupt and dangerous of them all', once again have clout.

The Army, too, complains of this. One major who leads raids in the Tamaulipas border town of Miguel Aleman claimed the police use their privileged position to tip off the narcos of the Army's whereabouts. 'We have been followed by the police every single moment,' he told the Associated Press. 'They have people every-where reporting on our every move, and that makes it hard to sur-prise them.'

In Matamoros I once requested to go along on a police patrol; my request was approved by a senior commander on the phone. But about half an hour later, a two-pickup-truck patrol showed up at the arranged meeting place; three policemen stood up on the truck's flatbed and pointed their semi-automatics at me before the vehicles screeched off, the cops hollering into the night. Whether intended as a threat or not, I interpreted it as one.

Newspapers throughout Mexico say that they have been pressured by organized crime to report what the narcos want published, or ignore certain incidents which they don't. Los Zetas, in particular, are believed to have made strong headway into the publishing industry. 'If you don't print a narco message from one group, they will punish you. Or the other side will punish you if you do publish it,' an editor in Durango told the *Los Angeles Times*. 'Or the government will punish you for printing anything. You don't know where the threat is going to come from.'

Alberto Velazquez, a reporter for *Expresiones de Tulum* in southeastern Mexico, was gunned down by a man on a motorcycle as he left a party. He had written articles that criticized local officials; his newspaper had received threats related to his work prior to his death. Velazquez was the twelfth journalist killed in Mexico in 2009.

Journalists are no longer really investigating anything in Sinaloa. Or in Tamaulipas, or in Ciudad Juarez. For good reason: at least forty-five journalists have died in Mexico since 2000, most of them for treading one foot too far into the realms of organized crime. The curtailment of reporting on the problem because of the risk is a serious threat to Mexican democracy.

Ismael Bojorquez and Javier Valdez have been reporting on the narcos in Sinaloa for several years now. When they launched their newspaper, *Rio Doce*, they didn't set out to cover organized crime, but quickly realized how much it appealed to readers. But reporting has been a tough slog. 'You know there's an imminent risk from what you write,' said Bojorquez, the weekly's editor. The fifty-three-year-old and his colleagues operate out of a small building in Culiacan. There's an electronic gate at the first floor entrance; Bojorquez has a windowless office in the back.

On 7 September 2009 *Rio Doce* received its first threat. A grenade was detonated outside their offices one night; no one was injured, and they didn't know who had planted it. Bojorquez and Valdez had their suspicions, however: they hadn't been writing about the local narcos much lately, instead focusing on outsiders who were now operating in Culiacan. It was probably the latter.

They've always been extremely careful about what they publish – rarely do they mention the names of alleged narcos, never any details that might give away someone's location to the authorities – but still, Bojorquez worries every time they publish something he thinks a narco might take a dislike to.

'When you sit and write, you think of your reader – his reaction to your story. In this case, it's the fucking ghost of the narco that enters your head. He's the one reading.'

Sources

Main Interviews

Former DEA Special Agent Michael Vigil; former DEA Special Agent Errol Chavez; former DEA Chief of Operations Michael Braun; former DEA Administrator Asa Hutchinson; DEA Chief of Intelligence Anthony Placido; anonymous US official in Mexico; former PGR adviser Ariel Moutsatsos; former federal prosecutor Samuel Gonzalez Ruiz; anonymous PGR official; anonymous Mexican federal police official; Gen. Noe Sandoval Alcazar; Air Force Maj. Valentin Diaz Reyes; Gen. Roberto de la Vega Diaz; Maj. Hugo de la Rosa; Josue Felix; human rights activist Mercedes Murillo; Sinaloa human rights commissioner Juan Jose Rios Estavillo; Badiraguato Mayor Martin Meza Otiz; unnamed local officials in Badiraguato; congressman Felipe Diaz Garibay; congressman Jose Luis Espinosa Pina; congressman Aaron Irizar Lopez; Manuel Clouthier Carrillo; Luis Astorga; Martin Amaral; Luis Ricardo Ruiz; UNODC regional representative Antonio Mazzitelli; Eduardo Buscaglia; Gustavo de la Rosa Hickerson; Jorge Hank Rhon; congresswoman Martha Tagle Martinez; congresswoman Yudit del Rincon; Jaime Cano Gallardo; Pedro Cardenas Palazuelos; Francisco Morelos Borja; Jaime Alberto Torres Valadez; Jorge Ramos; Carlos Murillo Gonzalez; former President Vicente Fox's spokesman Ruben Aguilar; Sinaloa police chief Josefina de Jesus Garcia Ruiz; Jorge Chabat; Victor Clark Alfaro; Jesus Blancornelas; about a dozen policemen and a dozen anonymous soldiers throughout Mexico; about two dozen unnamed sources, from ordinary citizens in Sinaloa to self-professed employees of Chapo and lower-level narcos; about a dozen local reporters throughout Mexico.

Books

Blancornelas, Jesus, *El Cartel*, Debolsillo, 2004.

Bowden, Mark, *Killing Pablo: The hunt for the world's greatest outlaw*, Penguin Books, 2001.

Grayson, George W., *Mexico: Narco-violence and a failed state?*, Transaction, 2009.

Oppenheimer, Andres, *Bordering on Chaos*, Little, Brown and Company, 1996.

Osorno, Diego Enrique, *El Cartel de Sinaloa*, Random House Mondadori, 2009.

Ravelo, Ricardo, *Los Capos*, Random House Mondadori, 2005.

Scherer, Julio, *Maxima Seguridad*, Random House Mondadori, 2002.

Shannon, Elaine, *Desperados: Latin drug lords, US lawmen and the war America can't win*, Penguin Books, 1988.

Prologue

(Epigraph) **'I'm a farmer.'** *Milenio* newspaper, 'They took us to jail to see Chapo', Ciro Gomez Leyva, 22.1.2008; author's interviews with journalists who were present. **You tell everyone ... You won't. They won't.** Author's interviews in Badiraguato. **Since a dramatic escape ... in Mexico and Latin America. Drug Enforcement Administration (DEA). The Mexican authorities want ... out of prison again.** Interview with the DEA's Michael Braun. **Chapo's enemies ... turned on him.** Statements by DEA, US State Department and PGR. **The war's toll ... the violence ebbing.** Numerous newspaper articles, the majority from *Reforma* and *El Universal*. **Chapo ... starting the war.** Author's interviews with DEA agents, PGR statements. **He grew up ... by the** 1990s. DEA, interviews with officials in Badiraguato. **Today ... organization.** *Forbes* magazine, 'The world's most powerful people', by Michael Noer and Nicole Perlroth, 11.11.2009. **Chapo's empire ... US cities.** US Department of Justice, 'Situation Report: Cities in Which Mexican DTOs

Operate Within the United States', 11.4.2008. **The cartel receives ... West Africa.** Interviews with Michael Braun, DEA and research by Edgardo Buscaglia, ITAM. **The Sinaloa cartel ... his childhood.** DEA, PGR interviews and statements. **Sinaloa's mountains ... stand in the way.** Interviews with officials in Badiraguato. **This is a land ... shoot first.** Interviews with locals in Badiraguato. **I met ... almost everyone is involved.** Interviews with officials and locals in Badiraguato. **How odd ... too dangerous.** Interviews with locals and officials in Badiraguato, September 2009. **In 2005 ... even exists.** *Los Angeles Times*, 'Mexico's master of elusion', by Richard Boudreaux, 5.7.2005. **Neither do ... they are born.** Author's interview with Meza Ortiz and radio interview conducted by Claudia Beltran, *Noroeste* newspaper, 8.12.2009. **Meza Ortiz ... counties in Mexico.** Government of Badiraguato. **The whole town ... Robin Hood-like auras.** Interviews with locals in Badiraguato, interview with Luis Astorga. **But with the drug war ... the old man said.** Interviews conducted in Badiraguato in 2008 and 2009.

Chapter 1

Articles used for reconstruction of escape and prison conditions: *El Universal*, ' "El Chapo" created a network of complicit [people]', by Francisco Gomez, 19.4.2001; *La Jornada*, 'The CNDH alerted Gertz about Puente Grande', by Victor Ballinas, Andrea Becerril and Juan Antonio Zuniga, 31.1.2001; *El Universal*, 'The search for Chapo intensifies', by Jorge Alejandro Medellin, 24.1.2001; *El Universal*, 'CNDH warns of more escapes from Puente Grande', by Bertha Fernandez, 24.1.2001; *El Universal*, 'Chapo enjoyed privileges: CNDH', by Sergio Javier Jimenez, 23.1.2001; *El Universal*, 'Search for narco is questioned', by staff writers, 23.1.2001; *El Universal*, 'They knew about all the anomalies', by Sergio Javier Jimenez, Mario Torres, Jorge Alejandro Medellin and Jana Beris, 23.1.2001; *El Universal*, 'El Chapo paid $2.5 million to escape', by Jorge Alejandro Medellin, 22.1.2001; *El Universal*,

'Indictment against "El Chapo" Guzman overturned', by Hernan Guizar, 13.10.2000; *El Universal*, 'They're searching for "Chapo" in Guatemala', by staff writers, 18.2.2001; *El Universal*, ' "El Chapo" could be in the country, says Macedo', by Jorge Alejandro Medellin, 15.2.2001; *El Universal*, 'Raids in search of "Chapo" ', by staff writers, 24.1.2001; *El Universal*, 'Injunction authorized for "Chapo;" they await orders to capture him', by Jorge Alejandro Medellin, 31.1.2001; *El Universal*, 'Gertz knew of possible escape: CNDH', by Fabiola Guarneros and Alejandro Torres, 31.1.2001; *El Universal*, 'Gertz urged to show his face', by Jorge Teheran, Jorge Herrera and Dora Elena Cortes, 1.2.2001; *El Universal*, 'Order of 73 arrested for the escape of "Chapo" ', by Jorge Alejandro Medellin, 23.2.2001; *El Universal*, 'DEA has 20 counts against Guzman', by Miguel Badillo and Dora Cortes, 25.1.2001; *Reforma*, 'CNDH denies intervention in Puente Grande prison', by Ivabelle Arroyo and Antonio Navarrete, 22.1.2001; *Reforma*, ' "El Chapo" pulled off a movie-style escape', by Antonio Navarrete and Denis Rodriguez, 21.1.2001; *Reforma*, 'Organized crime response is confirmed', by Laura Camachov, 21.1.2001; *Reforma*, ' "El Chapo" left prison as if it were his house', by Cecilia Gonzalez, 23.1.2001; *Reforma*, 'Investigation problems', by Alicia Calderon and Francisco Junco, 23.1.2001; *Reforma*, 'Internal disloyalty suspected in escape of "El Chapo" – Tello', by Antonio Navarrete and Denis Rodriguez, 21.1.2001; *Reforma*, 'They assure that "El Chapo" had a lot of information', by Jessica Perez, 23.1.2001; *Reforma*, ' "Chapo" will seek to regain power – Gutierrez Rebollo', by Isaac Guzman and Andres Zuniga, 29.1.2001; *Reforma*, 'Kids are joking around with the PFP; they're giving leads on "El Chapo" ', by Denis Rodriguez, 24.1.2001; *Reforma*, '[Authorities] recognize incapacity against organized crime', by staff writers, 22.1.2001; *Reporte Indigo*, 'Chapo's escape: From Puente Grande to Forbes', by staff writers, 21.3.2009; *Proceso*, ' "El Chapo," the perfect escape', by Ricardo Ravelo, January 2006; *El Cartel de Sinaloa*, by Diego Enrique Osorno, Random House Mondadori, 2009.

★

During the 1980s ... not go to the United States. Mark Bowden, *Killing Pablo*, Penguin Books, 2001, p. 51. Chapo, meanwhile ... partners in crime. Locals and journalists in Sinaloa. The day Chapo ... wives and girlfriends. *El Universal*, ' "El Chapo" created a network of complicit [people]', by Francisco Gomez, 19.4.2001. They feasted ... under Chapo's command. PGR statement, 1.2.2002. On at least ... long into the night. *El Universal*, ' "El Chapo" created a network of complicit [people]', by Francisco Gomez, 19.4.2001. Sometimes the fun ... Just imagine. Julio Scherer, *Maxima Seguridad*, Random House Mondadori, 2002, pp. 152–3, 160–2. To this day ... his internment. Minutes from the 146th session of the council of the National Human Rights Commission, CNDH. Mexico's prisons ... were rarely used. *El Universal*, ' "El Chapo" created a network of complicit [people]', by Francisco Gomez, 19.4.2001. Women inside ... at a moment's notice. *El Universal*, ' "El Chapo" created a network of complicit [people]', by Francisco Gomez, 19.4.2001. Chapo even received ... his libido. Interview with Carlos Vega of the PGR, 'America's Most-Wanted'. And then there was Zulema ... everything is OK. Scherer, *Maxima Seguridad*, pp. 9–36. Chapo would ... her sentence. *El Universal*, 'The narco with a woman's face', by Carolina Garcia, 31.1.2009. Chapo's relations ... investigated the complaints. *Wall Street Journal*, 'The drug lord who got away', by David Luhnow and Jose de Cordoba, 13.6.2009; Jalisco state human rights commission documents. Even though Chapo ... drug trafficking. Testimony before the Senate Committee on Banking, Housing and Urban Affairs by DEA Administrator Thomas Constantine, 28.3.1996. But by 1997 ... in Central America. Testimony before the Senate Caucus on International Narcotics Control by DEA Administrator Thomas Constantine, 14.5.1997. The following year ... he declared. Testimony before House of Representatives' Government Reform and Oversight Committee by DEA Administrator Thomas Constantine, 19.3.1998. In 1995 he had undergone ... legitimately. *Proceso*, 'El Ganon', by Ricardo Ravelo, February

2007. **According to ... one's entire life.** Scherer, *Maxima Seguridad*, pp. 9–36. **Apart from his brothers ... rejoin their ranks.** Protected witness testimony, published in *El Universal*, *Reforma* and *Proceso*. **There were also ... in October 2000.** Scherer, *Maxima Seguridad*, pp. 9–36. **The most interesting theory ... (PRI).** Author's interviews with Mexican journalists who cover organized crime. **Chapo hinted ... as yours.** Scherer, *Maxima Seguridad*, pp. 9–36. **Former federal ... claims as bogus.** Interviews with Gonzalez Ruiz and comment from US Embassy in Mexico City. **Nearly a year ... off the hook.** Interviews with former PGR officials and local journalists; *El Universal*, ' "El Chapo" created a network of complicit [people]', by Francisco Gomez, 19.4.2001; *La Jornada*, 'The CNDH alerted Gertz about Puente Grande', by Victor Ballinas, Andrea Becerril and Juan Antonio Zuniga, 31.1.2001. **In 1995 ... prophesied.** PGR. **On 12 October ... statement.** PGR statement, 12.10.2000. **By this time ... military manhunt.** *El Universal*, ' "El Chapo" created a network of complicit [people]', by Francisco Gomez, 19.4.2001. **The official story ... laundry cart.** Interviews with former PGR officials and local journalists; *El Universal*, ' "El Chapo" created a network of complicit [people]', by Francisco Gomez, 19.4.2001; *La Jornada*, 'The CNDH alerted Gertz about Puente Grande', by Victor Ballinas, Andrea Becerril and Juan Antonio Zuniga, 31.1.2001. **On 15 January 2001 ... to another facility.** Ricardo Ravelo, *Los Capos*, Random House Mondadori, 2005. **Lyrics from 'La Fuga del Chapo'.** Planeta deletras.com.

Chapter 2

Articles used for reconstruction of escape and pursuit: *El Universal*, 'Search for narco is questioned', by staff writers, 23.1.2001; *El Universal*, '500 police track "El Chapo" Guzman', by Pablo Cesar Carrillo, 31.1.2001; *El Universal*, 'The search for Chapo intensifies', by Jorge Alejandro Medellin, 24.1.2001; *El Universal*, 'CNDH warns of more escapes from Puente Grande', by Bertha Fernandez, 24.1.2001; *El Universal*, 'They're searching for "Chapo" in Guatemala', by staff writers, 18.2.2001; *El Universal*, ' "El Chapo" could be in the country, says Macedo', by Jorge Alejandro Medellin, 15.2.2001; *El Universal*, 'Raids in search of "Chapo" ', by staff writers, 24.1.2001; *El Universal*, 'Order of 73 arrested for the escape of "Chapo" ', by Jorge Alejandro Medellin, 23.2.2001; *Reforma*, 'Kids are joking around with the PFP; they're giving leads on "El Chapo" ', by Denis Rodriguez, 24.1.2001; *Reforma*, ' "El Chapo" left prison as if it were his house', by Cecilia Gonzalez, 23.1.2001.

As more than ... full swing. *El Universal*, '500 police track "El Chapo" Guzman', by Pablo Cesar Carrillo, 31.1.2001; *El Universal*, 'The search for Chapo intensifies', by Jorge Alejandro Medellin, 24.1.2001. **State human rights ... other things.** *Reforma*, 'CNDH denies intervention in Puente Grande prison', by Ivabelle Arroyo and Antonio Navarrete, 22.1.2001; *El Universal*, 'CNDH warns of more escapes from Puente Grande', by Bertha Fernandez, 24.1.2001; *Reforma*, ' "El Chapo" left prison as if it were his house', by Cecilia Gonzalez, 23.1.2001. **Tello Peon wondered why ... of their rights.** About a dozen articles on the escape and aftermath from *El Universal*, *Reforma* and *La Jornada*. **Mauricio Limon Aguirre ... had been sidelined.** *Reforma*, 'Investigation problems', by Alicia Calderon and Francisco Junco, 23.1.2001. **Those locals ... asked about one.** *Reforma*, 'Kids are joking around with the PFP; they're giving leads on "El Chapo" ', by Denis Rodriguez, 24.1.2001. **Tello Peon ... civil servant.** *Reforma*, '[Authorities] recognize incapacity against organized crime', by staff writers, 22.1.2001. **From that day ... most wanted man.** PGR. **In 2001 alone ... Reclusorio Preventivo Oriente.** PGR Annual Report, 2001. **Back in Guadalajara ... Mr Guzman Loera.** Ricardo Ravelo, *Los Capos*, Random House Mondadori, 2005. **The authorities ... be in luck.** *El Universal*, 'PGR closes in on "Chapo;" arrests brother and two bodyguards', by Jorge Alejandro Medellin, 8.9.2001; PGR Annual Report, 2001. **That autumn ... still no**

Chapo. Transcript of PGR press conference, 20.12.2001. **On another occasion ... deeply worrying.** *El Universal*, 'The other escapes of "El Chapo"', by Francisco Gomez, 20.5.2008; *El Universal*, 'He was hiding in Zinacantepec', by Teresa Montano Delgado, 11.9.2001; *El Universal*, '"El Chapo" takes advantage of errors to flee', by Teresa Montano Delgado, 8.10.2001; *El Universal*, '"El Chapo" is operating with total freedom throughout the country', by Francisco Gomez, 9.10.2004. **Rumours ... personal reasons.** Interviews with officials and journalists throughout Mexico; *El Universal*, 'Tello Peon, the illegal', by Ricardo Aleman, 30.3.2009; *Reforma*, '"Chapo" will seek to regain power – Gutierrez Rebollo', by Isaac Guzman and Andres Zuniga, 29.1.2001; *La Jornada*, 'Tello Peon, executive secretary of security system', by Claudia Herrera Beltran, 26.3.2009. **But as the year ... was still free.** PGR statements; author's interviews with former PGR officials.

Chapter 3

Lyrics from 'El Hijo de La Tuna'. Musica.com. **The hills ... like snow.** Mexican military aerial photos of the Sinaloan mountains, Google Earth images. **It was here ... in the nineteenth century.** Interviews with historians Luis Astorga and Martin Amaral. **And it was here ... 1957.** PGR. (Note: Sometimes Chapo's birthdate is listed as 25 December; that is incorrect.) **La Tuna had ... they'd inherited.** Interviews with locals in Badiraguato. The names of Chapo's kin come from an array of newspaper articles and statements from the Mexican authorities. **There's a famous ... promise.** George W. Grayson, *Mexico: Narco-violence and a failed state?*, Transaction, 2009, p. 269. **Most people ... 'Others are rich.'** Interviews with locals, officials, congressman Aaron Irizar Lopez, human rights commissioner Juan Jose Rios Estavillo. **Like most ... his life.** Julio Scherer, *Maxima Seguridad*, Random House Mondadori, 2002, p. 22. **But unlike his predecessors ... Sinaloans could grow.** Interviews with Luis Astorga. **Chapo's**

father ... same way today. Interviews with locals and officials in Badiraguato; interviews with Mexican military stationed in Sinaloa and throughout Mexico. Chapo's own father ... the United States. DEA. If you confuse ... in Sinaloa. Mendoza quoted in Diego Enrique Osorno, *El Cartel de Sinaloa*, Random House Mondadori, 2009, p. 27. Sinaloa wasn't always ... completely buried. Interviews with historian Martin Amaral. During the pre-Hispanic ... open to change. Sergio Ortega Noriega, *Breve Historia de Sinaloa*, Colegio de Mexico, 1999. Walking through ... you are there. Author's own impressions of Culiacan. Turning ... DEA agent. Interviews with anonymous DEA agent. The indigenous ... the New World. Noriega, *Breve Historia de Sinaloa*. In late 1810 ... independence. Mexican government's National Institute for Federalism and Municipal Development, INAFED. Since then ... among locals. Interviews with Astorga and Amaral. Legend had it ... revered symbol. Interviews with Jesus Manuel Gonzalez Sanchez. Violence is rife ... lot of attention. Interviews with Astorga, Amaral and Luis Ricardo Ruiz. The US government was ... the US market. *New York Times*, 'President orders wider drug fight; asks $155 million', by Dana Adams Schmidt, 18.6.1971; DEA *History Book*, '1970–1975' (pp. 3–23), '1975–1980' (pp. 24–42). Those who chose ... remained behind. Writings of Miguel Angel Felix Gallardo, published via his son Josue at miguelfelixgallardo.com; author's interviews with Astorga, Amaral, Ruiz, Irizar Lopez, Rios Estavillo and locals throughout Sinaloa. Eventually ... many battles. DEA *History Book*, '1975–1980' (pp. 24–42). Shortly after ... charge of it all. PGR. Even well into ... overseeing shipments. DEA interviews and congressional testimonies of DEA agents and administrators. According to ... was being offered. Interviews with local journalists, residents and officials of Badiraguato, Tamazula and Durango; interview with Astorga. The bosses ... in the United States. *Los Angeles Times*, 'Mexico's master of elusion', by Richard Boudreaux, 5.7.2005.

Chapter 4

Born on ... Institutional Revolutionary Party (PRI). Interviews with Josue Felix and Luis Astorga; George W. Grayson, *Mexico: Narco-violence and a failed state?*, Transaction, 2009. **The PRI ... all over Sonora.'** Interviews with Manuel Clouthier Carrillo; various newspaper articles; interviews with anonymous US state prosecutor. **El Padrino rose ... offered him protection.** Felix Gallardo's writings; Grayson, *Mexico: Narco-violence*. **El Padrino was a soft-spoken ... too much attention.** Interview with Josue Felix. **While still living ... Operation Trizo.** Interviews with Josue Felix and Luis Astorga. **Chapo learned ... and Griselda Guadalupe.** *Reforma*, ' "El Chapo" has six more children', by staff writers, 11.5.2008. **At the same time ... his own right.** Testimony before the US National Security, International Affairs and Criminal Justice Subcommittee of House Government Reform and Oversight Committee by DEA Administrator Thomas Constantine, 25.2.1997. **Chapo was ready ... for instance.** Interviews with DEA agents, past and present; *Reforma*, 'Investigation demanded into political-narco connections', by staff writers, 9.12.2009. **By the mid-1980s ... run it for them.** Interviews with DEA agents past and present. **At the time ... human chess game.** Transcript of a lecture at the DEA museum by the DEA's Michael Vigil, 2003; interviews with DEA agents past and present. **In late 1984 ... list went on.** Interviews with DEA agents past and present; transcript of a lecture at the DEA museum by the DEA's Michael Vigil, 2003; DEA's 'Biography of DEA employees killed in action'; transcript of a lecture at the DEA museum by former DEA Special Agent Robert Stutman, 2005; DEA *History Book*, '1985–1990' (p. 64); US Department of Justice. **So in 1987 ... Sinaloan city.** Interviews with Josue Felix and Luis Astorga. **El Padrino also decided ... one-man show.** Interview with Jesus Blancornelas, 2004; interviews with Astorga and security expert Jorge Chabat; Diego Enrique Osorno, *El Cartel de Sinaloa*, Random House Mondadori, 2009, p. 239; Ricardo Ravelo,

Los Capos, Random House Mondadori, 2005, pp. 85–108; writings of Miguel Angel Felix Gallardo. **On 8 April 1989 ... the betrayal.** Writings of Miguel Angel Felix Gallardo. **For decades ... Jorge Hank Rhon.** Interviews with Jose Ramos, Jorge Hank Rhon, Jesus Blancornelas and Victor Clark Alfaro since 2004; Tijuana government website. **Carlos Hank Gonzalez ... poor politician.** *New York Times*, 'Carlos Hank Gonzalez, 73, veteran Mexican politician', 13.8.2001. **A senior ... political system.** Statement before the Senate Foreign Relations Committee by Andrew A. Reding, director of the Americas Project at the World Policy Institute. **It quickly became ... fourteen of them.** Interview with Jorge Hank Rhon, 2004; interview with Jesus Blancornelas, 2004. **A father ... animals.** *La Jornada*, 'From the poor politician to poor politics', by Arturo Cano, 25.7.2004. **Hank Rhon's alleged. . . to violence.** *Insight* magazine, 'Family affairs', by Jaime Dettmer, 29.3.1999. **The Arellano Felix brothers ... from Sinaloa.** Interviews with former DEA Special Agent Errol Chavez; Mexican government statistics institute, INEGI. **Killing was sometimes ... such impunity.** Interviews with former DEA Special Agent Errol Chavez; interview with Jesus Blancornelas and Victor Alfaro Clark; *Guardian*, 'Blood brothers', by Julian Borger and Jo Tuckman; CBS News online report, '17 Indicted in Calif. murder-kidnap ring', culled from AP and CBS sources, 14.8.2009; various DEA testimonies before US Senate and House; Jesus Blancornelas, *El Cartel*, Debolsillo, 2004. **In 1994 ... before a court.** *La Jornada*, 'The murder of Colosio, the work of a narco or a lone assassin – PGR', by correspondents, 4.1.1999. **Hank Rhon ... as mayor.** Interview with Jorge Hank Rhon, 2004. **Indeed ... been accepted.** *Insight* magazine, 'DEA's "White Tiger" still on the prowl', by Jamie Dettmer, 29.10.2002. **Hector Felix Miranda ... after their trials.** Interview with Jesus Blancornelas, 2004, and various editions of his weekly, known as *Zeta*. **Hank was never ... allegations.** Interview with Jorge Hank Rhon, 2004. **The DEA ... to California.** DEA and PGR statements. **The eldest ...**

surrounding Ciudad Juarez. *New York Times*, 'Drug ties taint 2 Mexican governors', by Sam Dillon and Craig Pyes, 23.2.1997; *New York Times*, 'Drug Barons and plastic surgeons: Who's dead, who's hiding?', by Sam Dillon, 7.11.1997; *New York Times*, 'Court files say drug baron used Mexican military', by Sam Dillon and Craig Pyes, 24.5.1997; testimony before Senate Foreign Relations Committee by DEA Administrator Thomas Constantine, 8.8.1995; transcript of a lecture at the DEA museum by the DEA's Michael Vigil, 2003; *El Sol de San Juan de Rio*, 'Amado Carrillo's parties', by Sergio Arturo Venegas R., 26.11.2007; *El Universal*, 'The history of Amado Carrillo Fuentes "The Lord of the Skies"', by Jose Perez-Espino and Alejandro Paez Varela, 3.4.2009.

Chapter 5

Descriptions of Chapo's personality and manner of operating are drawn from interviews with DEA agents past and present, dozens of newspaper articles primarily from *El Universal* and *Reforma*, Ravelo's books, interviews with locals and self-alleged operatives in Sinaloa, PGR, Mexican military and federal police statements; *San Diego Union-Tribune*, 'U.S. indicts drug trafficker held in slaying of cardinal', by Stacy Finz, 29.9.1995. The document regarding his psychological mindset was published in various Mexican newspapers; I confirmed with three ex-federal police officials that it was indeed accurate. The events of the Guadalajara shooting have been pieced together from newspaper accounts and the PGR's own documents on the incident, as well as interviews with former officials.

The arrangement ... unyielding ambition. Interviews with DEA agents past and present. **He was ... alive.** Julio Scherer, *Maxima Seguridad*, Random House Mondadori, 2002, pp. 9–36. **His main adviser ... bad for business.** Ricardo Ravelo, *Los Capos*, Random House Mondadori, 2005; FBI Most-Wanted Fugitives bulletin; *Milenio*, 'The capture of El Chapo Guzman is a priority for the U.S.', by staff writers, 16.11.2008; *El Mexicano*, 'Ruffo and Franco Rios protected the Arellano Felix: "El Chapo"', by Nestor Ojeda, 8.7.2002. **In the Sierra ... trespassers coming.** Author's observations in Sinaloa; interviews with anonymous soldiers. **Occasionally ... any disturbances.** *La Voz de Tucson*, 'Arizona sheltering drug trafficking networks', by Samuel Murillo and Angel Larreal, 30.8.2006. **Miguel Angel Segoviano ... finally caught.** *Wall Street Journal*, 'The drug lord who got away', by David Luhnow and Jose de Cordoba, 13.6.2009. **At any one time ... to relay his orders.** Calculation of number of Chapo employees based on Mexican Defence Secretariat's calculations of organized crime membership in Mexico and military statements. **In Oaxaca ... it read.** *La Jornada*, 'The new geography of the narco', Alberto Najar, 24.7.2005; *El Pais*, 'One of the most-wanted head "narcos" captured in Mexico', by Francesc Relea, 19.1.2007. **In Guerrero ... and, naturally, Sinaloa.** *El Mexicano*, 'Ruffo and Franco Rios protected the Arellano Felix: "El Chapo"', by Nestor Ojeda, 8.7.2002. **Anyone could ... a word.** *La Voz de Tucson*, 'Arizona sheltering drug trafficking networks', by Samuel Murillo and Angel Larreal, 30.8.2006. **Chapo had first ... back to Sinaloa.** Indictment: United States vs. Joaquin Guzman, a.k.a. 'El Chappo [*sic*]', United States District Court, District of Arizona, 8.8.2001. **Another indictment ... US counterparts.** United States of America vs. Arlene Newland, Antonio Hernandez-Menendez, Santos Hernandez-Menendez, Nick Newland, United States Court of Appeals for the Ninth Circuit; Argued and submitted 15.9.1994, decided 14.7.1995. **This was ... underestimated.** Interviews with DEA Special Agent Errol Chavez. **Indeed, Chapo had ... Ciudad Juarez.** Ravelo, *Los Capos*; author's interviews with Jesus Blancornelas and Gonzalez Ruiz. **Like the other capos ... it worked.** Testimony before the House Committee on Government Reform by DEA Special Agent Errol Chavez, 13.4.2001. **It was slow ... to Agua Prieta.** Testimony before the House Government Reform and Oversight Committee by DEA Chief of Operations Donnie Marshall, 18.3.1998. **Chapo was**

getting ... deliveries. *San Diego Union-Tribune*, 'U.S. indicts drug trafficker held in slaying of cardinal', by Stacy Finz, 29.9.1995. **Chapo was also ... tankers.** 'America's Most-Wanted'. **In early May ... getting through.** United States of America vs. Felipe de Jesus Corona-Verbera, US Court of Appeals for the Ninth Circuit; Argued and submitted 15.10.2007, filed 7.12.2007; KOLD News, 'Drug tunnel architect faces 20 years', by Som Lisaius, date unknown; *Arizona Republic*, 'Architect of tunnel for smuggling drugs sentenced to 18 years', by Dennis Wagner, 22.8.2006. **And with each ... his ambition.** *Washington Post*, 'Drugs worth "billions" moved through tunnel', by Kevin Sullivan, 1.3.2002; author's interviews with DEA Special Agent Errol Chavez. **He thinks big ... Tons.** *Los Angeles Times*, 'Mexico's master of elusion', by Richard Boudreaux, 5.7.2005. **Cheap, disposable ... killed.** Interviews with DEA agents past and present. **This made it ... from Tijuana.** Interviews with DEA Special Agent Errol Chavez. **Chapo was ... Chapo's head.** *Los Angeles Times* magazine, 'Muerto, Inc.', by Michael Goodman, 1997. **In early 1992 ... was Jorge Hank Rhon.** Interviews with former federal officials; *Los Angeles Times* magazine, 'Muerto, Inc.', by Michael Goodman, 1997; *Reforma*, 'Witnesses testify that Arellano didn't participate in the shootout', by Fermin Vazquez, 25.5.1994; transcripts of lectures from former DEA special agents from DEA Museum. **That Chapo had eluded ... Jorge Ramos Perez. PGR. On 31 May ... been betrayed.** Transcript of lecture from former DEA special agents from DEA Museum. **It's unclear ... unprecedented levels.** Mark Bowden, *Killing Pablo: The Hunt for the World's Greatest Outlaw*, Penguin Books, 2001, p. 51; author's interviews with DEA agents past and present. **Once in the Mexican ... Arellano Felix brothers.** *El Mexicano*, 'Ruffo and Franco Rios protected the Arellano Felix: "El Chapo"', by Nestor Ojeda, 8.7.2002. **Francisco ... Ramon Arellano Felix.** 'Drug trafficking in Mexico: A first general assessment', by Luis Astorga, UNESCO. **$40 billion ... some estimates.** Interviews with experts and DEA statements. **By the new**

millennium ... in many U.S. cities. Testimony before House Government Reform and Oversight Committee by DEA Administrator Thomas Constantine, 19.3.1998. Along the south-western ... uncovered. DEA. Whereas before ... favourite. Interviews with Ismael Bojorquez. 'This guy ... too many families.' Statement from the office of President Vicente Fox, 30.5.2005.

Chapter 6

As the rain ... in blood, too. Interviews and observations with locals and officials in Badiraguato and Culiacan. One Friday night ... age two. *El Sol de Mazatlan*, 'Soldiers kill a family in Sinaloa de Leyva', by staff writers, 3.6.2007; *Reforma*, 'Two women and three children die in shootout', by staff writers, 3.6.2007; *Reforma*, 'Sedena pays $8 million for violations', by Benito Jimenez, 13.12.2009. in Santiago de los Caballeros ... the governor's office. Interviews with locals and officials in Badiraguato; Mexican Defence Secretariat; *Reforma*, 'Sedena pays $8 million for violations', by Benito Jimenez, 13.12.2009. Omar Meza ... increasingly popular. Interviews with Omar Meza; *Noroeste*, 'Corrido of massacre composed', by Sergio Lozano, 31.3.2008. But for the likes ... you killed. *New York Times*, 'Songs of love and murder, silenced by killings', by James McKinley Jr, 18.12.2007. One narco-corrido crooner ... twenty-eight times. *El Universal*, '[Authorities] confirm that a song killed Valentin', by Noemi Gutierrez, 27.11.2006. Chapo is a big ... his honour. Interviews with locals in Badiraguato and Culiacan. In one instance ... Chapo himself. *Los Angeles Times*, 'Mexico's master of elusion', by Richard Boudreaux, 5.7.2005; Deutsche Presse-Agentur, 'Mexican music group detained for playing for a drug trafficker', 15.11.2003; PGR. The members ... narco-culture. Notimex, 'Narco-corridos banned on public transport in Tijuana', by staff writers, 12.1.2009; *Milenio*, 'Narco-corridos banned on city buses in Nayarit', by staff writers, 11.1.2010. Yudit del Rincon ... out the door. Interviews with Yudit del Rincon; *Los Angeles Times*, 'In Sinaloa, the drug trade has infiltrated "every corner of life"', by Tracy Wilkinson, 28.12.2008. **Fighting the culture ... 'Los Gotcha'.** Various Mexican newspaper articles, 2007–9. **Several years back ... some apocryphal.** Interviews with locals and officials in Badiraguato. **Once ... thief's hands.** *Wall Street Journal*, 'The drug lord who got away', by David Luhnow and Jose de Cordoba, 13.6.2009. **But today ... the situation.** Interviews with locals and officials in Badiraguato. **In 2006 ... he said.** *El Pais*, 'In Chapo's domain', by Francesc Relea, 2.2.2007. **The narcos ... this code.** Interviews with locals and officials in Badiraguato and Culiacan. **Sinaloa consistently ... indebted to them.** Sinaloa state police; author's interviews with Sinaloa Police Chief Josefina de Jesus Garcia Ruiz and members of her staff; *Newsweek*, 'El Chapo: The most wanted man in Mexico', by Joshua Hammer, 18.6.2009; author's interviews with locals in Culiacan. **A group ... the law.** Interviews in Badiraguato. **The culture ... understand it.** Interviews with Martin Amaral. **The average ... is killed.** Sinaloa state police department. **On the outskirts ... well known.** Author's observations of the cemetery. **Years ago ... off a bridge.** Andres Oppenheimer, *Bordering on Chaos*, Little, Brown and Company, 1996, p. 299; interviews with journalists in Sinaloa. **A fresco ... the building.** Author's observations of the cemetery. **On another ... lodged in his head.** *Rio Doce*, 'Bloody war', by Cayetano Osuna, 7.9.2009; various articles from the Sinaloan newspapers *El Debate* and *Noroeste*. **Many ... No Names.** Interview with anonymous forensic specialist in Culiacan.

Chapter 7

General Noe Sandoval Alcazar ... spring up again. Author's observations of and interviews with the general in Culiacan, June 2008. **Mexico's military ... about 10,000.** Interviews with Luis Astorga; 'Drug trafficking in Mexico: A First General Assessment', by Luis Astorga, UNESCO. **In 1996 a general... high-energy**

man. *Los Angeles Times*, 'General Gutierrez to head up Mexico's war against drugs', by Mark Fineman, 6.12.1996. **Less than six . . . the drug cartels.** PGR statement, 13.8.1997; *El Universal*, 'Sentence confirmed for Gutierrez Rebollo', by Jorge Alejandro Medellin, 29.9.2000. **In the summer . . . drug business.** Observations of and interviews with General Sandoval. **In 2004 . . . actually catch him.** Interviews with locals and local journalists in Sinaloa and Durango. **Later that same year . . . National Security Committee.** *San Antonio Express-News*, ' "El Chapo" is Mexico's most wanted man', by Dane Schiller, 19.6.2005; *Los Angeles Times*, 'Mexico's master of elusion', by Richard Boudreaux, 5.7.2005.

Account of General Eddy's fight against Chapo: *El Universal*, 'The personal "war" between a general and "El Chapo" ', by Juan Velediaz, 13.10.2007; *Milenio*, 'Guzman Loera versus Hidalgo Eddy. The tale of a duel', by staff writers, 16.11.2008; *El Universal*, ' "El Chapo" leaves a trail of intimidation and death', by Juan Velediaz, 6.11.2006; *La Cronica*, 'General who tracked El Chapo decorated', by Daniel Blancas Madrigal, 10.2.2008; *Excelsior*, 'Archives of power: loyalties', by Martin Moreno, 12.2.2008; background information on 'The Empress' from US Department of the Treasury's Office of Foreign Assets Control (OFAC), statement issued 12.12.2007; *El Universal*, 'Account of capture of El Chapo Guzman still unconfirmed', by Javier Cabrera Martinez, 8.10.2007.

The military base . . . sent us soldiers. *El Sol de Sinaloa*, 'Excitement in Badiraguato ahead of troops' arrival', by Juan Manuel Pineda, 15.1.2007. **Several hundred . . . in the future.** *Milenio*, 'Guzman Loera versus Hidalgo Eddy. The tale of a duel', by staff writers, 16.11.2008. **The complaints . . . trashed the ranch.** Interviews with locals and officials in Badiraguato. **For General Sandoval . . . play dead.** *El Debate*, 'Noe Sandoval: There is no war in Sinaloa', by Rafael Gonzalez, 5.5.2008. **His strategy . . . narcos' necks.** Interviews with the general and his men in Sinaloa. **This was President Felipe Calderon's . . . be arrested.** Interviews with Luis

Astorga, Jorge Chabat and other rights and legal experts in Mexico. **General Sandoval's strategy ... the locals.** *Noroeste*, 'Granadazo in the barracks', by staff writers, 12.11.2008; *Noroeste*, 'Army takes Navolato ...', by staff writers, 12.11.2008; *Noroeste*, 'General "colds" mayor of Navolato', by Martin Gonzalez, 12.12.2008. **The helicopter landed ... and chuckling again.** Author's observations of and interviews with the general and his men in Sinaloa.

Chapter 8

While Chapo ... businesses flowing. PGR. El Mayo ... $20-million debt. *Los Angeles Times*, 'Coastal drug kingpin eyes Tijuana turf', by Chris Kraul, 19.3.2002. **First ... Michael Vigil.** Transcript of a lecture at the DEA museum by the DEA's Michael Vigil, 2003; *New York Times*, 'Drug barons and plastic surgeons: Who's dead, who's hiding?', by Sam Dillon, 7.11.1997. **The Arellano Felix brothers and the Gulf cartel ... as 'The Federation'.** Interviews with DEA special agents past and present. **They made ... Alfredo de la Torre.** California Southern District Drug Threat Assessment, December 2000; interviews with former DEA Special Agent Errol Chavez; testimony before the Subcommittee on Criminal Justice Oversight by Chief of International Operations William E. Ledwith, 16.5.2000. **The Arellano Felix brothers weren't keen ... Benjamin's brother.** *El Sol de Mazatlan*, 'It was on a Carnival Sunday that Ramon Arellano Felix died', by Luis E. Fernandez, 22.2.2009; CBS News/AP, 'Portrait of a Mexican drug lord', by Bootie Cosgrove-Mather, 24.10.2003. **El Mayo and Chapo ... the decade. DEA. El Mayo, meanwhile ... within US borders.** 'Organized crime and terrorist activity in Mexico, 1999–2002', by the Federal Research Division, Library of Congress, February 2003; *Milenio*, 'Principal money launderer for El Chapo Guzman extradited to United States', by Pedro Alfonso Alatorre Damy, 25.11.2008; *Noticieros Televisa*, 'Ismael Zambada Garcia, untouchable for 20 years', by Enrique Gil

Vargas, 1.8.2003; Notimex, ' "El Mayo" compared to Al Capone', by staff writers, 2.3.2004; *Frontera NorteSur*, 'Mexican drug lord Zambada had plastic surgery, visits US', by Agustin Perez Aguilar, 19.4.2004; *El Universal*, 'Madrazo accuses: Zedillo and Fox protected narcos', by Fidel Samaniego, 12.5.2009; Associated Press, 'How Mexico's new drug kingpin rose', by Will Weissert, 24.10.2003; author's interviews with former DEA Special Agent Errol Chavez. **Annually . . . the payload.** US Department of Justice, statement regarding Operation Trifecta indictments, 31.7.2003; interviews with DEA agents past and present. **Whereas Chapo . . . continues to flow.** US Department of the Treasury, Office of Foreign Assets Control (OFAC); the PGR office in Culiacan. **With the fall of . . . pushing their luck.** Interviews with former DEA Special Agent Errol Chavez and Jesus Blancornelas. **The Colombians . . . the DEA believed.** Interviews with former DEA Special Agent Errol Chavez; 'Organized crime and terrorist activity in Mexico, 1999–2002', by the Federal Research Division, Library of Congress, February 2003; US Department of the Treasury, Office of Foreign Assets Control (OFAC). **But Chapo . . . such a routine.** Testimony of protected witness, from *El Universal*, ' "El Chapo" is operating with total freedom throughout the country', by Francisco Gomez, 9.10.2004. **This was how . . . bars again.** Description of mindset drawn from interviews with DEA special agents; Zulema Hernandez's recollections in Puente Grande; newspaper articles; PGR statements. **On Friday . . . no one else.** *El Universal*, 'PGR raids residential neighbourhoods', by Javier Cabrera and Teresa Montano, 15.6.2002. **On Tuesday . . . no Chapo.** *El Universal*, ' "Chapo" tracked on outskirts of Atizapan', by staff writers, 3.7.2002. **The DEA's Chavez . . . just missed him.** Interviews with former DEA Special Agent Errol Chavez. **Chapo was also . . . best of intelligence.** *El Universal*, 'The Beltran Leyvas infiltrated SIEDO', by Silvia Otero, 13.8.2008; *El Universal*, 'Operation Cleanup rocks the PGR', by Francisco Gomez, 27.12.2008; *El Universal*, 'PGR officials linked to the Beltrans', by Silvia Otero, 13.8.2008; Reuters,

'Mexico presidential guardsman accused of drug ties', 27.12.2008; *Los Angeles Times*, 'Mexico acknowledges drug gang infiltration of police', by Tracy Wilkinson, 28.10.2008; *El Economista*, 'Corruption, key to the Beltran Leyvas' power', 18.12.2009; *Rio Doce*, 'El Barbas . . .', by staff writers, 21.12.2009. By 2003 Chapo was . . . the first time. Author's own conclusions based on interviews with DEA agents. Juan Garcia Abrego . . . Brownsville, Texas. PGR; Ricardo Ravelo, *Osiel: Life and tragedy of a capo*, Grijalbi Mondadori, 2009. The population of Matamoros . . . industrial plants. Government of Matamoros. Like Chapo . . . Gulf cartel. PGR. The United States . . . life in prison. *New York Times*, 'Mexican drug gang's reign of blood', by Sam Dillon, 4.2.1996; *New York Times*, 'U.S. jury convicts Mexican on drug charges', no byline, 17.10.1996; *New York Times*, 'At drug trial, Mexican suspect faces accuser', no byline, 20.9.1996. The fall of Garcia Abrego . . . key ally in the Gulf cartel. *El Universal*, 'Who is Osiel Cardenas?', by Francisco Gomez, 14.3.2003; *Proceso*, 'Osiel Cardenas: Seat of power, seat of blood', by Ricardo Ravelo, September 2009; Ravelo, *Osiel: Life and tragedy of a capo*; *Houston Chronicle*, 'Tracing the origins of the Gulf Cartel empire', by Dane Schiller, 3.1.2010. In 1997 Cardenas Guillen . . . burned them to death. 'Los Zetas: the ruthless army spawned by a Mexican drug cartel', by George W. Grayson, Foreign Policy Research Institute, May 2008; Dossierpolitico.com, 'Drug trafficking reorganizes with blood and fire', 20.6.2005; *El Universal*, ' "Los Zetas" from within', by Francisco Gomez, 31.12.2008; 'National Drug Threat Assessment 2008', National Drug Intelligence Center, October 2007. Chapo wasn't to be . . . supported them. *Noroeste*, 'Who is Edgar Valdez Villareal?', by staff writers, 30.9.2008; ' "El Chapo" is Mexico's most wanted man', by Dane Schiller, 19.6.2005; *Dallas Morning News*, 'Lieutenant in Mexican drug cartel a wanted man', by Lennox Samuels, 20.3.2006; *El Universal*, 'La Barbie, El Chapo's executioner', by Silvia Otero, 25.12.2005. The city of Nuevo Laredo . . . major arrests. *Milenio*, 'Los Zetas: Histories of nobody', by Diego Enrique

Osorno, 5.12.2007; *New York Times*, 'Rival drug gangs turn the streets of Nuevo Laredo into a war zone', by Ginger Thompson, 4.12.2005; ABC News/Nightline, 'Drug "war zone" rattles U.S.–Mexico border', 8.1.2006. **The latter had ... the Gulf cartel.** *San Antonio Express-News*, 'Prosecutors set to take on suspected Gulf Cartel leader', by Dane Schiller, 18.2.2007; transcripts of lectures by DEA agents from DEA museum; *Reforma*, 'U.S. wants Mexican capo', by Maribel Gonzalez, 15.12.2000. **In the early morning ... Cardenas Guillen's place.** *El Universal*, 'Osiel Cardenas falls', by Francisco Gomez, 15.3.2003; *Reforma*, 'Gulf cartel capo falls', by Juan Jose Ramirez and Abel Barajas, 15.3.2003; DEA statement, 21.3.2003. **Just months after ... Gulf cartel territory.** *El Universal*, ' "El Chapo" is operating with total freedom throughout the country', by Francisco Gomez, 9.10.2004. **Los Zetas ... simply intensified.** *Laredo Morning Times*/AP, 'Osiel pleads not guilty; used "Zetas" to control Nuevo Laredo in takeover', no byline, 10.2.2007. **After Chapo's visit ... law and order.** *La Jornada*, 'The new geography of the narco', by Alberto Najar, 24.7.2005. **When a humble ... and investigated.** *Washington Post*, 'Border police chief only latest casualty in Mexico drug war', by Mary Jordan and Kevin Sullivan, 16.6.2005; *New York Times*, 'Police chief gunned down on his first day', by Antonio Betancourt, 10.6.2005. **In 2009 an eerie ... happened to Mexico.** Author's reporting in Reynosa and Matamoros; *New York Times*, 'In Mexican city, drug war ills slip into shadows', by Marc Lacey, 12.6.2009.

Chapter 9

Although he ... had other ideas. *Los Angeles Times*, 'Mexico's master of elusion', by Richard Boudreaux, 5.7.2005. **Not only ... one's skin.** Interviews with former DEA Special Agent Errol Chavez. **Meth ... equipment.** White House Office of National Drug Control Policy, whitehousedrugpolicy.gov. **Jose de Jesus Amezcua Contreras ... coordinate shipments.** Various DEA congressional testimonies; White House Office of National Drug Control Policy. **Chapo seized ... worth of meth.** McClatchy newspapers, 'A madness called meth', 8.10.2000; interviews with DEA agents past and present. **Whereas ... own market.** Interviews with former DEA Special Agent Errol Chavez. **Chapo was expanding ... Gilberto Osuna.** PGR and DEA statements; Notimex, 'Chapo Guzman: Five years after his escape', by Gustavo Ramirez Ibarra, 18.1.2006. **He placed ... 'the Crystal King'.** *El Universal*, 'Ignacio Nacho Coronel Villareal, "El Chapo's financial brain"', by staff writers, 2.6.2008; *El Universal*, 'Nacho Coronel expands his "crystal" kingdom', by Juan Velediaz, 9.10.2008. **Chapo was also ... size up the turf.** *Proceso*, 'El Capo del PANismo', by Ricardo Ravelo, 15.3.2009. **Chapo knew that ... main Juarez rival.** *Noroeste*, 'The death of Rodolfo Carrillo', by Guadalupe Martinez, 11.9.2008; *EFE*, 'Death of Rodolfo Carrillo confirmed', no byline, 13.9.2004; *Noticieros Televisa*, 'Death of Rodolfo Carrillo Fuentes confirmed', by Enrique Gil Vargas, 12.9.2004. **After Rodolfo's death ... out of fear.** PGR press conference, 21.11.2005. **That New Year's Eve ... was Rodolfo Carrillo Fuentes.** *La Cronica*, 'Five lines of investigation in El Pollo's murder', by Ramon Sevilla, 4.1.2005; PGR statement issued 2.7.2008 ('Jose Ramirez Villanueva is sentenced to 42 years'); *El Universal*, 'El Pollo's assassin contradicts himself in statements', by Silvia Otero, 8.1.2005; *El Universal*, 'PGR takes case of the killing of Chapo's brother', by Francisco Gomez and Maria Teresa Montano, 2.1.2005. **Another huge blow ... of his father.** PGR statement, 15.2.2005. **Then in June ... best lawyer.** *El Universal*, 'Brother of El Chapo arrested at party', by Jorge Alejandro Medellin, Javier Cabrera and Giovana Gaxiola, 16.6.2005; *Noticieros Televisa*, 'Brother of "El Chapo" Guzman arrested', by Enrique Gil Vargas, 15.6.2005; *El Universal*, 'Charges against El Chapo's brothers without proof, they say', by Javier Cabrera Martinez, 18.6.2005. **Deep down ... criminal forfeiture.** DEA statement, 20.12.2004. **The DEA's agents ... more out there.** *Los Angeles Times*, 'Mexico's master of elusion', by Richard Boudreaux, 5.7.2005.

The Mexican authorities ... leads on Chapo. PGR press conference, 30.5.2005.

Chapter 10

Who sent you? ... policemen were killed. *El Universal*, 'Chief of anti-narco operations murdered', by staff writers, 8.5.2008; *Los Angeles Times*, 'With killing, Mexico drug war is seen as entering a new phase', by Hector Tobar, 18.5.2008; Notimex, 'Edgar Millan detained assassins before his death', no byline, 8.5.2008; *El Universal*, 'Profile: Edgar Eusebio Millan Gomez', by staff writers, 8.5.2008. Good cops ... Beltran Leyva brothers. Mini-profile of Genaro Garcia Luna drawn from interviews with anonymous federal agents and advisers who have worked with him, George W. Grayson, Jorge Chabat; *El Universal*, 'The SSP's engineer', by Alejandro Jimenez, 29.12.2008; *New York Times* magazine, 'The long war of Genaro Garcia Luna', by Daniel Kurtz-Phelan, 13.7.2008; *El Universal*, 'Calderon heads tribute to Edgar Millan', by Maria de la Luz Gonzalez, 9.5.2008; AFP, 'Narcos linked to "Chapo" Guzman arrested', no byline, 13.9.2003; *El Universal*, 'Garcia Luna: SSP is working to capture El Chapo', no byline, 13.3.2008; *Proceso*, 'Garcia Luna, incriminated', by Ricardo Ravelo, 23.11.2008; *El Debate*, 'Banners accuse officials of protecting Sinaloa cartel', by staff writers, 10.10.2008; author's interview with DEA Chief of Intelligence Anthony Placido; *Reforma*, 'Nine agents killed in a week', by Luis Brito, 10.5.2008; various television interviews featuring Garcia Luna; author's interviews with former PGR official. She and her husband ... exchange for information. Erica and Antonio's story drawn from interviews with 'Erica' and anonymous DEA agent. Other articles used for the Garay bust and background: *Rolling Stone*, 'The making of a narco state', by Guy Lawson, 4.3.2009; *El Universal*, 'Ex drug czar accused of receiving $450,000 from drug trafficking', by Maria de la Luz Gonzalez, 21.11.2008; *La Jornada*, 'Noe Ramirez received $450,000 a month from the Sinaloa cartel, reveals Medina Mora', by

Gustavo Castillo Garcia, 22.11.2008; *New York Times*, 'In Mexico drug war, sorting good guys from bad', by Marc Lacey, 1.11.2008. **President Calderon ... 'costly' war.** President Calderon speech in Tecoman, Colima, 17.4.2007. **For the first time ... was adhered to.** Author's reporting in Ciudad Juarez and Culiacan. **With US support ... don't follow them.** *Los Angeles Times*, 'Fixing Mexico police becomes a priority', by Ken Ellingwood, 17.11.2009; interviews with DEA agents past and present. **Top federal cop ... his colleagues.** 'Source of leak that allowed for murder of Millan investigated', by Maria de la Luz Gonzalez, 10.5.2008. **Just months ... extradition to Mexico.** *El Universal*, 'Two agents linked to Ye Gon case murdered', by Maria de la Luz Gonzalez, 2.8.2007; *Washington Post*, 'Justice Dept. wants charges against Mexican man dropped', by Del Quentin Wilber, 23.6.2009; *Washington Post*, 'Mexico, the DEA, and the case of Zhenli Ye Gon', by Jorge Carrasco, 29.10.2008; Reuters, 'Mexico asks U.S. to extradite suspected meth maker', 13.7.2007. **Thirty-five-year-old ... This is what makes Sinaloa.** Interviews in Culiacan; *Los Angeles Times*, 'In Sinaloa, the drug trade has infiltrated "every corner of life"', by Tracy Wilkinson, 28.12.2008. **General Sandoval ... can be trusted.** *El Universal*, 'Sinaloans warned of fake Mexican Army', by Javier Cabrera Martinez, 18.7.2009; *Noroeste*, 'Josefina de Jesus Garcia Ruiz: "I feel safe in the streets"', no byline, 5.6.2008. **Late one night ... be alive today.** Interviews with anonymous DEA agent and 'Erica'; transcript of a lecture at the DEA museum by DEA Regional Director for the North & Central Americas Region, David Gaddis, 1.4.2009.

Chapter 11

Lyrics from 'El Hijo de La Tuna'. Musica.com. **At 8.30 p.m. .... long-time close allies.** *El Universal*, 'Son of Chapo attacked with bazooka in commercial centre', by staff writers, 9.5.2008; *El Universal*, 'Official sources confirm death of El Chapo's son', by staff writers, 9.5.2008; *El Universal*, 'PGR confirms death of El Chapo's son', by staff writers, 9.5.2008; *La Jornada*, 'Sinaloa, in danger on account of violence following murder of Chapo's son', by Javier Valdez Cardenas, 10.5.2008; *El Universal*, 'Son of The Empress killed in shootout', by staff writers, 9.5.2008; *El Universal*, 'Those killed in commercial centre are identified', by Javier Cabrera Martinez, 9.5.2008; *Reforma*, 'El Chapo has six more children', by staff writers, 11.5.2008; *Newsweek*, 'El Chapo: The most wanted man in Mexico', by Joshua Hammer, 18.6.2009. **The brothers ... history in Sinaloa.** Description of 'Mochomo', his activities and the relationship between Chapo and the Beltran Leyva brothers is drawn from author's interviews with locals and officials in Culiacan, as well as the following articles, most of which focus on his brother Arturo: *Rio Doce*, 'El Barbas . . .', by staff writers, 21.12.2009; *El Universal*, 'Profile of Arturo Beltran Leyva', by staff writers, 16.12.2009; *EFE*, 'Profile: Arturo Beltran Leyva', no byline, 17.12.2009; *Rolling Stone*, 'The war next door', by Guy Lawson, 13.11.2008; *El Universal*, 'Profile: Carlos Beltran Leyva', by staff writers, 2.1.2010; *La Jornada*, 'Army disarms police in Tamaulipas', by staff writers, 23.1.2008. **On 21 January 2008 ... to be interrogated.** *El Universal*, 'PGR captures suspected leader of Sinaloa cartel', by Carlos Aviles, 21.1.2008; *El Universal*, 'Mochomo, a Sinaloa cartel operative, falls', by Carlos Aviles and Javier Cabrera, 22.1.2008; *Reforma*, 'Beltran caught without a single shot being fired', by staff writers, 22.1.2008; Notimex, 'Alfredo Beltran Leyva, head of the Sinaloa cartel, falls', no byline, 21.1.2008; *Milenio*, 'Sedena rejects links between more soldiers and Alfredo Beltran Leyva', no byline, 31.10.2008. **Like all Chapo's sons ... Frida Sofia Guzman Munoz.** Description of Chapo's relationship with family drawn from author's interviews with DEA agents past and present, the PGR, interviews with locals and officials in Sinaloa; and newspaper articles, including the following: *El Universal*, '"El Chapo" created a network of complicit [people]', by Francisco Gomez, 19.4.2001; *Reforma*, 'El Chapo has six more children', by staff writers, 11.5.2008. **Edgar was ... past generations.** *Proceso*, 'The narco-juniors', by Alejandro Gutierrez, 5.6.2005; author's interviews with Luis Astorga. **One** alleged narco-junior ... drug operations. Interview with anonymous narco-junior in Mexico City. Chapo's son Edgar ... the authorities. *Reforma*, 'El Chapo has six more children', by staff writers, 11.5.2008. Chapo's son Ivan Archivaldo ... rounded up. *La Jornada*, 'Defence says El Chapito is a "hostage" of the state', by Gustavo Castillo and Israel Davila, 10.6.2005; *El Universal*, 'Chapito goes back to La Palma prison', by Carlos Aviles, 20.7.2005; statement by the Federal Judiciary Council (CFJ), 5.2.2008; PGR statement, 15.2.2005; PGR statement, 8.6.2005; PGR statement, 21.10.2005. Often they were ... losing this war. Reuters, 'Savvy young heirs give Mexico drug cartels new face', by Mica Rosenberg, 8.4.2009; *El Universal*, 'El Mayo Zambada's son caught', by Maria de la Luz Gonzalez, 19.3.2009; *El Universal*, 'PGR confirms arrest of Vicente Carrillo Leyva', by Maria de la Luz Gonzalez, 2.4.2009; *El Universal*, 'Profile: Vicente Carrillo Leyva', by staff writers, 2.4.2009; *Reforma*, 'Son of Amado Carrillo captured', by staff writers, 2.4.2009; *Reforma*, 'Carrillo located because of his wife', by Antonio Baranda, 3.4.2009. Perhaps, but ... known better. Interviews with sources in Sinaloa; Eduardo Medina Mora interview with *EFE*, March 2009. He and Alfredo ... the drug lord. Sedena statement/press conference, 19.3.2009; Indictment: United States vs. Joaquin Guzman-Loera, Ismael Zambada-Garcia, Jesus Vicente Zambada-Niebla, Alfredo Guzman-Salazar [et al.], United States District Court, Northern District of Illinois, 20.8.2009. At the time ... Michoacan. *La Jornada*, 'El Chapo "hidden" in the mountains between Colima and Michoacan ...', by Alfredo Mendez, 12.5.2008. According to some ... is more likely. Interviews with locals and officials in Sinaloa. The Sinaloa organization ... smoothly and safely. Interviews with DEA and security experts; Ravelo's books, various *Proceso*, *El Universal* and *Reforma* articles; *La Jornada*, 'The new geography of the narco', by Alberto Najar, 24.7.2005. However, bad blood ... increasing pressure. Indictment: United States v. Joaquin Guzman-Loera, Ismael Zambada-Garcia, Jesus Vicente Zambada-Niebla, Alfredo Guzman-Salazar [et al.], United States District Court, Northern

District of Illinois, 20.8.2009; Sedena statement, 28.10.2009. **Shortly before ...The killings continued.** Interviews with local journalists and correspondents for *El Universal*; *Noroeste*, '1167 killed: Narcoviolence marks 2008', by Guadalupe Martinez, 1.1.2009. **Chapo and El Mayo ... the Federation.** *El Universal*, 'The pact between the Gulf cartel and the Beltrans', by staff writers, 19.5.2008. **In mid-May 2008 ... and Chapo.** Interviews with US officials. **On 30 May ... the United States.** Statement by Ambassador Tony Garza, 30.5.2008. **They also ... than ever before.** *Noroeste*, '1167 killed: Narcoviolence marks 2008', by Guadalupe Martinez, 1.1.2009; interviews with locals and officials in Sinaloa.

Chapter 12

The seventeen-year-old brunette ... up in the Sierra. Account of wedding from *Proceso*, 'The top capo's wedding', by Patricia Davila, 7.11.2007; additional descriptions from photographs supplied by the government of Canelas, author's interviews with locals in Tamazula, Durango, and anonymous Durango officials. **For the authorities ... Chapo always gets away.** Interviews with US and Mexican authorities. **Journalists, too ... they are seeing him.** *Los Angeles Times*, 'Mexico's master of elusion', by Richard Boudreaux, 5.7.2005. **Deciphering which ... less and less.** Interviews with DEA agents past and present, members of the Mexican military, the PGR, locals and officials in Sinaloa. **One cool November ... true to his word.** Article by Javier Valdez, *Rio Doce*, translation courtesy of borderreporter.com. **It's always ... was ever found.** PGR; *Los Angeles Times*, 'Mexico's master of elusion', by Richard Boudreaux, 5.7.2005; *San Antonio Express-News*, '"El Chapo" is Mexico's most wanted man', by Dane Schiller, 19.6.2005; *Wall Street Journal*, 'The drug lord who got away', by David Luhnow and Jose de Cordoba, 13.6.2009. **In cities like Culiacan ... for the locals.** *Newsweek*, 'El Chapo: The most wanted man in Mexico', by Joshua Hammer, 18.6.2009; author's interviews with locals in Sinaloa and Durango. **The**

reverence ... furious. Interviews with anonymous DEA agent. The Mexican government ... up in court. *Guardian*, 'El Chapo: the narcotics king who made it into Forbes magazine', by Jo Tuckman, 14.3.2009; author's interviews with several Mexican security experts. Josue Felix ... a symbol. Interviews with Josue Felix. But this has ... Chapo never came. Author's observations and interviews with locals and officials in Sinaloa and Durango.

Chapter 13

Congressman Felipe Diaz Garibay ... narco-terrorism. Interviews with congressman Felipe Diaz Garibay. On 6 September 2006 ... who had done it. *New York Times*, 'With beheadings and attacks, drug gangs terrorize Mexico', by James McKinley Jr, 26.10.2006. Propaganda banners ... alleged links to La Familia. Television images from Morelia, 15–20 September 2008; Associated Press, 'Banners hung in Mexico blame hit men for attack', by Gustavo Ruiz, 20.9.2008; *Houston Chronicle*, 'Three arrested in Morelia grenade attack', by Dudley Althaus, 26.9.2008. 'When we went in ... assassins took control.' *New York Times* magazine, 'The long war of Genaro Garcia Luna', by Daniel Kurtz-Phelan, 13.7.2008. Originally the paramilitary ... his close-knit crew. 'Los Zetas: The ruthless army spawned by a Mexican drug cartel', by George W. Grayson, Foreign Policy Research Institute, May 2008. As Los Zetas expanded ... to be Zetas. Author's reporting throughout Mexico and interviews with anonymous DEA agent. Guatemala was ... Guzman is in Honduras. Reuters, 'Guatemala checks shootout dead for Mexican drug lord', by Mica Rosenberg, 26.3.2008; Reuters, 'Guatemala says Mexico drug lord not in shootout dead', by Mica Rosenberg, 28.3.2008; Notimex, 'Guatemala: "El Chapo" didn't die in shootout', no byline, 28.3.2008. The methods of killing ... the same way. Interviews with locals, officials and experts in Michoacan, 2007–9; interviews with Luis Astorga; George W. Grayson, 'La Familia Michoacana: A deadly Mexican cartel revisited,' Foreign Policy

Research Institute, August 2009; interviews with anonymous DEA agent. **The plane crashed ... suspicious eyebrow.** Author's recollections of 4.11.2008. **On 27 November 1989 ... cartel boss.** Mark Bowden, *Killing Pablo: The Hunt for the World's Greatest Outlaw*, Penguin Books, 2001, p. 59. **For most Mexicans ... died in the drug war.** Author's reporting 2007–8. **A bombing attempt ... be a target.** Reuters, 'Mexican troops fight Sinaloa drug cartel', by Mica Rosenberg and Anahi Rama, 14.5.2008; *El Universal*, 'It targeted the SSP-DF', by Icela Laginas and Alberto Cuenca, 16.2.2008. **That included ... Mexican history.** Associated Press, 'Mexico honors soldiers beheaded by drug cartels', no byline, 22.12.2008; Agence France-Presse, 'Mexican army vows crackdown after soldiers beheaded', no byline, 22.12.2008. **We're going to ... the drug war.** Author's reporting in Ciudad Juarez. **Since Chapo ... die in 2009.** Homicide tallies from *El Universal*, *Reforma* and *Milenio*. **The soldiers faced ... for the adrenalin.** Author's reporting throughout Mexico in 2007–9; interviews with anonymous DEA agent; *Dallas Morning News*, 'Protests may be Mexican drug cartels' latest tactic to fight military presence', by Laurence Iliff, 19.2.2009. **Residents ... counter-drug official.** *Washington Post*, 'U.S. forces asylum on Mexican human rights activist Gustavo de la Rosa', by William Booth, 22.10.2009. **Since its founding ... (the other side).** Author's reporting in Ciudad Juarez. **But even when ... recent as yesterday.** *Washington Post*, 'U.S. forces asylum on Mexican human rights activist Gustavo de la Rosa', by William Booth, 22.10.2009. **One Saturday night ... on the US radar.** Interviews with officials and locals in Ciudad Juarez. **Barrio Azteca controls ... affiliated to Los Aztecas.** National Drug Intelligence Center reports; author's interviews with Ciudad Juarez prison officials. **Organized crime ... the murders.** *New York Times*, '17 killed in Mexican rehab center', by Marc Lacey, 25.9.2009; *Milenio*, 'Five killed in massacres in rehabilitation centres for addicts', no byline, 25.9.2009; *Dallas Morning News*, 'Mexican drug cartel finishing off rival gang, experts say', by Alfredo Corchado and Angela Kocherga, 4.9.2009; author's interviews with officials in Ciudad Juarez. **Back in Sinaloa ... boss of bosses.** Author's reporting in Sinaloa. **Attorney General ... in Afghanistan.** *Wall Street Journal*, 'The drug lord who got away', by David Luhnow and Jose de Cordoba, 13.6.2009. **In April 2009 ... 'You'll never get Chapo.'** *El Universal*, 'Archbishop: "El Chapo" lives in Durango', by staff writers, 22.4.2009; *El Universal*, 'Soldiers executed in Durango . . .', by Monica Perla Hernandez, 18.4.2009.

Chapter 14

'The growing assault ... homeland security alone.' US Joint Forces Command, 'The Joint Operating Environment (JOE)', pp. 38–40, 25.11.2008. **Almost immediately ... effectively ignored.** Interviews with Shannon O'Neil, Council on Foreign Relations, and Roberta S. Jacobson, US State Department deputy assistant secretary for Canada, Mexico and NAFTA. **But with the rising ... new administration.** McClatchy newspapers, 'Drug violence pushes Mexico to top of U.S. security concerns', by Marisa Taylor, 24.3.2009; *Los Angeles Times*, 'Calderon seeks to dispel talk of "failing state"', by Ken Ellingwood, 25.1.2009; National Drug Intelligence Center, 'National Drug Threat Assessment 2009', December 2008. **Mexican drug traffickers ... cell operations.** Interviews with DEA agents past and present; DEA statement following Operation Impunity II, December 2000. **Some in the DEA ... our concern.** Testimony before the House Appropriations Committee by DEA Special Agent Joseph M. Arabit, 24.3.2009. **Indeed ... 'non-traditional places'.** Interview with anonymous DEA agent. **Places like ... into our area.** Interview with Sheriff Chris Curry, NBC 13 WVTM, NBC's affiliate for Birmingham, Alabama; DEA statement, 17.9.2008. **In Columbus ... sport badges.** *Washington Post*, 'From Mexico, drug violence spills into U.S.', by Manuel Roig-Franzia, 20.4.2008; *Los Angeles Times*, 'Border drug war is too close for comfort', by Scott Kraft, 19.2.2009. **The case of Rey Guerra ... sometimes**

they can. *Los Angeles Times*, 'On the borderline of good and evil', by Scott Kraft, 3.4.2009. **Further embarrassment ... not drug trafficking.** *Nogales International*, 'Documents paint picture of a good agent that went bad', by Michel Marizco, 15.9.2009; *Nogales International*, 'Obstruction charges now set for Cramer', by Michel Marizco, 8.12.2009; *Los Angeles Times*, 'Former U.S. anti-drug official's arrest "a complete shock" ', by Sebastian Rotella, 17.9.2009. **More cases ... new face of crime.** National Drug Intelligence Center, 'National Drug Threat Assessment 2009', December 2008; statement by the office of Senator Dick Durbin, 17.3.2009. **The Calderon administration ... into consideration.** Associated Press, 'Mexico president denies country a "failed state" ', by Traci Carl, 26.2.2009; *Los Angeles Times*, 'Calderon seeks to dispel talk of "failing state" ', by Ken Ellingwood, 25.1.2009; author's interviews with US officials in Mexico and academics in Sinaloa at the time. **In April 2009 ... sigh of relief.** MSNBC.com, 'Obama: Mexico drug war "sowing chaos" ', no byline, 16.4.2009; *El Universal*, 'Calderon and Obama to close border to weapons', by staff writers, 16.4.2009. **The US drug market ... very near.** United Nations Office on Drugs and Crime (UNODC). **The DEA estimates ... and launder.** DEA; testimony before the House Committee on Oversight and Government Reform by DEA Chief of Intelligence Anthony Placido et al., 9.7.2009; RAND Drug Policy Research Center. **In recent years ... north of the border.** Factcheck.org, 'Counting Mexico's guns', 17.4.2009. **It's a huge ... cop killers.** Mexican Defence Secretariat. **In a single raid ... their arsenal.** *New York Times*, 'In drug war, Mexico fights cartel and itself', by Marc Lacey, 29.3.2009. **The cartels are using ... guerrilla fighting.** *Los Angeles Times*, 'Drug cartels' new weaponry means war', by Ken Ellingwood and Tracy Wilkinson, 15.3.2009. **US authorities ... year before.** Bureau of Arms, Tobacco and Firearms (ATF). **Others warned ... like pancakes.** *New York Times* magazine, 'The long war of Genaro Garcia Luna', by Daniel Kurtz-Phelan, 13.7.2008. **There had already ... flashpoint.** Associated Press, 'Feds: Gun, cash seizures up at Mexican border', by Elliot

Spagat, 3.11.2009. **The Flores brothers ... worried about dying.** *Washington Post*, 'U.S. guns behind cartel killings in Mexico', by Manuel Roig-Franzia, 29.10.2007; Denise Dresser, at launch of Woodrow Wilson International Center for Scholars' Mexico Institute report, available at http://mexicoinstitute.wordpress.com/. **Under Obama ... within Mexico. DEA. The DEA ... Nuevo Laredo.** *Newsweek*, 'America's role in Mexico's drug war', by Jerry Adler, 8.12.2009. **It authorized ... US border.** Testimony before the House Appropriations Committee by DEA Special Agent Joseph M. Arabit, 24.3.2009. **In March 2009 ... allies-turned-rivals.** *Los Angeles Times*, 'Sinaloa cartel may resort to deadly force in U.S.', by Josh Meyer, 6.5.2009. Indictment: United States vs. Joaquin Guzman-Salazar [et al.], United States District Court, Northern District of Illinois, 20.8.2009.

Chapter 15

US officials ... in an hour. DEA statement, 25.2.2009. **The Sinaloa cartel wasn't ... in the Southern Cone.** Interviews with US officials in Central America; PGR assessment; *El Universal*, 'Sinaloa cartel fights Colombians for Peru plaza', by Jose Melendez, 18.2.2009; *Los Angeles Times*, 'Mexico's drug lords look south', by Chris Kraul, 25.3.2009; *La Nacion*, 'Another blow for the Sinaloa cartel in the country', by Gustavo Carabajal; *EFE*, 'Argentina denies Mexican drug cartel has foothold . . .', no byline, 14.11.2008. **Former DEA Chief ... bite us in the ass.** Interviews with Edgardo Buscaglia and Michael Braun; testimony before the Senate Committee on Foreign Relations by Michael Braun, 23.6.2009. **The cartels ... the jungles of Colombia.** Statements from the Mexican Navy, Army and PGR. **Colombian police ... tons of cocaine.** *New York Times*, 'Drug subculture', by David Kushner, 23.4.2009. **These first makeshift ... to build.** Joint Interagency Task Force South Fact Sheet, published by US Southern Command. **The incident ... US intelligence.** BBC News, 'Mexican navy seizes cocaine sub', no byline, 18.7.2008.

US Admiral ... US Southern Command. Joint Interagency Task Force South Fact Sheet, published by US Southern Command. Taking note ... evade detection. *Navy Times*, 'Legislation targets drug-smuggling subs', by Amy McCullough, 30.7.2008. With the spotlight ... ton of cocaine. US Department of Justice Audit Report, February 2007; CNN, 'Drug smugglers becoming more creative, U.S. agents say', by Deborah Feyerick, Michael Cary and Sheila Steffen, 16.4.2009; Reuters, 'Cocaine haul found hidden in frozen sharks', no byline, 17.6.2009. A forty-year-old ... Mexico City. PGR. A woman ... $30,000. PGR; *Houston Chronicle*, 'Cocaine Jesus statue seized by Texas agents', by Dane Schiller, 30.5.2008. Women have long ... a part of it. Author's observations and reporting based on interviews with officials and locals in Sinaloa. In late December 2008 ... Culiacan since. PGR; interviews in Sinaloa and Michoacan; interviews with Martha Tagle Martinez. In Ciudad Juarez's ... going on vacation. *Los Angeles Times*, 'Women play a bigger role in Mexico's drug war', by Tracy Wilkinson, 10.11.2009; author's interviews with female prisoners and prison officials in Ciudad Juarez and Culiacan. To some young women ... 'La Reina'. Interviews with inmates in Santa Martha Acatitla women's prison. Sandra Avila Beltran ... the business. *El Universal*, 'A Queen of low profile and an esoteric Tiger', by Silvia Otero, 5.10. 2007; *Newsweek*, 'Underworld Queenpin', by Joe Contreras, 11.10.2007. Once in prison ... here in the prison. Author's reporting in Santa Martha Acatitla; PGR.

Chapter 16

They had spotted ... didn't arrive in time. *Proceso*, 'El Chapo: The arranged escape', by Ricardo Ravelo, January 2009. Patrols ... now be routine. Telephone interviews with authorities in Durango. Attorney General Eduardo Medina Mora ... drug-related crime. Author's observations of Medina Mora at press conferences and televised meetings; interviews with DEA agents past and present; quotes from *Wall Street Journal,* opinion piece by Mary Anastasia O'Grady, 25.2.2008. **Garcia Luna, too … in the world.** Author's observations of Garcia Luna's press conferences and interviews; quotes from *New York Times* magazine, 'The long war of Genaro Garcia Luna', by Daniel Kurtz-Phelan, 13.7.2008. **But in May … government.** PGR statement, 30.5.2009. **There had been … the same reason.** Author's interviews with soldiers in Sinaloa; Sedena (Mexican Defence Secretariat). **Guerrero had always … could be overthrown.** Interviews with generals and soldiers in Guerrero; interviews with local journalists in Sinaloa; *La Jornada,* 'Chapo and La Barbie linked to execution in Acapulco', by Misael Habana and Gustavo Castillo, 4.8.2005. **Chapo was taking … most trusted allies.** PGR. **In Culiacan … to contradict that.** PGR; interviews with anonymous DEA agent in Mexico. **As the feds … feared him.** Interviews in Sinaloa. **General Sandoval … and Nacho Coronel.** Las Trancas accounts from Sedena, *Rio Doce, El Universal* and *Reforma;* author's interviews with several local journalists who were on the scene. **We're going to … moving all the time.** Interviews with anonymous DEA agent in Mexico. **Chapo had also … of ammunition.** Sedena and PGR. **On 18 December 2008 … was dead.** PGR. **Chapo still … matter of time.** Interviews with anonymous DEA agent in Mexico. **Throughout 2009 … in the year.** *Wall Street Journal,* 'The war on drugs is a failure', by Fernando Henrique Cardoso, Cesar Gavira and Ernesto Zedillo, 23.2.2009. **Former foreign minister … US to sustain.** Ruben Aguilar Valenzuela and Jorge Castaneda, *El Narco: La Guerra Fallida,* Punto de Lectura, 2009; *Newsweek,* 'America's role in Mexico's drug war', by Jerry Adler, 8.12.2009. **Some Mexican experts … such an agreement.** Mexican media reports and pundit commentary. **Even President Calderon … distant third.** Associated Press, 'Mexican president says crime third priority', by Mark Stevenson, 7.1.2010. **Residents of Culiacan … yet to come.** Author's reporting in Culiacan. **Mexico's jails, too … from Juarez and Los Zetas.** PGR, federal police and Sedena. **Matamoros** prison ... thirty injured. Author's reporting in Matamoros. At the state prison ... twenty-six injured. *El Universal*, 'Riot in Durango leaves at least 19 dead', by Monica Hernandez and Enrique Proa, 15.8.2009; follow-up from PGR statements. And in the most ... as federal agents. Associated Press, 'Gang frees 50 inmates from Mexican prison', by Alexandra Olson, 17.5.2009; follow-up from PGR statements. The Mexican government ... prison system. *El Universal*, 'Jorge Tello Peon: Evaluating the police is impossible', by Francisco Gomez, 19.9.2009. Ciudad Juarez and ... worked for Chapo. Interviews in Culiacan, Ciudad Juarez and Matamoros. 'El Padrino' Felix Gallardo ... only repression. Miguel Angel Felix Gallardo's writings, published online. Construction of 'Don Neto' Fonseca's ... are numbered. Author's own observations. Rafael Caro Quintero ... now work for him. PGR; DEA statements; interviews with anonymous DEA agent in Mexico. El Mayo's brother and son ... newspaper *Reforma*. PGR; *Reforma*, 'Zambada dynasty weakened', by staff writers, 23.11.2009. El Mayo's comments in *Proceso*, 'In El Mayo Zambada's lair', 4.4.2010. On 11 December 2009 ... rival was dead. PGR; *El Universal*, 'Arturo Beltran Leyva dies in Cuernavaca', by staff writers, 16.12.2009. In Nogales, Sonora ... *posada* [holiday party]. borderreporter.com. El Barbas had posthumously ... were murdered. PGR. El Barbas was buried ... his grave. Reporting from locals. Less than two weeks ... self-preservation. PGR; reporting from locals. Chapo was winning ... a vengeance. PGR. As Los Zetas ... the 'never ending war'. Author's own analysis from local reporting. But Chapo was ... like sitting ducks. *Dallas Morning News*, 'Mexican drug cartel finishing off rival gang, experts say', by Alfredo Corchado and Angela Kocherga, 4.9.2009. Shortly after ... the world. Associated Press, 'Sinoloa cartel wins Juarez turf war', by Alicia A. Caldwell and Mark Stevenson, 9.4.2010. In early 2009 ... to Chapo's people. PGR. He clearly wasn't ... matter of time. Interview with former DEA Chief of Operations Michael Braun. Back in Culiacan ... death or jail. Sandoval speech published in *Noroeste* online. Sandoval's comments about Chapo were made to BBC correspondent Katya Adler in early 2010. **One of Sandoval's ... just a farmer.** Reporting by Marc Lacey of the *New York Times* specifically for this book. **Chapo, however ... prostate cancer.** Interviews with locals and journalists in Sinaloa. **He can't spend ... being killed.** Reporting by Marc Lacey of the *New York Times* specifically for this book. **Chapo trusted ... never be caught.** Interviews with locals in Sinaloa. **In Mexico City ... will ever fall.** Interview with anonymous DEA agent.

Index

Acknowledgements

Many thanks to Joel Rickett at Viking for editing guidance and encouragement, not to mention coming up with the overarching theme of the book in the first place.

Thanks also to Marc Lacey, William Booth, Anne-Marie O'Connor, Tom Buckley, George Grayson, Brian Rausch, Blake Lalonde and Francisco Candido for encouragement, advice and moral support, as well as reporting help in some instances.

Thanks to Richard Ernsberger, Stryker McGuire, Marcus Mabry, Rod Nordland, Sam Seibert, Chris Dickey, Scott Johnson, Babak Dehghanpisheh, Andy Nagorski, Michael Meyer, Fareed Zakaria, Joe Contreras, Nisid Hajari and Karen Fragala for support in the past, and for helping me improve my journalism while I was at *Newsweek*.

Roger Sewhcomar, thanks for always encouraging me to write over one more pint. My other friends, you know who you are.

My gratitude goes out to all the sources who helped me tell this story whose names I can't mention for their own safety.

And thanks also to all those sources who opened up, knowing that I was a journalist, possibly risking their lives in so doing, in order to help recount what is happening in Mexico today. Apologies to the people I had to lie to in order to gain better access.

Last, but of course not least, thanks to my family for their support.